Balkan Yearbook of European and International Law

Volume 2022

The Balkan Yearbook of European and International Law publishes peer-reviewed scholarly articles, notes, comments and book reviews on private and public European and International Law. The yearbook contains summaries and analyses of recent decisions by national and international courts and arbitral or other tribunals. The yearbook has one section with a special hot topic or focus as well as sections about European and international law in each volume. Moreover, it presents book reviews to recent publications from the region or with a major impact for the region. The yearbook focuses on recent developments of European and International Law and presents a forum for scholarly discourse on European and International Law from the perspective of the region of South-East Europe. However, the publication is not exclusive in that regard: contributions from the perspective of the wider world are also strongly encouraged and welcomed.

Ivana Kunda • Zlatan Meškić • Enis Omerović •
Dušan V. Popović
Editors

Balkan Yearbook of European and International Law 2022

Springer

Editors
Ivana Kunda
Rijeka, Croatia

Zlatan Meškić
Riyadh, Saudi Arabia

Enis Omerović
Riyadh, Saudi Arabia

Dušan V. Popović
Belgrade, Serbia

ISSN 2524-8715 ISSN 2524-8723 (electronic)
Balkan Yearbook of European and International Law
ISBN 978-3-031-29431-0 ISBN 978-3-031-29432-7 (eBook)
https://doi.org/10.1007/978-3-031-29432-7

This Springer imprint is published by the registered company Springer Nature Switzerland AG
The registered company address is: Gewerbestrasse 11, 6330 Cham, Switzerland

Preface

As the Balkan Yearbook of European and International Law is reaching its fourth edition for the year of 2022, we are pleased to confirm that BYEIL has been admitted to the Scopus, the Elsevier's abstract and citation database, including its three previous issues. This achievement is of course owed not only to the editors' efforts and professionalism of the personnel in Springer, but also to all the contributors and reviewers whom we owe much appreciation. In keeping with the standards of this publication, we are presenting before you nine articles, each of which brings new perspective on various legal issues.

Prompted by the discussions on the rules enacted in the European Union in the context of cooperation in civil matters and extent to which they respond to the need of the cross-border European families in organising their property relations, the special section of this year is devoted to family property in private international law. First, debates concerning the Succession Regulation and more recently, on the Twin Regulations on property regimes in marriage and registered partnership, have made us think also about the national laws which remain outside their scope. This concerns both EU Member States and third States. In total, six articles offer views on different aspects of family property in cross-border cases. The opening article provides a comprehensive discussion of legal regulation of family relations in Bosnia and Herzegovina and complexities related to internal conflict of laws among three separate territorial units. Expectedly, these complex issues spill over to situations of conflict of laws beyond those within Bosnia and Herzegovina, where nationality as a connecting factor refers to its law as a whole. The following contribution is focused on the treatment of the Certificate of Succession in Turkish law, from the perspective of international jurisdiction and applicable law when a certificate is requested before Turkish authorities, as well as the recognition of such foreign Certificate in Turkey. The author points out to several issues, showing that despite the Turkish courts' position, some authors tend to favour the opposite views questioning certain arguments and established practices.

The third article is showcasing a situation of Lithuania, an EU Member State which has not participated in the enhanced cooperation established by the Twin Regulations. Building on the Lithuanian substantive and procedural law, the authors make important conclusions about the private international law issues arising in matters of couple's property. They find Lithuanian private international law inadequate for the intense cross-border family lifestyles in European Union of today, hence they recommend that Lithuania joins the Twin Regulations. Next two among the family property articles turn the focus towards Croatia, a Member State which participates in the enhanced cooperation established by the Twin Regulations. These articles examine the areas left outside the scope of the Regulations and the extent to which the Regulations still come in play due to particular national conflict of law rules, respectively. The former article offers an insight into the projected approach which the Croatian courts will take when seized with a property dispute arising out of a same-sex marriage or in relation to divorce of such marriage. The latter examines in detail the issues of international jurisdiction, applicable law and recognition and enforcement in cases of *de facto* couples, which although not falling under the scope of the Twin Regulations, end up being subject to them due to referencing technique applied by the Croatian legislator. The special section closes with a contribution which brings to the front the Greek perspectives on law and policy concerns in mediating family property disputes. Seeing mediation as a valuable tool in resolving family property disputes, the author warns about the deterring effect which the multiplicity of legal instruments and their fragmentation on both international and EU level may have over choosing mediation over judicial proceedings.

In the section on EU law, this year's volume offers a fresh look at the topic extensively discussed in the literature, the effects of Brexit over the EU trademark. In addition to commenting on the adequacy of the rules, now with some time distance and practical experience gained, the author is paying attention also to the possible future development in terms of corresponding UK trademarks and UK legal framework.

The section on international law has two accounts written by young scholars with passionate approach to their topics. The overall assessment of political and legal environment in the former Yugoslavia and Bosnia and Herzegovina today is at the centre of attention in the article debating the state of the rule of law in Bosnia and Herzegovina. Given that the rule of law is an international standard, this article is placed in this section despite some references to European law which would also qualify it for the other general section of BYEIL. Pointing to the circumstances the author sees as obstacles on the way to achieve this ideal legal-political standard in Bosnia and Herzegovina, he concludes by contending that any improvement is conditioned on deepening the focus towards the causes of the problems and not just the problems themselves. The other article tackles a thorny issue of legal nature of cryptoassets. The analysis starts from the technical characteristics of cryptoassets as the author attempts to develop an overview of the rights attributed to those assets in different legal systems. The result of the comparative analysis is that the existing differences steam from the very character of a particular legal systems as such. In these cases, as well as in some other, extension by analogy of the conclusions on legal nature from one field to another, or from one instrument to another, has to be exercised with caution.

Rijeka, Croatia — Ivana Kunda
Riyadh, Saudi Arabia — Zlatan Meškić
Riyadh, Saudi Arabia — Enis Omerović
Belgrade, Serbia — Dušan V. Popović

Contents

Editors and Contributors

Editors

Ivana Kunda University of Rijeka, Faculty of Law, Rijeka, Croatia.

Zlatan Meškić Prince Sultan University, Riyadh, Saudi Arabia.

Enis Omerović Prince Sultan University, Riyadh, Saudi Arabia.

Dušan V. Popović University of Belgrade, Faculty of Law, Belgrade, Serbia.

Contributors

Jasmina Alihodžić University of Tuzla, Faculty of Law, Tuzla, Bosnia and Herzegovina

Anita Duraković University 'Džemal Bijedić' in Mostar, Faculty of Law, Mostar, Bosnia and Herzegovina

Jura Golub Josip Juraj Strossmayer University of Osijek, Faculty of Law, Osijek, Croatia

Vassiliki Koumpli Hellenic Institute of International and Foreign Law, Athina, Greece
Metaxas and Associates Law Firm, Athina, Greece

Agnė Limantė Law Institute of the Lithuanian Centre for Social Sciences, Vilnius, Lithuania

Ines Medić University of Split, Faculty of Law, Split, Croatia

Iza Razija Mešević University of Sarajevo, Faculty of Law, Sarajevo, Bosnia and Herzegovina

Benjamin Nurkić University of Tuzla, Faculty of Law, Tuzla, Bosnia and Herzegovina

Kristina Pranevičienė Vilnius University, Faculty of Law, Vilnius, Lithuania

Zeynep Derya Tarman Koç University Law School, Istanbul, Turkey

Danijela Vrbljanac University of Rijeka, Faculty of Law, Rijeka, Croatia

Part I
Special Section on Family Property Private International Law

Interstate and Cross-Border Family Relations in Bosnia and Herzegovina: The Intricacies of a Multi-Layered Legal System

Anita Duraković and Jasmina Alihodžić

1 Introduction

The Constitution of Bosnia and Herzegovina divided competencies between the state and the entities. It starts from the enumeration of the competencies of the institutions of Bosnia and Herzegovina (Article III/1) with the presumption of competencies in favor of the entities (Article III/3.a). Thus, the area of private-legal relations was brought under the jurisdiction of the Republika Srpska (hereinafter: RS) and the Federation of Bosnia and Herzegovina (hereinafter: FBH), i.e., its cantons. Pursuant to the aforementioned provisions of the Constitution of Bosnia and Herzegovina, the Constitution of Republika Srpska determines the competencies of this entity in the field of private law relations (Article 68 of the Constitution of RS).[1] In terms of competencies in the field of private law relations, the situation is significantly different in the FBH and in RS. The concept of division of competencies between the FBH and its cantons accepted by the Constitution includes three types of competencies, namely the exclusive competence of the Federation, the common competence of the Federation and the cantons, and the competence of the cantons. The exclusive competencies of the Federation and the common competencies are explicitly enumerated.[2] The cantons have all the competencies that are not explicitly entrusted to the federal government, while the Constitution of the Federation of BH

[1] This article has been amended by Amendments XXXII, CVI, LVIII and LXXV.

[2] Articles III/1 and 2 of the FBH Constitution.

A. Duraković (✉)
University 'Džemal Bijedić' in Mostar, Faculty of Law, Mostar, Bosnia and Herzegovina
e-mail: anita.durakovic@unmo.ba

J. Alihodžić
University of Tuzla, Faculty of Law, Tuzla, Bosnia and Herzegovina
e-mail: jasmina.alihodzic@untz.ba

I. Kunda et al. (eds.), *Balkan Yearbook of European and International Law 2022*,
Balkan Yearbook of European and International Law 2022,
https://doi.org/10.1007/978-3-031-29432-7_1

uses a methodology according to which only some of the competencies of the cantons are listed *exempli causa*.[3] Following the provisions of the Constitution of the Federation of BH, it could be concluded that the area of private law relations is not even within the competence of the Federation, but within the competence of the canton. However, the above provisions of the Constitution of the Federation of BH must be interpreted in the context of the entire legal system of Bosnia and Herzegovina, and its Constitution. In accordance with this Constitution, ensuring the single and free market is a legitimate goal and a given value for all holders of power and levels of its organization in Bosnia and Herzegovina.[4] In this regard, the "fragmentation" of competencies in areas that are the *conditio sine qua non* for establishing a single market, such as the area of private law relations, bringing them to the cantonal level could be considered contrary to the provisions of the Constitution of Bosnia and Herzegovina.[5] Accordingly, and having in mind the existing division of competencies between the entities/cantons, and the special legal status of Brcko District of Bosnia and Herzegovina, the area of family law relations is regulated by family laws of the Federation of BH, Republika Srpska and Brcko District of BH.[6]

The occurrence of interstate conflict of laws is normal and regular in all multi-legal order states such as Bosnia and Herzegovina. Conflicts of laws can occur in almost all areas of private law, but it is most pronounced in the area of family law, because the differences between internal legislations in these areas are the largest and most common.[7] Parties to family law relations should know in advance the law applicable for their interstate conflict of laws. If the same legal situation is governed by the same law, regardless of whether the body decides in Sarajevo, Banja Luka or Brcko, the level of legal certainty arising from the predictability of applicable law would increase significantly, which is extremely important for participants in legal transactions. Full legal certainty in this regard is provided by the 1979 Resolving Conflicts of Law and Jurisdiction in Status, Family and Inheritance Relations Act (hereinafter: the ZRSZN),[8] which applies to the entire territory of Bosnia and Herzegovina and was taken over from the former Socialist Federal Republic of Yugoslavia (hereinafter: the former SFRY).[9] Namely, with the Constitutional

[3] Article III/4 of the FBH Constitution.

[4] Line 4, Article I/4 of the Constitution of BH.

[5] More on this issue and the decisions of the Constitutional Court of BH which can be applied by analogy to the Federation of BH in: Alihodžić (2012), pp. 219–221; Alihodžić and Begić (2013), pp. 336–338.

[6] See the Revised Statute of the Brčko District of Bosnia and Herzegovina, which entered into force on 6 May 2008 (Official Gazette of the Brčko District of BH No. 17/08), Amendments to the Statute of the Brčko District of Bosnia and Herzegovina adopted by the Supervisor's Order of 21. December 2009, Official Gazette of the Brcko District of BH no. 39/09), Art. 8. and Art. 22.

[7] Stanivuković and Živković (2004), p. 224.

[8] Official Gazette SFRY 9/79 i 20/90 (hereinafter: ZRSZN).

[9] Official Gazette RBH 2/92 i 13/94, Official Gazette of Serbs' People in BH 21/92 and Official Gazette BD BiH 1/2000.

Amendments of 1971 and then the new Constitution of 1974, the former SFRY significantly expanded the legislative competence of republics and provinces in many areas, especially in the matter of civil and family relations. This opened the possibility for one and the same relationship to be regulated differently in individual republics or provinces. Different substantive solutions within the former SFRY as a state with a complex legal order required the adoption of a single act at the level of the Federation that would solve the problem of interstate conflict of laws. The legislative activities ended with the adoption of the ZRSZN,[10] which was then, after the dissolution of the SFRY, taken over into the legal system of Bosnia and Herzegovina.[11] Although this Act was adopted with the intention of regulating the inter-republican and inter-provincial conflict of laws in the former SFRY, it is applied by analogy in Bosnia and Herzegovina as it is today.[12] The ZRSZN is applied in the matters falling within its scope, not only when there is an inter-entity conflict of laws in Bosnia and Herzegovina, but presumably also the conflict of law rules of Bosnia and Herzegovina[13] or another country refer to the law of Bosnia and Herzegovina without indicating its exact territorial unit.

In this paper, different legislative solutions to certain family law issues are explained because they regularly result in a conflict of laws between different territorial units. The relevant provisions of the ZRSZN that offer a solution to internal authorities when applying the law of Bosnia and Herzegovina as the applicable law will be pointed out and analyzed, especially with relation to the nationality principle as a connecting factor. The focus will further turn to a specific problem that foreign authorities may face in a situation where choice of law provisions refers to the law of Bosnia and Herzegovina, as a law of the state with more than one legal system. However, due to limited volume no issues of procedural nature will be dealt with in this paper, although regulated by family legislation and the ZRSZN.

[10] More about the history of the enactment of the ZRSZN in: Alagić (1971), pp. 73–77; Blagojević (1973), pp. 5–22; Blagojević and Puhan (1974), pp. 223–243; Varadi (1975), pp. 122; Jezdić and Pak (1982), pp. 20–21; Varadi (1987), pp. 358–360.

[11] Muminović believes that the adoption of this law in 1992, when the legal order of RBH was *de iure* unique, can be attributed to a legislative error, but that in today's conditions the possibility of applying this law *per analogiam* is not excluded. Muminović (1999), p. 235.

[12] The original text of this law was amended according to the constitutional structure and legislative competence established by the Constitution of Bosnia and Herzegovina, the constitutions of the entities and cantons, and the Statute of the Brcko District, as well as other applicable laws in Bosnia and Herzegovina. Šaula (2008), pp. 287–301.

[13] See: Dissolution of Conflict of Laws with Regulation of other Countries in Certain Relations Act, Official Gazette SFRY, no. 43/82, 72/82; Official Gazette, RBH 2/92, 13/94; Official Gazette BH, no. 53/10 (hereinafter: PIL Act).

2 Family Legislation in Bosnia and Herzegovina

Family legislation in Bosnia and Herzegovina has gone through several stages of development. Immediately after the Second World War, in 1946, the Marriage Basic Act[14] was passed, which contained solutions unique to the former SFRY. The second phase in the evolution of family legislation occurs after the 1971 Constitutional Amendments, which transferred the legislative competence for regulating family issues from the federation to the republics and provinces. This resulted in the enactment of eight different family laws which normatively, in different ways approached the subject of family law. The then Republic of Bosnia and Herzegovina passed its family law in 1979—the Family Act of the Socialist Republic of Bosnia and Herzegovina,[15] which was taken over for the entire territory of Bosnia and Herzegovina after the dissolution of the former SFRY.[16] The last phase in the evolution of Bosnia and Herzegovina's family legislation began with the signing of the Dayton Peace Agreement in 1995, which in Annex IV—the Constitution of Bosnia and Herzegovina, entrusted the authority to regulate family issues to the entities. Accordingly, three family laws are in force in different territorial entities in Bosnia and Herzegovina: the Family Act of the Republika Srpska[17] from 2002 (hereinafter: the PZ RS), the Family Act of the Federation of Bosnia and Herzegovina from 2005[18] (hereinafter: the PZ FBH), and the Family Act of the Brcko District from 2007[19] (hereinafter: the PZ BDBH).These laws differ in terms of the normative regulation of certain family law issues, and thus open the door widely to the problem of interstate conflict of laws. Some of the most important differences in relation to marital law, matrimonial property regime of spouses, parental responsibility, determination of paternity and maternity, maintenance and adoption will be analyzed below, while a comprehensive analysis would go beyond aim of this paper.

2.1 Marriage and Dissolution of Marriage

The first difference, which is rather linguistic than legally relevant, relates to the term that family laws in BH use for persons who are married to each other: the PZ FBH

[14] Official Gazette FPRY, No. 29/1946, 36/1948, 44/1951, 18/1955, Official Gazette SFRY, No. 12/1965, Official Gazette No. 52/1971, 11/1978.

[15] Official Gazette SR BH, No. 21/1979, 44/1989.

[16] Official Gazette RBH, No. 2/1992, 13/1994, Official Gazette of Serbs' People in BH, No. 9/99 and Official Gazette of BD, No. 1/2000.

[17] Official Gazette of Republika Srpska, No. 54/2002, 41/2008, 63/2014, 56/2019 – Decision of the Constitutional Court.

[18] Official Gazette of the FBH, No. 35/2005, 41/2005 – correction, 31/2014, 32/2019 – Decision of the Constitutional Court.

[19] Official Gazette of the BD BH, No. 23/2007.

uses the term *bračni partneri*, the PZ RS calls them *bračni supružnici*, and the PZ BDBH uses the term *bračni drugovi*, all three terms referring to *spouses*. Importantly, what they have in common is the definition of marriage as a legally regulated union of life of a man and a woman,[20] and the principles on which marriage is based: free will, equality of marital partners, mutual respect and mutual assistance[21] (with a difference that the PZ FBH and the PZ BDBH also state the obligation of fidelity[22]).

There are slight differences in the form of marriage. Namely, in addition to the civil form of marriage and the obligation to conclude a marriage before the civil registry official,[23] which is contained in all three family laws,[24] the PZ FBH provides for a religious form of marriage, i.e., gives spouses the possibility of marriage before a religious official, but only after presenting an excerpt from civil marriage registers.[25] Furthermore, all three laws allow, in exceptional cases, marriage by proxy, with different deadlines for this special power of attorney: 60 days from the date of certification according to the PZ FBiH and the PZ BDBH, and 90 days according to the PZ RS.[26]

Regarding the conditions for the validity of marriage (the PZ FBH), i.e., marital disorders (the PZ RS and the PZ BDBH), all three family acts agree that pre-existing marriage.[27] inability to reason,[28] kinship,[29] infancy[30] and lack of will[31] are obstacles to marriage. However, there are some differences in the standardization of certain marital disorders.[32] Thus, the PZ FBH, unlike the other two family acts, provides that, exceptionally, a court in non-litigious proceedings may allow a person who is incapable of reasoning to conclude a marriage if it determines that he or she is able to understand the meaning of marriage and the obligations arising from it and that marriage is obviously in his or her interest.[33] A marriage between adopter and adoptee from simple adoption (*nepotpuno usvojenje*) is not allowed under the PZ FBH sine simple adoption is explicitly stated as an irreversible marital obstacle.[34] On

[20] Art. 6 PZ FBH, art. 4 par. 1 PZ RS, art. 4 par. 1 PZ BDBH.

[21] Art. 4 par. 2 and art. 39 and 40 PZ RS, art. 4 par. 2 and art. 29 PZ BDBH.

[22] Art. 30 PZ FBiH, art. 29. par. 2. PZ BDBH.

[23] Art. 7 par. 1. and 2. PZ FBiH, art. 14. PZ RS, art. 6. par. 1. PZ BDBH.

[24] Art. 7 par. 3. PZ FBiH.

[25] Art. 7 par. 3. PZ FBiH.

[26] Art. 24 PZ FBH, Art. 23. PZ RS, art. 15 PZ BD BH. In the Federation of BH and the Republika Srpska, it is specified that the power of attorney is certified before a court or a notary, while in the Brcko District of BH it is not stated where this power of attorney is certified.

[27] Art. 10 PZ FBH, art. 31 PZ RS, art. 21 PZ BDBH.

[28] Art. 11 PZ FBH, art. 32 PZ RS, art. 22 PZ BDBH.

[29] Arts. 12-14 PZ FBH, arts. 33-35 PZ RS, arts. 23-25 PZ BDBH.

[30] Art. 15 PZ FBiH, art. 36. PZ RS, art. 26. PZ BDBH.

[31] Art. 16 PZ FBiH, art. 30. PZ RS, art. 20. PZ BDBH.

[32] See more on this issue: Traljić and Bubić (2007), pp. 45–59.

[33] Art. 11 par. 2 PZ FBH.

[34] Art. 13 PZ FBH.

the other hand, PZ RS and the PZ BDBH consider simple adoption as a ground for prohibition of marriage,[35] however, the court may, in non-litigious proceedings, allow these persons for justified reasons and at their request, to conclude a marriage.[36] All three family laws stipulate that the court may, exceptionally, in a non-litigious procedure, allow marriages to relatives by marriage (in-laws) if it finds that there are justified reasons,[37] with the Republika Srpska requiring the court to obtain the opinion of the guardianship authority before making a decision.[38] The age limit for marriage is 18 years, with the possibility that the court may in non-litigation, exceptionally and if it is in his or her interest (the PZ FBH), or for justified reasons (the PZ RS and the PZ BDBH) allow marriage to a person who has reached 16 years of age if it finds that there are justifiable reasons that the person is physically and mentally capable of performing the rights and duties arising from the marriage and that the marriage is in his or her interest.[39] In the Republika Srpska, the opinion of the guardianship authority is additionally required.[40]

Regarding the dissolution of marriage, there are noticeable differences in the family legislation in Bosnia and Herzegovina. In the matter of annulment of marriage, they are of a smaller scope and refer to the circle of persons authorized to file a lawsuit for annulment of marriage. In the Federation of BH and in the Brcko District of BH, the right to sue for annulment of marriage belongs to marital partners and the guardianship authority,[41] while in the Republika Srpska, in addition to the above, this right, in certain cases, belongs also to the public prosecutor's office.[42] Regarding divorce, all three family laws allow for divorce, and provide that a spouse may request a divorce if the marital relationship is severely and permanently disrupted, with the PZ RS providing for the intolerance of living together as a subjective element.[43] Divorce proceedings are initiated by a divorce lawsuit as regulated in all three laws. In the Federation of BiH, spouses can also apply for a consensual divorce.[44] It is based on the consensual will of the spouses to divorce them, and may be used by all spouses, regardless of whether it is a childless marriage or a marriage with children over which the parents exercise parental care. On the other hand, the PZ RS regulates the possibility of consensual divorce and divorce by joint application, and the difference is reflected in the fact that the possibility of consensual divorce is limited to marriages without children, and divorce by joint application is

[35] Marital prohibition is a circumstance whose existence at the time of marriage does not result in the annulment of the marriage, but it only delays the conclusion of the marriage while it exists.

[36] Art. 37 PZ RS, art. 27 PZ BDBH.

[37] Art. 14 par. 2 PZ FBH, art. 35 par. 2 PZ RS, art. 25 par. 2 PZ BDBH.

[38] Art. 35 par. 3 PZ RS.

[39] Art. 15 par. 2 PZ FBH, art. 36 par. 2 PZ RS, art. 26 par. 2 PZ BDBH.

[40] Art. 36 par. 3 PZ RS.

[41] Art. 36-38 PZ FBH, arts. 34-36 PZ BDBH.

[42] Art. 49 PZ RS.

[43] Art. 41 PZ FBH, Art. 52 PZ RS, art. 39 PZ BDBH.

[44] Art. 42 PZ FBH.

available in case of marriage with children over whom parents exercise parental care.[45] The PZ BDBH knows only of a consensual application for divorce if the spouses have joint minor or adopted children or children over whom parental rights have been extended.[46,47]

2.2 *Matrimonial Property*

Generally, in the family legislation in Bosnia and Herzegovina, the community of property regime has been accepted as the default matrimonial property regime, but there are differences in terms of terminological and legal definition of property of spouses. The PZ FBH calls the property of marital partners the matrimonial property (*bračna stečevina*), the PZ BDBH the marital property (*bračna tekovina*), and the PZ RS uses the term of the property of spouses (*imovina bračnih supružnika*). Matrimonial property in the PZ FBH and marital property in the PZ BDBH are, by their legal nature, co-ownership in equal parts,[48] while according to the PZ RS, the property of spouses is, by its legal nature, joint property.[49] The RS's Rights *In Rem* Act defines joint ownership as: "Ownership of two or more persons (joint ventures) on the same thing whose shares are not determined but are determinable."[50] The PZ RS determines the shares in the joint property of the spouses, one half each.[51]

Although it seems that the solutions adopted in the PZ FBH and the PZ RS, with regard to the part belonging to the spouses (equal parts/shares and one half each) are identical, there are still significant differences. Unlike the PZ FBH and the PZ BDBH, the PZ RS provides that each spouse may request the court to determine that a larger part of the joint property belongs to him or her, if he or she proves that his or her contribution to the acquisition of joint property is obviously greater than the contribution of the other spouse.[52] According to this provision, there is a rebuttable legal presumption in the PZ RS that each spouse owns one half in their joint property. The court will determine the size of the spouse's share according to his or her contribution to the joint property, taking into account not only the personal income and earnings of each spouse, but also the assistance of one spouse to another, household and family work, taking care of and upbringing of children, as well as any

[45] Art. 54 i 55 PZ RS.

[46] Art. 40 PZ BDBH.

[47] On divorce in BiH see more in: Duraković (2016), pp. 174–178.

[48] Art. 252 par. 1 PZ FBH, art. 229 par. 1 PZ BDBH.

[49] Art. 270 par. 3-6 PZ RS.

[50] Rights *In Rem* Act RS (Official Gazette RS No. 124/08, 95/11), art. 43 par 1.

[51] Art. 272 par. 1 PZ RS. See more in: Radić (2016), pp. 177–252.

[52] Art. 273 par. 1 PZ RS.

other form of work and cooperation in the management, maintenance and increase of joint property.[53]

While the PZ FBH and the PZ BD do not regulate the possibility of allocating property that serves personal needs, personal belongings of the spouse, property for the profession, or property for which one of the spouses would have a personal interest, the PZ RS stipulates that when dividing the joint property, the spouse's share will primarily include items that are used to perform his or her profession. Also included in the spouse's share are things acquired through work during the marital union that serve exclusively his or her personal use. If the value of the listed items is disproportionately high in relation to the value of the entire joint property, the spouse who should receive the above items has two options: to compensate the other spouse for the appropriate value or to cede other items to the other spouse. Failure to do so will result in the division of these items as well as other joint property.[54]

Spouses are given the possibility of regulating marital and property relations through a marriage contract. The marriage contract in Bosnia and Herzegovina was first regulated by the PZ RS in 2003, and subsequently in the PZ FBH in 2005 and in the PZ BDBH in 2007. With the 2008 amendments to the PZ RS, the standardization of the marriage contract in the family legislation in Bosnia and Herzegovina makes is almost equal in all territorial entities.[55] With regard to the choice of applicable law for a marriage contract, the autonomy of the spouses is limited. Spouses cannot agree on the application of the law of another state to property relations.[56] This provision is interpreted in a way to apply in the case when both spouses are citizens of Bosnia and Herzegovina.[57]

2.3 *Parental Responsibility*

The regulation of the relationship between parents and children is based on the principles guaranteed by the constitution and international instruments—the principle of protection of children, respect for private and family life, prohibition of discrimination and the principle of equality of parents. In accordance with these principles, the basic rule in all three family acts is that the contents of parental care are exercised by the parents jointly, by agreement and on an equal footing.[58] The

[53] Art. 273 par. 2 PZ RS.

[54] Art. 274 PZ RS.

[55] Regarding the marriage contract, the PZ RS Civil Code contained a provision by which the marriage contract is certified by a court or a notary. It follows that the contract could have been drawn up by a lawyer or the spouses themselves and the court or notary would have only certified the marriage contract. Unlike PZ RS, according to PZ FBH marriage contract must be notarized. With the amendments to the PZRS from 2008, the solution from the PZ FBH was taken over.

[56] Art. 260 PZ FBH, art 271 par. 7 PZRS-e, art. 237 PZ BDBH.

[57] See more in: Alihodžić and Krešić (2014), pp. 441–443.

[58] Art. 141 PZ FBH; art. 85 PZRS; art. 124 par. 1 PZ BD.

definition of parental care in BH legislation is, however, not uniform. The differences that exist in the applicable laws are terminological and essential in nature. Thus, in the PZ FBH and the PZ BDBH the term "parental care" (*roditeljsko staranje*) was accepted, and in the PZ RS the term "parental right" (*roditeljsko pravo*). Parental care is explicitly regulated as a set of responsibilities, duties and rights of parents that they have in order to protect the personal and property rights of the child.[59] On the other hand, the PZ RS does not contain an explicit definition of parental rights, but only regulates the equality of mother and father in terms of exercising parental rights and duties, and parents' exercise of parental rights by agreement.[60]

The principle of joint, consensual and equal care for the personal and property rights of the child is not exercised in the same way when the child's parents live together and when they no longer live together or when such a union has never been established. When parents live together, parental care is, as a rule, exercised without the intervention of the competent authorities (a court or guardianship authority).[61] In the event that there is no consensus between the parents on the exercise of parental care despite the fact that they still live together, acting in the interest of the child, the legislator prescribed the possibility of intervention by the competent authorities. Thus, according to the PZ FBH, if there is a dispute between parents about parental care, the decision is made by the court in a non-litigious procedure at the application by the parent, the child who is able to understand the meaning and legal consequences of their actions, or guardianship authority in whose territory the child has his or her domicile. Conversely, according to the PZ RS and the PZ BDBH, this matter is decided by the guardianship authority.[62] The exercise of parental care in Bosnia and Herzegovina in the case of a separate life of the parents, can be defined as joint[63] and individual. According to the PZ FBH, the court will, as a rule, always opt for joint parental care, except in cases where it is contrary to the best interests of the child.[64] In the PZ RS and the PZ BDBH, the issue of exercising parental care in the case of separate life of parents is regulated somewhat differently. Namely, the basic rule is that parental care/right is exercised by the parent with whom the child lives, i.e., in case of divorce and annulment of marriage, the parental right is exercised by the parent to whom the child is entrusted for protection and upbringing.[65] The PZ

---

[59] Art. 129 PZFBH; art. 122 par. 1 PZBD.

[60] Art. 85 PZ RS.

[61] Korać Graovac (2017), pp. 56.

[62] Art. 85 par. 2 PZRS and 124 par. 3 PZ BDBH. The PZ RS regulates only the actual and not the territorial competence of the guardianship authority, while the PZ BDBH explicitly regulates that it is the guardianship authority in the place of child's domicile.

[63] The introduction of the model of joint parental care in our legislation is a consequence of the implementation of the child's right to live with both parents, which is a prerequisite for the realization of the full range of other children's rights. See more in: Radić (2014), pp. 103–106.

[64] Art. 142 par. 3 PZ FBH.

[65] Art. 86 par. 2 and 3 PZ RS, art. 125 PZ BDBH.

FBH and the PZ BDBH introduce special new duties: taking care of a child, meeting his or her normal needs and protection from all forms of vice such as drugs, alcohol, vagrancy, robbery, theft, prostitution, begging, as well as all forms of juvenile delinquency, and violence, injury, economic exploitation, sexual abuse and all other antisocial phenomena.[66] Regarding the care of education, parents are, according to the PZ FBH and the PZ BDBH, obliged to take care of regular primary and secondary education of the child, and if possible, his or her higher education,[67] while the duty of parents under the PZ RS is limited to regular primary education and only if possible, to further education.[68]

There are also certain differences in the legal status of minors. All three family acts state that full legal capacity is acquired at the age of majority—18, or by marriage before coming of age. PZ FBiH and PZ BDBH provide the possibility of acquiring legal capacity to a minor over the age of 16 who has become a parent.[69] Furthermore, there are differences in the age for limited legal capacity. While PZFBH and PZBDBH prescribe that a minor acquires limited legal capacity at the age of 14,[70] The PZ RS does not adopt the division of minors according to the degree of legal capacity, hence it can be concluded that all minors are legally incapable and cannot act independently in legal transactions.[71] The PZ FBH states that a minor who has reached the age of 14 may enter into legal transactions by which he or she acquires rights, while a minor may enter into transactions with which he or she disposes of property or assumes obligations only with the consent of his or her parents.[72] In the PZ RS in this case the minimum age is 15 years,[73] and in the PZ BDBH 16.[74]

2.4 *Maternity and Paternity*

All three family acts are on the same footing about the main rule for maternity and paternity: the child's mother is the woman who gave birth to him or her,[75] and the father is the husband of the child's mother.[76]

---

[66] Art. 134 par. 2 PZ FBH, art. 117 par. 2 PZ BDBH.

[67] Art. 136 par. 2 and 3 PZ FBH, art. 119 par. 2 and 3 PZ BDBH.

[68] Art. 83 par. 2 and 3 PZ RS.

[69] Art. 157 par. 3 PZ FBH, art. 139 par. 3 PZ BDBH.

[70] Art. 157 par. 5 PZ FBH, art. 139 par. 5 PZ BDBH.

[71] The act regulates the obligations and rights of parents to represent their minor children (art. 84 para. 1 PZRS), i.e., authorizes the guardian to represent the ward (art. 92 PZRS), and to conclude legal transactions in his name and on his behalf (art. 203, par, 1 PZRS).

[72] Art. 137 par. 2 PZ FBH.

[73] Art. 84 par. 3 PZ RS.

[74] Art. 120 par. 3 PZ BDBH.

[75] Art. 53 PZ FBH, art. 109 par. 1 PZ RS, art. 49 PZ BD.

[76] Art. 54 PZ FBH, art. 109 par 2 PZ RS, art. 50 par. 1 PZ BD.

There are some differences, however, with regard to the paternity of a child born in the mother's later marriage. The PZ FBH stipulates that if a child is born in a later marriage of the mother, but before the expiration of 300 days from the termination of her previous marriage, the husband of the mother from a later marriage will be considered the child's father.[77] The PZ RS stipulates, however, that if a child is born in a later marriage of the mother, but before the expiration of 270 days after the termination of the previous marriage, the husband of the mother from the previous marriage will be considered the child's father, unless the husband of the mother from the later marriage, upon to her consent, acknowledges the child.[78] The PZ BDBH does not specifically regulate this situation.

Furthermore, the registration of paternity acknowledgment in the birth register requires the consent of a child older than 14 years according to the PZ FBiH,[79] or 16 years according to the PZ RS and the PZ BD BiH.[80] The right of a child to file a lawsuit to establish paternity and maternity is not limited in time according to the PZFBH,[81] while the PZ RS and the PZ BDBH provide for a deadline—up to 25 years of age of the child.[82] All three family acts give the right to file this lawsuit to the guardianship authority, but the deadlines within which this right can be exercised are different. The PZ FBH and the PZ BDBH provide that this lawsuit can be filed until the child reaches 18 years of age,[83] while the PZ RS sets the period of 1 year after the birth of the child if the mother has indicated before the registrar a man, whom she considers to be the father of the child.[84]

2.5 Maintenance

All three family acts stipulate that mutual support of marital and extramarital partners, parents and children and other relatives is their duty and right.[85] There are certain differences regarding the persons who may take the role of the maintenance debtor and the manner this duty is realized.

Thus, the maintenance of a minor child from grandparents is explicitly regulated by the PZ FBH and the PZ BDBH,[86] while the PZ RS does not have explicit provisions on mutual support of grandparents and grandchildren, but the provisions

---

[77] Art. 54 par. 2. PZFBH. Read more in: Bubić and Traljić (2007), pp. 34–37.

[78] Art. 109 par. 4. PZRS.

[79] Art. 63 PZFBH.

[80] Art. 119 par. 1 PZ RS, art. 52 par. 3 PZ BD.

[81] Art. 72 PZFBH.

[82] Art. 123 par. 1 PZ RS and art. 60 PZ BD.

[83] Art. 72. PZ FBH and art. 64 PZBD.

[84] Art. 125 PZ RS.

[85] Art. 213 PZ FBH, art. 231 PZ RS, art. 192 PZ BDBH.

[86] Art. 222 par. 1 PZFBH and art. 201 par. 1 PZBDBH.

on maintenance between other relatives in the direct line apply to this obligation,[87] When a minor child cannot realize the right to parental support, this duty, according to the PZ FBH and the PZ BDBH, burdens the stepmother or stepfather under certain conditions, regardless of whether the child has other blood relatives who are able to support him,[88] while according to the PZ RS this duty of stepmother or stepfather is subsidiary not only in relation to the child's parent but also in relation to other blood relatives who are obliged by law to support him.[89] Termination of incomplete (simple) adoption results in the termination of mutual rights and duties of the adopter and the adoptee.[90] The exception is provided only in relation to the mutual obligation of maintenance in the PZ FBH and the PZ BDBH. The obligation of the adopter to support the adoptee even after the termination of adoption will exist if the adoptee is a minor and has no blood relatives who are obliged by law to support him or are unable to support him and can last up to 1 year from the termination of adoption.[91] There is a difference in family legislation regarding the relatives who are under certain conditions obliged to support an adult relative for the purpose of regular schooling. According to the PZ FBiH and the PZ BDBH, in addition to parents, this obligation exists only for grandparents.[92] In Republika Srpska, the legislator opted for a solution according to which the obligation to support an adult child who is in regular schooling is exclusively that of the parents.[93]

Maintenance in all cases is determined according to the abilities of the debtor and the needs of the creditor.[94] The general active presumption (presumption on the part of the maintenance creditor) is standardized as incapacity for work, i.e., inability to find employment, lack of sufficient means of maintenance or inability to earn them from one's own property.[95] According to the general rule on the manner of determining maintenance in the PZ FBiH and the PZ BDBH, the court has to oblige the maintenance debtor to pay future monthly amounts of support expressed in a specified amount of money.[96] The PZ RS stipulates that maintenance is determined as a percentage or as a fixed amount if the income is earned abroad, provided that the percentage cannot be less than 15% for each creditor, and the percentage for all persons seeking support cannot exceed 50%.[97] If the maintenance debtor does not

[87] Art. 239 PZ RS.

[88] Art. 220 par. 1 PZ FBH, art. 199 par. 1 PZ BD.

[89] Art. 237 par. 1 PZ RS.

[90] Termination of incomplete adoption and its effects are regulated by the provisions of arts. 120-123 PZ FBH, arts. 171-173 PZ RS and arts. 103 and 104 PZ BDBH.

[91] Art. 122 par. 1 and 3 PZ FBH; art. 105 par. 1 and 3 PZ BDBH.

[92] Art. 222 par. 1 PZ FBH, art. 201 par. 1 PZ BDBH.

[93] Art. 233 par. 1 in relation to art. 239 PZ RS.

[94] Art. 214 PZ FBH, art. 232 par. 1 PZ RS, art. 193 PZ BDBH.

[95] See for example: art. 219 par. 1 and art. 224 PZ FBH; art. 236 par. 1 and art. 241 PZ RS; art. 198 par. 1 and art. 203 PZ BDBH.

[96] Art. 244 PZ FBH, art. 221 PZ BDBH.

[97] Art. 261 PZ RS.

receive income, the court will order payment of future monthly maintenance in specified amounts of money determined as a percentage of guaranteed personal income in Republika Srpska,[98] while under the PZ FBH the court seized with the maintenance proceedings will take into account the data published by the Federal Minister of Labor and Social Policy concerning the average needs of the person requesting maintenance, given the cost of living.[99]

2.6 *Adoption*

All three family acts differentiate between two types of adoption: full and incomplete (simple).[100] Certain differences are present in terms of the conditions for establishing adoption. Under the PZ FBH and the PZ BDBH, a child cannot be adopted before the expiration of three months from his or her birth, and if it is a child of minor parents, it can be adopted after 1 year after the birth if he or she is unlikely to be raised in families of parents or other close relatives.[101] Under the PZ RS, there is no minimum age limit, but from the provision of Art. 3 of the Instructions of the Ministry of Health and Social Welfare on the procedure of adoption of children[102] it may be concluded, by extensive interpretation, that at least 40 days must elapse from the day of the child's birth.[103] According to the PZ FBH and the PZ BDBH, the maximum age limit for adoptees is 10 years, while in the Republika Srpska only a child up to the age of five can be fully adopted.[104] In case of incomplete adoption, the FBH and the BDBH provide that a child up to the age of 18 may be adopted, if the child is older than 10 and if he is able to understand the meaning of adoption, his or her consent is required.[105] There are no such provisions in the RS PZ.

Regarding the eligibility on the part of the adopter, the PZ FBH and the PZ BDBH are uniform in prescribing that the adopter can only be a person aged between 25 to 45 and who is at least 18 years older than the adoptee (with certain exceptions).[106] Under the PZ RS, there is no age limit for an adopter, but it is required that the adopter is at least 18 years older than the adoptee.[107] According to the PZ FBiH and the PZ BDBH, in case of full adoption, besides the spouses jointly and stepmother or stepfather of the child being adopted,[108] extramarital partner who

[98] Art. 260 par. 2 PZ RS.

[99] Art. 235 par. 4 PZ FBH.

[100] Art. 91 par. 2 PZ FBH, art. 149 PZ RS, art. 76 par. 2 PZ BDBH.

[101] Art. 94 PZ FBH, Art. 79 PZ BDBH.

[102] Official Gazette RS, br. 27/2004.

[103] Read more in: Šaula (2010), p. 59.

[104] Art. 157. PZ RS.

[105] Art. 103. PZ FBH, Art. 87. par. 1. i 2. PZ BDBH.

[106] Art. 96 PZ FBH, Art. 81 PZ BDBH.

[107] Art. 151 par. 2 PZ RS.

[108] Art. 102 par. 1 PZ FBH, Art. 158 PZ RS, Art. 86 par. 1 and 2 PZ BDBH.

has been living out of wedlock with the child's parent for at least 5 years is also are eligible as adoptive parent.[109] In the case of incomplete adoption, the range of persons who can adopt is much wider: spouses who jointly adopt, one spouse with the consent of the other, the stepmother or stepfather of the adopted child, an unmarried person and extramarital partners living in an extramarital relationship lasting at least 5 years.[110] Such a possibility is not envisaged in the PZ RS. The PZ FBH and the PZ BDBH impose an obligation on adoptive parents to inform the child that he or she has been adopted, with the Federation of BH specifying that this should be no later than when the child reaches the age of seven, or immediately after the adoption, if the child is older than that age.[111] Such an obligation is not prescribed by PZ RS.

3 Internal Conflict of Laws of Bosnia and Herzegovina Before Domestic Authorities

In a situation where one family relationship is connected with several territorial units in Bosnia and Herzegovina, the issue of choosing the applicable law is raised. The problem of interstate conflict of laws in Bosnia and Herzegovina is regulated by ZRSZN. It contains rules for resolving conflicts of laws in the field of personal status, family law and succession between the territorial entities, i.e., between cantonal laws or the law of the Brcko District of BH, and the laws of another entity or canton.[112] The rules of the ZRSZN refer to the law of the territorial unit that is to be applied in the case of a private law relationship that is connected to either two or all three territorial units, such as divorce of a FBH citizen and a RS citizen before he authorities of the Brčko District of BH. The ZRSZN also applies in situations with an element external to Bosnia and Herzegovina, which are resolved by domestic authorities, when the national choice of law rule refers to the law of Bosnia and Herzegovina as applicable.[113] Therefore, issues of relationship between choice of law rules for international cases, on the one hand, and choice of law rules for internal cases, on the other, may arise in the process of determining the applicable substantive law.

From a nomotechnical perspective, there is no difference between the ZRSZN and the Bosnian and Herzegovinian PIL Act: choice of law rules in both acts have a typical structure consisting of a legal category and a connecting factor. However, there is a difference in among the selected connecting factors. In the field of personal status, family relations and succession, the ZRSZN takes the *lex domicilii* as the

[109] Art. 102 par. 2 PZ FBH, Art. 86 par. 3 PZ BDBH.

[110] Art. 104. PZ FBH, Art. 87. par. 3 and 4 PZ BDBH.

[111] Art. 92 par. 2 PZ FBH, Art. 77 PZ BDBH.

[112] Art. 1 ZRSZN.

[113] Art. 2 ZRSZN.

basic connecting factor, whereas the *lex nationalis* appears as a subsidiary solution.[114] The notion of "domicile" is defined in the same way by the law of Bosnia and Hercegovina and the law of the Republika Srpska, hence the issue of qualification does not arise. Domicile is located in the municipality or district in which a citizen resides with the intention of living there permanently.[115] Citizenship, as a subsidiary criterion, is regulated by the Constitution of BH,[116] the Citizenship of BH Act,[117] the Citizenship of the Federation of BH Act,[118] and the Citizenship of the RS Act.[119] The basic principle is that all persons who have the citizenship of Bosnia and Herzegovina, also have the citizenship of one of the entities.[120] In order to solve the problem of dual entity citizenship, entity laws stipulate that by acquiring new entity citizenship, the previous entity citizenship is lost *ex lege*.[121]

There is, however, lack of regulations in the Brcko District of BH because this territorial unit does not envisage special citizenship, in addition to citizenship of Bosnia and Herzegovina, for its citizens; they have the right to choose (and change) among the entity citizenships.[122] Citizens of Bosnia and Herzegovina domiciled in the Brcko District of BH acquire the citizenship of one of the entities, either on the basis of law or upon request of their choice.[123] This means that citizenship, as a connecting factor in the interstate conflict of laws in Bosnia and Herzegovina, will never refer to the family law of the Brcko District of BH. Only entity family laws (the PZ FBH and the PZ RS) can be applied based on this connecting factor. The right to choose and change entity citizenship opens the door wide to circumventing the law, i.e., the fraudulent behavior of the parties. It is possible that a well-informed party chooses another entity citizenship with the intention of assuring the application of one entity's laws instead of those that would otherwise be applicable if no change had taken place. These facts call into question the justification of entity citizenship as a connecting factor. Therefore, *de lege lata,* some authors advocate against application of entity citizenship as a connecting factor, stating that although this creates

[114] Such choice of the then SFRY legislator was quite logical, given that accepting citizenship as the basic connecting factor would have had meant exclusion of the possibility to apply two out of eight legislations in the former SFRY, because there was no provincial citizenship (in Vojvodina and Kosovo), and citizenship as a connecting factor would never indicate the law of one of these two provinces. Varadi (1987), p. 363; Blagojević and Puhan (1974), pp. 235–236. There is a similar situation within BH, because there is no citizenship of the Brčko District of BH.

[115] Art. 3 par. 7 of the Domicile and Residence of BH Citizens Act, Official Gazette of BiH, no. 32/2001, 56/2008, 58/2015. and Art. 4. of the Residence and Stay of Citizens Act, Official Gazette of RS, no. 53/93, 67/93, 48/94, (17/99, 33/99).

[116] Art. I, point. 7 Anex 4 to the General Framework Agreement for Peace in BH.

[117] Official Gazette BH, No., 22/2016 – consolidated text.

[118] Official Gazette FBH, No. 34/2016 i 98/2016 – correction.

[119] Official Gazette RS, No. 59/2014.

[120] Art. I/7 a) BiH Constitution.

[121] Meškić (2017), p. 66.

[122] Art. 12 par. 2 Part II Statute BD BiH.

[123] Art. 30 Citizenship of BH Act, Art. 28 Citizenship of FBH Act, Art. 30 Citizenship of RS Act.

legal uncertainty, it leads to the application of *lex fori* as a solution that is justified because it satisfies the closest connection principle and the principle of equality of laws that might be applied.[124] In addition, the internal procedural rules on territorial jurisdiction contained in the three acts allow for several alternative fora, and the parties can easily avoid the application of otherwise applicable law by seizing the court in another territorial unit. This opens up opportunities for unwarranted forum shopping. Furthermore, choice of law rules for internal cases rely to a much greater extent than those for international case on the *lex fori* as a connecting factor or some other decisive connection which leada to the same result. However, the *fraus legis* as a reason for evading the application of law is not sanctioned by internal conflict of law rules.[125] The ZRSZN also excludes the *renvoi,* which presupposes the existence of not only more substantive systems but also more choice of law systems of the same rank, and has no importance in the case of establishing unified choice of law rules for all legal areas. Finally, the public policy clause is also left out.[126] The reason is that as much as the substantive solutions may differ among territorial units, those in one territorial unit cannot be in conflict with the basic principles of the legal order of another territorial unit because the laws of territorial units must be harmonized with the basic principles set by the Constitution of Bosnia and Herzegovina.

In the context of family relations, the applicable law is primarily related to the domicile/common domicile/last common domicile of the person(s), and secondarily to the citizenship/common citizenship of the territorial unit in case the person does not have domicile/common domicile/last common domicile in the territory of Bosnia and Herzegovina. This rule is for material conditions to conclude the marriage of the citizen of Bosnia and Herzegovina;[127] personal and property relations of marital partners;[128] divorce;[129] the relationship between parents and children;[130] maintenance between relatives;[131] deprivation, extension or return of parental care;[132] establishing or disputing paternity or maternity;[133] adoption[134] and placing a person under guardianship.[135]

---

[124] Meškić (2017), op. cit. p. 69. See also: Meškić et al. (2018), p. 639.

[125] The reasons that led the legislator against the introduction of *fraus legis* as a general institute, relate to the fact that the differences between individual legislations were not so great, because all legislations were subject to federal law and that due to high mobility of population, change of residence is not always motivated by fraud so re-examining the newly created connecting factors would seriously undermine legal certainty. Varadi (1975), p. 91.

[126] Relevant to this point is that Savigny considered that *ordre public* was not necessary in interstate context. Von Savigny (1849), p. 34.

[127] Art. 13 ZRSZN.

[128] Art. 16 ZRSZN.

[129] Art. 18 ZRSZN.

[130] Arts. 21 and 22 ZRSZN.

[131] Art. 26 ZRSZN.

[132] Art. 27 ZRSZN.

[133] Art. 28 ZRSZN.

[134] Arts. 29 and 30 ZRSZN.

[135] Art. 33 ZRSZN.

As a subsidiary solution, in the event that the applicable law cannot be applied under the above connecting factors, limited party autonomy is available in certain cases. The parties may choose the applicable law among the entity laws for the form of marriage, when the marriage is concluded before the diplomatic-consular mission of Bosnia and Herzegovina abroad,[136] and for personal and property relations of spouses who have neither a common domicile nor a common entity citizenship.[137]

A possible alternative is to apply the *lex fori*. Besides, the *lex fori* as a connecting factor gets a very prominent place in the ZRSZN. Pursuant to Art. 6 of the ZRSZN, *lex fori* (the law of the territorial unit whose authority has jurisdiction to decide the case) is applied in all cases in which the ZRSZN (or another act) does not determine the applicable law. The *lex fori* appears, not only as a subsidiary connecting factor, but also as a rule for certain issues of personal status, family relations and succession. In addition to this provision of a general nature in Art. 6, the application of the law of the territorial unit to which the competent authority hearing the case belongs or before which the relationship is established or has been established in the past is explicitly prescribed for form of marriage;[138] personal and property relations of spouses of different entity citizenship and domicile in the impossibility of reaching an agreement on the choice of applicable law;[139] personal and property relations of spouses, one of whom is a foreigner;[140] divorce of the marriage concluded abroad, if the spouses have neither a common domicile nor the common entity citizenship;[141] divorce where one or both spouses are foreigners.[142]

The ZRSZN takes into account substantive fairness, opting in certain cases for the application of more favorable law. Thus, for relations between parents and children, if they do not have common entity domicile or common citizenship, the applicable law will be that of the territorial unit in whose territory the domicile of the parent or child is located, or the law of the territorial unit of which the parents or child is a national, if that law is more favorable to them.[143] The application of more favorable law is also envisaged in the matter of maintenance between parents and children—the applicable law is the law of the territorial unit in whose territory the children or parents are domiciled or the law of the territorial unit whose citizen is the maintenance creditor.[144]

The set system of choice of law rules in the ZRSZN seems closer to the solutions in the EU than those in the Private International Law Act in Bosnia and Herzegovina. In a situation where choice of law rule refers to the law of Bosnia and Herzegovina,

[136] Art. 15, par. 2 ZRSZN.
[137] Art. 16 par. 2 and 3 ZRSZN.
[138] Art. 15 par. 1 ZRSZN.
[139] Art. 16, par. 3 ZRSZN.
[140] Art. 17 ZRSZN.
[141] Art. 19 ZRSZN.
[142] Art. 20 ZRSZN.
[143] Art. 22 par. 3 ZRSZN.
[144] Art. 23 ZRSZN.

and it concerns a foreign citizen or a stateless person, the ZRSZN provides solutions for certain family matters. As a rule, the law of the territorial unit in whose territory the person has domicile/common domicile applies (e.g., conclusion of marriage,[145] divorce,[146] relations between parents and children,[147] deprivation, extension or return of parental rights,[148] establishing or disputing paternity and maternity,[149] adoption,[150] and placing under guardianship[151]), and in the absence of domicile, it will be the *lex fori* in cases of marriage, divorce or adoption.

4 Internal Conflict of Laws of Bosnia and Herzegovina Before Foreign Authorities

When a foreign choice of law rule refers to the law of Bosnia and Herzegovina as a whole, a foreign authority may encounter a dilemma in determining the applicable substantive law that would regulate a particular family relationship because Bosnia and Herzegovina, as a state, consists of several territorial units, each of which is competent to independently regulate the family law matters. Thus, the foreign authority will have to select among three legal systems for family law, which as explained above differ in many aspects.

In doing so the foreign authority will first of all be bound by its own legal system in selection of the general principle which applies in these situations: the one-step principle according to which direct choice is made by a choice of law rule that refers to a state with more than one legal system, or the two-step principle which refers to internal choice of law rules of the foreign country. The one-step principle prevails in the doctrine, except in the case when the law of a state with more than one legal system is referred to by the choice of law rule, which uses nationality as a connecting factor.[152] This is well illustrated by looking at these situations from the perspective of the EU regulations on family matters, which approach this problem in two ways depending on whether the reference is made by means of connecting factor capable of territorial anchoring or nor, the latter being nationality.

The Rome III Regulation[153] accepts the one-step system for connecting factors capable of indicating exact territorial unit: any reference to the law of a state with

[145] Art. 14 ZRSZN.

[146] Art. 20 ZRSZN.

[147] Art. 24 ZRSZN.

[148] Art. 27 par. 2 ZRSZN.

[149] Art. 28, paragraph 2 ZRSZN.

[150] Art. 30 ZRSZN.

[151] Art. 33, par. 2 ZRSZN.

[152] Muminović (2006), p. 91.; Varadi et al. (2003), p. 178.; Jezdić (1980), p. 19.

[153] Council Regulation (EU) No 1259/2010 of 20 December 2010 implementing enhanced cooperation in the area of the law applicable to divorce and legal separation, Official Journal of the European UnionL 343/10, 29. 12. 2010.

more than one legal system is interpreted as a reference to the law in force in the respective territorial unit, and any reference to habitual residence in a state with more than one legal system is interpreted as a reference to habitual residence in a territorial unit. However, when reference is made to the nationality of the state with more than one legal system the Rome III Regulation employs the two-step principle: the situation is resolved, first by the internal conflict of law provisions of the state with more than one legal system, and only in the absence of such provisions, the choice of territorial unit is left to the parties, and in the absence of such a choice the closest connection principle applies. In the last described situation, the reference is made to the law of the territorial unit with which both parties or one of them is most closely connected.[154]

If referring to the law of Bosnia and Herzegovina as the applicable law, and given the division of competencies to legislate private law relations there, and the exclusion of *renvoi*, the result is the following: any reference to the law of Bosnia and Herzegovina refers to substantive family law in force in one of the two entities or the district (the PZ FBH, the PZRS or the PZ BDBH) and any reference to habitual residence in Bosnia and Herzegovina refers to habitual residence in the entity or district in which the habitual residence is located in a particular case. In fact, the one-step principle is suitable for application in all situations of territorial conflict of laws, except when reference to the law of a state with more than one legal system is made my means of nationality.[155] Thus, only in the case of nationality as a connecting factor will the ZRSZN be applied.

The one-step principle can cause certain problems if the parties have chosen the applicable law.[156] For instance, if the parties have chosen Spanish law as the applicable law, and not the law of a certain territorial unit within it, the question arises whether the chosen law should be "saved" by taking the law of the territorial unit within Spain with which it has the closest connection or to neglect the voluntary choice of law and to reach for objective connecting factors. The answer to this question may depend on the facts on which the chosen law is based. If the parties have chosen as applicable the law of the state of the court, then only the law of the territorial unit in which the court is located will be applicable. In the case of the choice of the law of the state of their habitual residence, the applicable law shall be that of the territorial unit in which both have their habitual residence. If their habitual residence is in different territorial units, voluntary choice becomes inoperative.[157] In the context of Bosnia and Herzegovina as a state to which the reference is made by means of choice of law clause, the choice of law of the state of which the parties are nationals may be problematic if the parties do not have the common entity nationality within Bosnia and Herzegovina. In such instances, the exact the territorial unit whose law is to be applied could be resolved by the internal conflict of law

[154] Art. 14. Council Regulation (EU) No 1259/2010.

[155] Stanivuković and Živković (2008), pp. 317, 320.

[156] See art. 5 of the Council Regulation (EU) No 1259/2010.

[157] Mayer (2019), pp. 736–738.

provisions in Bosnia and Herzegovina, i.e., the ZRSZN. If, on the contrary, the parties choice of law of Bosnia and Herzegovina would prove ineffective, objective connecting factors should be resorted to,[158] taking into account the fact that the parties need to know exactly the legal and social consequences of the chosen applicable law.[159]

The Regulation on the Matrimonial Property Regime,[160] the Regulation on the Property Consequences of Registered Partnerships[161] and the Maintenance Protocol[162] accept the two-step principle as primary one, which means that the internal choice of law rules of the state with more than one legal system determine the territorial unit whose law applies.[163] In the absence of these internal rules, the one-step principle applies.[164]

Given the scope of the rules in the ZRSZN, the determination of applicable law in family matters is left to its provisions whenever Bosnia and Herzegovina is referred to in general by nationality as a connecting factor. The ZRSZN solves the described problems in such a way that if the law of another state indicates that the rights and obligations of a national of Bosnia and Herzegovina should be regulated according to the law of Bosnia and Herzegovina, applicable is the law of the territorial unit in whose territory he or she is domiciled. In the absence of a domicile, the law of the entity of which he or she is a national becomes applicable.[165] This provision refers only to the nationals of Bosnia and Herzegovina. Situations when a foreign choice of law provision refers to the law of Bosnia and Herzegovina, in a situation when a foreign citizen whose status is being disputed before a foreign court has domicile or habitual residence in Bosnia and Herzegovina, remains out of its reach. In this situation, it is possible to apply only the one-step principle, since there are no internal conflict of law rules governing this issue.

---

[158] See the same opinion in: Basedow (2011), p. 33; Hau (2013), p. 255.

[159] Preamble, point 18. of the Council Regulation (EU) No 1259/2010.

[160] Council Regulation (EU) 2016/1103 of 24 June 2016 implementing enhanced cooperation in the area of jurisdiction, applicable law and the recognition and enforcement of decisions in matters of matrimonial property regimes, Official Journal of the European Union L 183/1, 8. 7. 2016.

[161] Council Regulation (EU) 2016/1104 of 24 June 2016 implementing enhanced cooperation in the area of jurisdiction, applicable law and the recognition and enforcement of decisions in matters of the property consequences of registered partnerships, Official Journal of the European Union L 183/30, 8. 7. 2016.

[162] Council Decision of 30 November 2009 on the conclusion by the European Community of the Hague Protocol of 23 November 2007 on the Law Applicable to Maintenance Obligations, Official Journal of the European UnionL 331/17, 16. 12. 2009. Pogledati: Explanatory Report by Bonomi (2013), p. 36. Read more in: Geuenich (2017), pp. 252–255.

[163] Art. 33. par. 1. Council Regulation (EU) 2016/1103, art. 33. par. 1. Council Regulation (EU) 2016/1104, čl. 16. Protocol.

[164] Art. 33. par. 2. Council Regulation (EU) 2016/1103, art. 33. par. 2.Council Regulation (EU) 2016/1104.

[165] Art. 3 ZRSZN. As stated above, the citizens of the Brcko District of BH have the nationality of one of the other two entities.

5 Conclusion

The complex state system of Bosnia and Herzegovina and the constitutional division of legislative competences when it comes to private law relations result in a multi-layered legal system in family matters. On the substantive level, the family matters are regulated by three family acts: the PZ FBH, the PZ RS and the PZ BDBH. Comparison among the provisions contained in these acts reveals significant terminological and, more importantly, substantial differences in regulation of certain family law institutes. This in turn leads to an internal conflict of laws. In a situation where one family law relationship is connected with several territorial units in Bosnia and Herzegovina, the domestic authority needs to determine the applicable law.

The rules of internal conflict of laws in Bosnia and Herzegovina are contained in the ZRSZN. In the field of personal status, family relations and succession, the ZRSZN uses as primary connecting factor the *lex domicilii*, while the *lex nationalis* appears on a subsidiary level. Given that the citizens of the Brcko District of BH may have the nationality of one of the other two entities, nationality as a connecting factor in the internal conflict of laws in Bosnia and Herzegovina will never refer to the family law of the Brcko District of BH, but only to the family law of FBH or RS. This coupled with the right to choose and change entity nationality, opening the door to *fraus legis*, raises questions as to the justification of entity nationality as a connecting factor. Therefore, some authors argue for the non-application of entity nationality as a connecting factor in favor of the application of the *lex fori* considering that justified by the closest connection principle and the principle of equality among legal systems. Furthermore, the ZRSZN takes into account material justice, opting in certain cases for the application of more favorable law. Taken on the whole, the system of choice of law rules in the ZRSZN is closer to the solutions in the EU than those in the Bosnian and Herzegovinian PIL Act.

When a foreign choice of law provision refers to the law of Bosnia and Herzegovina as a state with more than one legal system, the foreign authority encounters a problem of determining the law of which territorial unit within Bosnia and Herzegovina should apply to a particular family matter. The solution depends on which of the two generally accepted principles is accepted by foreign legislation. If the one-step principle is given preference, reference to the law of Bosnia and Herzegovina would lead to the substantive family law in force in one of the two entities or the district (FBH, RS or BDBH). Any reference to habitual residence in Bosnia and Herzegovina shall relate to habitual residence in one of the two entities or the district. In short, the one-step principle is suitable for application in all situations of territorial conflict of law, except when reference to the law of a state with more than one legal system is made through nationality as a connecting factor. Only in the case of nationality as a connecting factor will the ZRSZN be called in action.

If the parties have chosen the law of Bosnia and Herzegovina as applicable, and not the law of a certain territorial unit within it, the application of the law may depend on the facts on which the party autonomy is based. If the parties have chosen the law of the state of the court or the law of domicile or habitual residence, the law of the territorial unit of the court or domicile or habitual residence, respectively, will apply. The choice of the law of the state of which the parties are nationals, but who do not have a common entity nationality, can be problematic. In such a case, the choice is left to the internal conflict of law rules in the ZRSZN. However, if parties' choice is not effective, objective connecting factors should apply, taking into account the fact that the parties need to know exactly the legal and social consequences of the chosen applicable law. In states that accept the two-step principle, the choice of applicable law is left to the internal conflict of law rules of the state concerned, and in the absence of these rules, the one-step principle applies. In the context of Bosnia and Herzegovina, this would mean that the determination of applicable law in particular case is subject to the provisions in the ZRSZN. The ZRSZN applies only to the rights and obligations of the nationals of Bosnia and Herzegovina and refers to the law of the territorial unit in whose territory the national has his or her domicile, and in the absence of domicile, to the law of the entity of which he or she is a national. Situations when a foreign conflict of law rule refers to the law of Bosnia and Herzegovina as a whole, and which concern a foreign citizen with domicile or habitual residence in Bosnia and Herzegovina, remain outside the ZRSZN's reach. Then, it is possible to apply only the one-step principle, given the absence of internal conflict of law rules on the issue.

References

Alagić D (1971) Rešenja unutrašnjih sukoba zakona u uporednom zakonodavstvu, Godišnjak PF u Sarajevu, pp 57–78

Alihodžić J (2012) Razvoj evropskog međunarodnog privatnog prava: pravci reforme zakonodavstva u Bosni i Hercegovini, pp 219–221

Alihodžić J, Begić Z (2013) Pravne pretpostavke za reformu međunarodnog privatnog prava u Bosni i Hercegovini, Zbornik radova s Međunarodne naučne konferencije Pravni i ekonomski aspekti procesa integracije BiH u EU, Mostar, pp 335–353

Alihodžić J, Krešić B (2014) Interlokalni sukob zakona u oblasti imovinskih odnosa bračnih partnera u Bosni i Hercegovini: Osvrt na buduća komunitarna koliziona pravila, Zbornik radova sa II Međunarodne konferencija Bosna i Hercegovina i Euroatlanske integracije. Bihać:439–454

Basedow J (2011) Das internationale Scheidungsrecht de EU, Anmerkungen zur Rom III – Verordnung, Borić, T., Lurger, B., Schwarzenegger, P., Terlitz, U., Öffnung und Wandel – Die internationale Dimension des Rechts II, FS für Willibald Posch, Wien, pp 29–54

Blagojević B (1973) Regulisanje sukoba republičkih odnosne pokrajinski zakona sa zakonima drugih republika odnosno pokrajina. Pravni život br. 1:5–23

Blagojević B, Puhan I (1974) Teze i obrazloženje na Nacrt Zakona o sukobu zakona i sukobu nadležnosti u unutrašnjem pravu SFRJ. Naša zakonitost br. 2:223–243

Bonomi A (2013) Protocol of 23 November 2007 on the Law Applicable to Maintenance Obligations, Explanatory Report, Edited by the Permanent Bureau of the Conference, The Hague, Netherlands

Bubić S, Traljić N (2007) Roditeljsko i starateljsko pravo, Sarajevo

Duraković A (2016) Međunarodno privatno pravo razvoda braka u Europskoj uniji i Bosni i Hercegovini, Mostar

Geuenich B (2017) Die Bestimmung des andwendbare Recht in Falle des internationaleprivatrechtlicen Verweisung auf einen territorialen Mehrrechtsstat, Tübingen
Hau W (2013) Zur Durchführung der Rom III – Verordnung in Deutschland. FamRZ 4:247–259
Jezdić M (1980) Međunarodno privatno pravo I, Beograd
Jezdić M, Pak M (1982) Međunarodno privatno pravo III, Beograd
Korać Graovac A (2017) Od zajedničkog do samostalnog ostvarivanja roditeljske skrbi i natrag – kako zaštititi prava djece i roditelja, Godišnjak Akademije pravnih znanosti Hrvatske, vol. VIII, posebni broj, 2017, Akademija pravnih znanosti Hrvatske, Zagreb, pp 51–73
Mayer O (2019) Parteiautonomie bei Mehrrechtsstaaten. RabelsZ 83:722–759
Meškić Z (2017) Rješenje unutrašnjeg (interlokalnog) sukoba zakona u građanskopravnim stvarima u BiH s obzirom na nepostojanje državljanstva Brčko Distrikta, Zbornik radova sa XII Savjetovanja iz oblasti građanskog prava, Bistrica, 18. – 21. okobar, pp 61–75
Meškić Z, Duraković A, Alihodžić J (2018) Bosnien und Herzegowina als ein Mehrrechtsstaat. IPRax 6:633–642
Muminović E (1999) O uzajamnom odnosu načela najuže veze, autonomije volje i favorabilnosti mjerodavnog prava u vezi s potrebom zakonodavnog djelovanja države Bosne i Hercegovine u materiji međunarodnog privatnog prava. Godišnjak Pravnog fakulteta u sarajevu, Sarajevo, pp 229–242
Muminović E (2006) Međunarodno privatno pravo, Sarajevo
Radić D (2014) Najbolji interes djeteta i pravo djeteta da živi sa roditeljima, Zbornik radova Dani porodičnog prava "Najbolji interes djeteta u zakonodavstvu i praksi", Pravni fakultet Univerziteta "Džemal Bijedić" u Mostaru, Mostar, pp 100–114
Radić D (2016) Imovinski odnosi u braku, Banja Luka
Šaula V (2008) Osnovi međunarodnog privatnog prava Republike Srpske, Banja Luka
Šaula V (2010) Unutrašnji sukob zakona u materiji porodičnog prava u Bosni i Hercegovini, Godišnjak Pravnog fakulteta Univerziteta u Banja Luci, br. 31/32:49–67
Stanivuković M, Živković M (2004) Međunarodno privatno pravo – opšti deo, Beograd
Stanivuković M, Živković M (2008) Međunarodno privatno pravo – opšti deo, Službeni glasnik, Beograd
Traljić N, Bubić S (2007) Bračno pravo, Sarajevo
Varadi T (1975) Međunarodne i unutrašnje kolizione norme, Beograd
Varadi T (1987) Međunarodno privatno pravo, Novi Sad
Varadi T, Bordaš B, Knežević G (2003) Međunarodno privatno pravo, Novi Sad
Von Savigny FC (1849) System des heutigen römischen Recht VIII, Berlin

Applicative Problems Regarding the Turkish Certificate of Succession

Zeynep Derya Tarman

1 Introduction

A Certificate of Succession is defined as a certificate of authority, which is given by the court of peace[1] or notary upon the request of the heirs, and which enables the heirs to have actual dominance over the estate values by proving their title of heirship and thus to dispose of the rights in the estate.[2] Although the Certificate of Succession is essentially requested through non-contentious jurisdiction, it is also possible to request it through a contentious jurisdiction. In this regard, the document given as a result of contentious jurisdiction is called a final court judgment. In this paper, the Certificate of Succession *involving a foreign element* requested through non-contentious jurisdiction will be examined.

In practice, there are cases where a Certificate of Succession is needed by a Turkish citizen as well as a non-Turkish citizen residing in Turkey or those who do not reside in Turkey for various reasons. Determining the competent authority to grant a Certificate of Succession requested by those who do not reside in Turkey is a debated issue under Turkish law. International jurisdiction to granting a Certificate of Succession is a controversial issue in the Turkish doctrine. Additionally, certain issues arise also with regards to the law applicable to succession in the case of a same-sex marriage. The fact that same-sex marriage is regulated in various legal systems, but neither under Turkish substantive law nor under the Turkish Private

[1]There are different kinds of civil courts which can be classified as peace courts (*sulh hukuk mahkemesi*), basic civil courts (*asliye hukuk mahkemesi*) and specialised courts.

[2]Serozan and Engin (2021), p. 477; Kocayusufpasaoğlu (1987), p. 580.

Z. D. Tarman (✉)
Koç University Law School, Istanbul, Turkey
e-mail: ztarman@ku.edu.tr

I. Kunda et al. (eds.), *Balkan Yearbook of European and International Law 2022*, Balkan Yearbook of European and International Law 2022,
https://doi.org/10.1007/978-3-031-29432-7_2

International Law and Procedural Law Act[3] (PILA), may result in the surviving spouse not being recognized as a legal heir under the Certificate of Succession. Finally, the Certificate of Succession involving a foreign element may also prove to raise issues in the recognition and enforcement proceedings under Turkish law. Where a Certificate of Succession is obtained from a foreign judicial or administrative authority, it may not be recognized in Turkey due to it not being a final decision. On the other hand, the recognition of the parts of a Certificate of Succession relating to immovable properties in Turkey is not possible as Turkish courts have exclusive jurisdiction on rights *in rem* relating to immovable properties in Turkey.

After briefly dwelling on the legal nature of the Certificate of Succession, the abovementioned issues will be elaborated upon, starting with the courts in Turkey which are competent to issue the Certificate of Succession in a case with a foreign element. The focus will then shift to the issue of determining the applicable law in the issuance of a Certificate of Succession. Lastly, the questions related to recognition of Certificate of Succession issued by a foreign authority will be examined in particular regarding the condition for the recognition under Turkish law and their consequent legal effect in Turkey.

2 Certificate of Succession in Turkish Law

This chapter contains brief account of the legal nature of the Certificate of Succession in Turkish law and discusses authorities competent to issue such certificate.

2.1 Definition and Legal Nature of a Certificate of Succession

According to the Turkish Civil Code[4] (hereinafter: TCC), art. 575, death, absence or presumed death of a natural person, triggers the opening of the succession and the estate is determined according to this moment. In accordance with art. 599 of the TCC, as a rule, the heirs of the deceased shall be entitled to the whole of the estate *ipso jure* without the need to make any declarations as to acceptance. Although the heirs jointly own the estate, in order for the heirs to transact with third parties and to prove that they have the right to dispose of the rights in the estate, they need to obtain the Certificate of Succession defined in art. 598 of the TCC.[5] A Certificate of Succession is the document showing the legal heirs of the deceased and the respective shares of these persons.[6] This document is given to the heir upon his or her

[3] OG 4 February 2011 No.27836.

[4] OG 22 November 2002 No.24607.

[5] Baran-Çelik (2019), p. 442; Serozan and Engin (2021), pp. 477–478.

[6] Antalya and Sağlam (2015), p. 346.

request. While not being in the nature of a finalized decision, the Certificate of Succession still enables the heirs—by proving their title—to obtain actual dominance over the movables and to acquire the registry possession and right to disposal over the immovables.[7] Under Turkish law, the persons who have the right to request a Certificate of Succession are legal and appointed heirs. In addition, under certain conditions, the creditors of the legator or heir, the testator and the land registry office may have a right to demand a Certificate of Succession as well.[8]

In Turkish law the Certificate of Succession is a document that allows the heir to prove his or her title as a heir and constitutes the presumption of the existence of the right of inheritance, but the contrary can always be claimed and proven.[9] Since the decisions regarding the issuance of the Certificate of Succession do not constitute a final decision, the invalidity of this document can always be claimed.[10] For these reasons, the succession documents are considered as a mere presumption of the heir's title until contrary is proven in a legal procedure. In other words, a Certificate of Succession given in a non-contentious jurisdiction does not determine the title of heir in terms of substantive law in a definitive way. On the other hand, a Certificate of Succession given through a contentious jurisdiction constitutes a final judgment in material terms and carries the nature of a final decision, along with its effects.

2.2 *Competent Authorities to Issue a Certificate of Succession*

2.2.1 The Courts and/or Notaries

In Turkish law, the competent authorities in issuing a Certificate of Succession are regulated under art. 598 of the TCC. In 2011, the law was changed (see art. 598, par. 1 of the TCC), and, in addition to the civil courts of peace, notaries have now also been authorized to issue this document,.[11] According to the relevant regulation of Notary Act[12] regarding the notaries' authority to issue a Certificate of Succession, the notary public shall examine the population records and determine whether the person concerned is a legal heir upon such request.[13] However, the right to request a Certificate of Succession from a notary is reserved for Turkish citizens only. In accordance with Article 71/B of the Notary Act, notaries are not authorized to issue a Certificate of Succession requested by foreigners. For this reason, foreigners can

---

[7] Serozan and Engin (2021), p. 489; Kocaağa (2005), p. 85.

[8] Ruhi (2014), pp. 14–15. Serozan and Engin (2021), p. 477.

[9] Antalya and Sağlam (2015), p. 443; Serozan and Engin (2021), p. 479.

[10] Antalya and Sağlam (2015), p. 350; Serozan and Engin (2021), p. 479.

[11] Serozan and Engin (2021), p. 478.

[12] OG 5 February 1972 No. 14090.

[13] Serozan and Engin (2021), p. 478.

only request the Certificate of Succession from the courts of peace.[14] There is also a similar provision to the one mentioned in art. 37 of the Land Registry Act. According to this provision, the transfer of ownership procedures for foreigners are regulated in accordance with the Certificate of Succession issued by the courts. Although the Notary Act and the Land Registry Act makes a distinction between the courts and notaries as competent authorities based on the requestee being a Turkish or a non-Turkish citizen, the relevant regulation on the application of Notary Act regulates this issue slightly differently and restricts the authority of the notaries to a greater extent. Accordingly, the art. 5 of the Regulation on the Issuance of a Certificate Succession[15] excludes the notary publics from the authority to issue certificates of succession not only where the requestee is a non-Turkish citizen but in all cases where the succession involves a foreign element. However, under the principles of Turkish constitutional law, a regulation cannot introduce a rule that restricts the rights granted under an act. Hence, the Land Registry Act and the Notary Public Act should be taken as a basis with regards to the authority of the notaries in issuing a Certificate of Succession.[16] Nevertheless, as the restriction regarding the notaries' competence to issue a Certificate of Succession is broader under the said Regulation compared to the relevant acts itself, this may cause hesitations with regards to the determination of the competent authority in making a request for a Certificate of Succession in practice.

The instances in which the applicant is a Turkish citizen, but the case involves a foreign element, render the competence of the notaries as controversial. For example, where the deceased is a foreign citizen or where certain other heirs have a foreign nationality—even if the requestee is a Turkish citizen—the competence of the notaries can be challenged if the Regulation is considered. On the other hand, if the heir requesting a Certificate of Succession has multiple nationalities, one of which is a Turkish nationality, their right to request a Certificate of Succession from the notaries becomes also dubious. Under Turkish law, if a Turkish citizen also holds a foreign nationality, Turkish citizenship will be taken as the basis in relation to the "determination of the applicable law". [17] However, due to the expression used under the relevant Regulation which deprives the notaries from issuing certificate of "succession involving foreign elements", in the current practice the heirs are prevented from applying to notaries for the issuance of certificates of succession in any case involving a foreign element.[18]

[14] Şanlı et al. (2021), p. 633.

[15] OG 04 October 2011 No. 28074.

[16] The fact that this provision narrows the applicability of the rule stipulated in art. 71/B of the Notary Act is criticized under the Turkish doctrine, see: Şanlı et al. (2021), p. 496; Çelikel and Erdem (2021), p. 633.

[17] Çelikel and Erdem (2021), p. 68; Şanlı et al. (2021), p. 37.

[18] On the website of the Notaries Union of Turkey, the instances where the Certificate of Succession cannot be given by the notaries are listed. Accordingly, one of the instances where a Certificate of Succession cannot be given by the notaries is listed as the case where the descendent or any of the

Pursuant to art. 28 of the Turkish Citizenship Act,[19] those who are Turkish citizens by birth but renounce their Turkish citizenship by obtaining permission to leave, their descendants up to the third degree shall continue to benefit from the same rights granted to Turkish citizens, except for the exceptions listed in the article in an exhaustive manner. Since the rights of inheritance are not listed among the exceptions in this article, those who are Turkish citizens by birth and renounce their Turkish citizenship by obtaining permission to leave will be able to benefit from their rights of inheritance just as the Turkish citizens. These persons in terms of their legal status are also categorized as "blue card holders" named after the blue card they receive showing their special status. According to some opinions in the doctrine, since blue card holders have the right to benefit from rights of inheritance, just like Turkish citizens, they have the right to request a Certificate of Succession from a notary.[20] However, another view in the doctrine emphasizes that blue card holders cannot request a Certificate of Succession from notaries due to their status of a foreigner (albeit a special one) as a consequence of renouncing their Turkish citizenship.[21] In addition, where a blue card holder requests a Certificate of Succession from a notary, since the succession would involve a foreign element, these persons shall also be required to make a request to the court if the abovementioned Regulation is relied on. It is submitted here, however, that it is not possible for blue card holders to request a Certificate of Succession from a notary, for a more practical reason: their birth records being closed when they lose their Turkish citizenship.

Hence, when a foreigner needs to obtain a Certificate of Succession, request shall be directed to the court of peace by a single heir or several heirs without naming an adverse opponent. As stated above, a decision by a court on the issuance of a Certificate of Succession does not constitute a final decision.[22] On the other hand, the Certificate of Succession can also be subjected to a contentious jurisdiction, where the annulment of the Certificate of Succession or its re-issuance is requested. In such proceedings, since the previously granted Certificate of Succession does not

---

heirs has more than one citizenship; see: Turkish Notaries Union, (https://portal.tnb.org.tr/Sayfalar/MirascilikHiz.aspx).

[19] OG 12 June 2009 No. 27256.

[20] Baran-Çelik (2019), pp. 493–494. A similar discussion is made with regards to the blue card owners and the foreigner-specific security deposit obligation pursuant to art. 48 of the PILA. For the view that blue card holders should not be considered as foreigners and should be exempted from the foreigner-specific security deposit obligation pursuant to art. 48 of the PILA, see: Acun-Mekengeç (2017), pp. 28–29.

For a decision by the 8th Civil Chamber of the Court of Cassation stating that it is possible for blue card holders to obtain a Certificate of Succession from a notary public, see: 8th Civil Chamber of the Court of Cassation Case no. 2014/15452, Decision no. 2014/16450 Date: 19.09.2014 (Lexpera).

[21] Altınkaya (2020), pp. 70 ff. In addition, on the website of the Turkish Notaries Union, the legator or any of his/her heirs having renounced their Turkish citizenship is listed among the instances where the Certificate of Succession cannot be granted by the notaries, see: Turkish Notaries Union, (https://portal.tnb.org.tr/Sayfalar/MirascilikHiz.aspx).

[22] Dursun (2020), p. 194; Şanlı et al. (2021), p. 641.

constitute a final decision, it cannot be raised as a final decision objection but may constitute a discretionary evidence before Turkish courts.[23] Additionally, in the case of annulment or re-issuance of the Certificate of Succession, the jurisdictional rules determining the competent court are separate from the issuance of the Certificate of Succession for the first time in a non-contentious jurisdiction, and are determined according to art. 11, par. 3 of the Turkish Code of Civil Procedure [24] (hereinafter: TCCP).

2.2.2 Competent Courts in Issuing the Certificate of Succession Involving a Foreign Element

Although notaries competence to issue the Certificate of Succession is controversial when such certificate is requested by blue card holders or persons with multiple nationalities one of which is a Turkish nationality, the notaries are competent as the courts are to issue a Certificate of Succession not involving a foreign element.[25] However, if the heirs or the legator are connected to a foreign country, the foreign element in the proceedings for requesting the Certificate of Succession would mean that the courts are exclusively competent to issue the Certificate of Succession.

The determination of the competent court may vary depending on whether the Certificate of Succession issued in a case involving a foreign element is subject to contentious or non-contested proceedings. In Turkish law, the Certificate of Succession is a document that is requested from the court without naming an adverse opponent and is given as a result of non-contentious jurisdiction (art. 382, par. 2 of the TCCP).[26] Under art. 383 of the TCCP, the competent court in non-contentious jurisdiction matters is the civil court of peace. In accordance with art. 384 of the TCCP, among the courts of peace within Turkey, the competent court for a non-contentious proceeding is the peace court situated at the place where the person requesting the document or one of the interested parties resides. In addition, if there is an objection during the issuance of the Certificate of Succession, or if there is a request for the re-issuance or annulment of the Certificate of Succession and the issuance of a new Certificate of Succession, this will be subjected to the contentious jurisdiction. Hence, the jurisdictional rules to determine the competent court for the issuance of a Certificate of Succession involving a foreign element based on the

[23] Çelikel and Erdem (2021), p. 801; Şanlı et al. (2021), p. 641. However, in order to be considered as discretionary evidence, the document must contain an Apostille annotation in accordance with The Hague Convention Abolishing the Requirement of Legalization for Foreign Public Documents, or it must be approved by the Turkish consulate in accordance with art. 244/p.1 of the TCCP.

[24] OG 4 February 2011 No. 27836.

[25] There is a foreign element in cases where there is an issuance of testamentary disposition in a foreign country; the deceased or heirs are foreigners; the requestee's domicile or habitual residence is situated in a foreign country; the presence of some or all of the property in relation to the succession is situated in a foreign country.

[26] Serozan and Engin (2021), p. 478.

contentious and those based on the non-contested proceedings vary. Since the focus of this paper is the Certificate of Succession with a foreign element issued in a non-contentious jurisdiction, the issuance of the Certificate of Succession through a contentious jurisdiction will not be examined, unless where relevant in relation to the topic in the focus.

In international procedural law, the rules of jurisdiction are the rules that determine whether the courts of a particular state are competent to resolve a dispute involving a foreign element. In Turkish law, the international jurisdiction of Turkish courts is regulated under the PILA. The PILA envisages special rules of jurisdiction with regards to specific issues under its arts. 41–46. The disputes that do not fall within the scope of application of the PILA special rules of jurisdiction, the general rule for international jurisdiction is applied which is specified under art. 40 of the PILA. Accordingly, where there are no special rules, the rules of domestic law determining the jurisdiction will be applied as the general rule for international jurisdiction.[27]

It is controversial in the doctrine whether art. 43 of the PILA—on the jurisdiction of Turkish courts in cases relating to succession—or art. 40 of the PILA—on the general international rule of jurisdiction leading to the application of the Turkish domestic civil procedure rules of jurisdiction—will be applicable in proceedings following the request for a Certificate of Succession involving a foreign element. According to some, art. 40 of the PILA has to be taken into account in determining the international jurisdiction of Turkish courts. According to this view, art. 43 of the PILA by its title "succession cases" indicates that it is only applicable in contentious proceedings. As the request for a Certificate of Succession is a non-contentious proceeding, it shall not fall under the application of art. 43 of the PILA. Hence, the competent authority must be determined according to PILA art. 40 which triggers the application of the rules of the domestic civil procedure in the issuance of a Certificate of Succession, i.e., art. 384 of the TCCP.[28] Accordingly, the peace court of the place of residence where the person requesting the Certificate of Succession (or one of the relevant persons resides) will be the competent court in these proceedings. On the other hand, the opposing view is that art. 43 of the PILA shall be applied in all matters related to succession, including matters subject to non-contentious jurisdiction.[29] Accordingly, pursuant to art. 43 of the PILA, the court of the last place of residence of the deceased in Turkey, if the last place of residence is not in Turkey,

[27]Çelikel and Erdem (2021), p. 566; Şanlı et al. (2021), pp. 389–390.

[28]Çelikel and Erdem (2021), pp. 631, 632; Şanlı et al. (2021), p. 495; Tekinalp (2020), p. 411; Doğan (2022), p. 67; Can and Tuna (2019), p. 125; Özkan and Tütüncübaşı (2020), p. 85; Akıncı (2020), p. 142; Bilkay (2021), pp. 905–929.

[29]Ekşi (2013), p. 28; Güngör (2021), p. 249; Tanrıbilir (2018), p. 129. For the opinion of the Court of Cassation regarding the Certificate of Succession see 14th Civil Chamber of the Court of Cassation Case/Decision no. 1997/6013, Date: 01.06.2015, (lexpera.com.tr.) "*The international jurisdiction of Turkish courts in succession cases with a foreign element is regulated under Article 43. Accordingly, the cases related to the succession can be heard in the court of the last place of residence of the deceased in Turkey, and in case the last place of residence is not in Turkey, the*

the court of the place where the assets included in the estate are located will have international jurisdiction. Art. 43 of the PILA is a cascading rule, hence, the jurisdiction of the court of the place where the assets included in the estate are located will only arise if the deceased does not have his or her last place of residence in Turkey.

It is submitted here that, although the title of art. 43 of the PILA explicitly refers to "succession cases", this provision should not be interpreted to be applicable to contentious proceedings only, but should determine the jurisdiction of Turkish courts for all succession matters involving a foreign element. In addition, there is no rule of jurisdiction regulating particularly the issuance of a Certificate of Succession. Therefore, the competent court for issuing a Certificate of Succession should also be determined according to art. 43 of the PILA as for all other succession matters.

Besides, if applied in the proceedings of Certificate of Succession, art. 40 of the PILA would often prove unworkable, such as when a person making the request (or the persons concerned) is not a Turkish resident. In such situations it would be impossible to establish a competent court in Turkey based on art. 40 of the PILA. To illustrate the point, a person residing abroad requests a Certificate of Succession before the Turkish courts, with reference to art. 40 of the PILA. The jurisdiction of Turkish courts would be determined according to art. 384 of the TCCP, according to which, "[u]nless the law provides otherwise, the court of the place where the person making the request for non-contentious judicial works or one of the relevant persons resides is competent." Therefore, if the person who is requesting the Certificate of Succession does not reside in Turkey, a competent court cannot be established in Turkey according to this provision. On the other hand, when the art. 43 of the PILA is relied on as a ground for jurisdiction, even in the case where the last place of residence of the deceased is not Turkey, competence of a Turkish court would be established, in the location of the assets included in the estate.

3 The Law Applicable to the Certificate of Succession Involving a Foreign Element

The Certificate of Succession is a document that names the heirs and their respective shares in the estate. When a Certificate of Succession involving a foreign element is requested from a Turkish court, the law applicable to the issuance of the Certificate of Succession will be determined according to the PILA as discussed below. However, particular challenges are posed when a deceased spouse was in a same-sex marriage.

---

court of the place where the assets which are included in estate is located is authorized, therefore, the judgment has to be annulled.".

3.1 *Special Rule in the PILA*

When a Certificate of Succession involving a foreign element is requested from a Turkish court, the law applicable to the issuance of the Certificate of Succession will be determined according to art. 20 of the PILA.[30] According to this provision, succession shall be governed by the national law (*lex nationalis*) of the deceased. In determining the law applicable to succession relations with a foreign element, legal systems have evolved in two branches. While one division subjected movable and immovable properties to separate laws, the other division subjected the estate, as a whole, to a single law.[31] The latter system is also known as the "unitary system" and is accepted under Turkish law as well, according to which the estate as a whole is subject to a single law under art. 20, par. 1 of the PILA.[32] Accordingly, the national law of the deceased governs the law applicable to succession. Since the determination of the respective shares is also subject to the succession status, the law to be applied to the respective shares will be determined according to art. 20, par. 1 of the PILA. Nevertheless, the second sentence of art. 20, par. 1 envisages an exception to the 'unitary system' by stating that Turkish law will be applied to the immovables in Turkey. Hence, if the deceased is a foreign citizen and leaves immoveable assets in Turkey, the Turkish judge will apply two separate laws when issuing the Certificate of Succession. The national law of the deceased will be applied to all estates other than immovables located in Turkey, and Turkish law will be applied to immovables located in Turkey.

While determining the applicable law pursuant to art. 20, par. 1 of the PILA, art. 4, par. 1 subpar. (b) should also be considered. Where the deceased has more than one nationality, one of which is a Turkish nationality, his or her Turkish nationality will prevail, and Turkish law will apply as the national law, regardless whether the deceased had a closer connection with his foreign nationality. Hence, Turkish law will be applicable in the issuance of a Certificate of Succession in all cases in which the deceased has more than one nationality, one of which is Turkish. Pursuant to art. 4, par. 1 subpar. (c) of the PILA, for those who have more than one nationality neither of which is Turkish, the nationality of the state with which they have the closest relationship will prevail, and the law of that state will govern the issuance of the Certificate of Succession as the applicable law.

When issuing the Certificate of Succession, determination of the statutory heirs, their respective shares, property falling within the scope of the estate, the causes and consequences of disinheritance, and reserved shares are subject to the law provided by art. 20, par. 1 of the PILA.[33] Although the nationality of the heirs is irrelevant to determining the respective shares, the restrictions imposed by the foreigners' law in terms of immovable ownership rights in Turkey should be taken into account. There

[30]Çelikel and Erdem (2021), p. 345; Şanlı et al. (2021), p. 265 et al.; Tekinalp (2020), p. 236.

[31]Çelikel and Erdem (2021), p. 346; Şanlı et al. (2021), p. 264.

[32]Çelikel and Erdem (2021), p. 346; Şanlı et al. (2021), p. 264; Ekşi (2014), p. 122.

[33]Süral (2016/2017), p. 373.

are certain restrictions regarding the acquisition of immovable property by a foreign person in Turkey. Accordingly, pursuant to art. 35 of the Land Registry Act, the President determines the which country's citizens have the right to acquire immovables in Turkey. In addition, the Military Forbidden Zones and Security Zones Act envisages certain restrictions in terms of the location of the immovable property which a foreigner can acquire. As a matter of fact, in many of its decisions, the Court of Cassation has ruled that under the Certificate of Succession it is essential to specify whether the foreign heirs can acquire immovables in the estate or not, taking into account the rules of the Turkish Foreigners Act.[34]

In contrast to the substantive elements of the Certificate of Succession, naming the legal heirs of the deceased and their respective shares in accordance with the law determined by art. 20, par. 1 of the PILA, the Certificate of Succession is subject to the law of the court issuing it (*lex fori*) with regards to its formal validity.

3.2 Death of a Spouse in a Same-Sex Marriage

In succession cases involving a foreign element particularly challenging is the situation of determining the succession rights following the death of a spouse in a same-sex marriage. Although, same-sex marriages have been legally accepted and regulated in many legal systems either with or without registration, the absence of provisions under both Turkish substantive law and conflict of laws rules together with the strict approach to the public policy exception result in the invalidity of same-sex marriages from a Turkish legal perspective, whilst such marriages are most probably recognized as valid in terms of the foreign law applied to marriage.[35]

Where one of the spouses dies in a same-sex marriage, the surviving spouse's request for a Certificate of Succession in Turkey brings in legal problems as the validity of that marriage constitutes a preliminary issue in the issuance of the Certificate of Succession. Although there is no consensus under the Turkish doctrine as to how to determine which law governs the preliminary issue, one view favors the conflict of laws rules of the court where the main issue is being heard (*lex fori*), whilst the other prefers the conflict of laws rule that governs the main issue to be tried (*lex cause*).[36]

Where the *lex fori* principle is preferred in terms of determining the applicable law to the preliminary issue, the preliminary issue shall be handled independently of the law applicable to the issuance of Certificate of Succession. There is no special conflict of laws rule governing the material validity of a same-sex marriage under the PILA. However, taking into account the interests of the parties, it would be an appropriate to apply by analogy the conflict of laws rule for marriage, i.e., art.13 of

[34] Şanlı et al. (2021), p. 264, fn. 300; Ekşi (2014), p. 123.

[35] Tarman (2021), p. 318.

[36] Çelikel and Erdem (2021), p. 133; Şanlı et al. (2021), pp. 105–106.

the PILA. In accordance with art. 13, par. 1 of the PILA, marriage capacity and the conditions of marriage are subject to the national law of each spouse at the time of marriage. Since the marriage conditions sought under Turkish law require the parties to be of different sexes, the same-sex marriage made by Turkish nationals will be materially invalid under Turkish law. On the other hand, since the validity of the marriage of, for instance, two Dutch citizens will be subjected to Dutch law pursuant to art. 13, par. 1 of the PILA, it should be accepted that there is a valid marriage between two Dutch citizens unless the public policy clause prevents the implementation of the authorized foreign law.

Where the principle of *lex causae* is preferred in terms of the applicable law to the preliminary issue, the validity of the marriage will be determined in accordance with the law applicable to the main issue, in other words to the issuance of the Certificate of Succession. In this case, regarding the movable properties, if the national law of the deceased has legalized same-sex marriages, there will be a materially valid marriage. Nevertheless, Turkish public policy might still be raised as a ground in terms of the validity of the marriage. In case the deceased is a foreign citizen and leaves immovable in Turkey, the Turkish court will apply Turkish law in accordance with art. 20, par. 1 of the PILA and this will result in the invalidity of the same-sex marriage and in the surviving spouse not being recognized as a potential legal heir.

It is submitted here that, in the above example in which following the death of one of spouses who are Dutch citizens, the property of the decedent is located in Turkey and there is a valid same-sex marriage according to the national laws of each spouse at the time of marriage, the Certificate of Succession requested by the surviving spouse from Turkish authorities should recognize him or her as the potential heir (unless the applicable law indicates otherwise for other reasons). However, in case the deceased is a foreign citizen and leaves immovable property located in Turkey, the Turkish court will apply Turkish law in accordance with art. 20, par. 1 of the PILA. Since same-sex marriage is not regulated under Turkish law and the surviving spouse will not be recognized as an heir. The same consequences may occur in determining the law applicable to succession regarding the movable properties of the deceased foreign person, since even if the national law of the deceased person entitles the Turkish spouse as an heir, the public policy exception as stipulated under art. 5 of the PILA can present an obstacle to that. Pursuant to art. 5 of the PILA, the application of a provision of the law of any state specified by the PILA may be refused if such application is manifestly incompatible with the Turkish public policy and, if necessarily, Turkish law shall be applied. Hence, where a same-sex marriage is valid in accordance with the applicable foreign law, Turkish law might still prevail rendering such marriage invalid if it is considered that recognizing the validity of a same-sex marriage is manifestly contrary to Turkish public policy. In this case, the surviving spouse cannot be an heir. When the interests of the parties are considered and the intervention of public policy is considered an exceptional tool only, the institution of same-sex marriage should not constitute a violation of Turkish public policy.[37] On the other hand, if the national law of the deceased is Turkish law, the marriage will be invalid since Turkish family law requires them to be of different sexes as a condition of marriage. As a result, the surviving foreign spouse will not be considered an heir where the national law of the deceased is Turkish law.

If a foreigner dies and leaves no heirs behind, the Turkish State is the last heir for estates located in Turkey pursuant to art. 20, par. 3 of the PILA.

4 Recognition of Certificates of Succession Issued in Foreign Countries

The legal effect of a court decision is limited to the country in which they were granted. For this reason, in order for a decision granted by a foreign state court to be valid in Turkey, it must either be recognized and/or enforced depending on the nature of the decision.[38] Recognition of the foreign court judgments means recognition of the *res judicata* effect of that judgment in Turkey.[39] Therefore, these decisions have no execution effect. For a foreign court judgment which is not subject to enforcement such as declaratory judgments, or judgments about formative rights, a recognition decision shall suffice. On the other hand, an enforcement decision grants the foreign judgment an execution force in Turkey. Foreign court decisions ordering something to be done, not to be done, or to be given, are subjected to enforcement proceedings[40] as these decisions have the ability to be enforced, therefore, they must be executed separately in order to satisfy the plaintiff.[41] Finally, an enforcement decision also includes the recognition, as enforcement means that both the execution force and the *res judicata* effect of that judgment are accepted in Turkey.

4.1 Relevant Legal Sources

The recognition and enforcement of foreign court judgments in Turkey have been regulated under art. 50 and so forth of the PILA. However, Tukey is party to a number of bilateral and multilateral agreements dealing with the recognition and enforcement rules that provide for a facilitated procedure.[42] Pursuant to art. 90 of the

[37] Ekşi (2014), p. 130.
[38] Çelikel and Erdem (2021), p. 711; Şanlı et al. (2021), p. 620.
[39] Çelikel and Erdem (2021), pp. 623, 713; Şanlı et al. (2021), p. 620.
[40] Çelikel and Erdem (2021), pp. 624, 625, 713; Şanlı et al. (2021), p. 620.
[41] Çelikel and Erdem (2021), pp. 624, 625, 713; Şanlı et al. (2021), p. 620.
[42] Ekşi (2014), p. 136.

Turkish Constitution and art. 1, par. 2 of the PILA, the provisions of international agreements to which Turkey is a party shall prevail over the national rules on the matters that fall under their scope. In this context, the Consular Agreement between Turkey and Germany regarding the recognition of the Certificate of Succession[43] is significant. Article 17 of the Agreement reads as follows: "A document issued by a competent authority of the State of which the testator is a citizen in accordance with the law of succession and in particular the law of the heirs or the executor of the will, shall suffice to prove this law for the movable estate in the other state." According to one view, this provision has been interpreted that this article should be understood to refer to the Certificate of Succession, granted in accordance with the German legal procedure, and which shall be accepted as evidence in terms of movable properties when a request is made from the Turkish courts for the Certificate of Succession.[44] However, other believe the this article shall be interpreted as to refer to the Certificate of Succession issued by the German authorities but recognized under Turkish law in terms of movable properties included in the estate.[45] Along with the said discussions in interpreting this article, and considering the Turkish population living in Germany, the doctrine points out the need to update the text of the agreement, along with the it also the clarify of such provisions, whilst the text of the agreement should be adapted to contemporary Turkish language.[46]

It is important to note that there are two other consular agreements containing similar provisions on recognition and the jurisdiction of Turkish courts regarding Certificates of Succession: art. 16 of the Consular Agreement between Turkey and Poland dated 31 May 1927 and art. 21 of the 2nd chapter of the Consular Agreement between Turkey and Italy dated 7 April 1931.[47]

4.2 *Recognition Under the PILA*

Recognition of a foreign Certificate of Succession before Turkish courts involves legal issues that require particular attention. Since the Certificate of Succession is a decision that only determines the heirs and their distributive shares, it does not have an execution force and hence shall be subjected to recognition.[48] For this reason, in order for the decisions regarding the Certificate of Succession taken from a foreign court to be effective in Turkey, they must be recognized by a Turkish court. It is important to note that art. 58, par. 2 of the PILA, highlights that the foreign court

[43] Official Gazette, no. 1514, 8 June 1930.

[44] For the view that the Agreement does not allow the recognition of the certificates of succession, see: Nomer (2021), p. 552.

[45] Bilkay (2021), p. 910 ff.

[46] Bilkay (2021), p. 910.

[47] For detailed information, see Bilkay (2021), p. 910.

[48] Çelikel and Erdem (2021), p. 801.

decisions in non-contentious proceedings shall produce effects in Turkey also subject to their recognition.

The provisions of the PILA regarding the enforcement proceedings are also applicable in recognition proceedings except for the condition set forth under art. 54(a) concerning reciprocity. Accordingly, in order for a recognition decision to be made, the prerequisites stated in art. 50, par. 1 of the PILA and the conditions stated in art. 54, par. 1 of the PILA (with reference to art. 58, par. 1 of the PILA) must be fulfilled.

4.2.1 Prerequisites for Recognition

Art. 50 of the PILA requires that the decision must be granted in a civil action, by a state court and be final under the law of the state in which it was given. The below discussion focuses on finalization and state court as the essential prerequisites.

Finalization

Art. 50 of the PILA stipulates that only foreign court judgments, which are final according to the law of the state of the court that issued the judgment, shall be allowed to be recognized and/or enforced before the courts of Turkey. This prerequisite creates problems in terms of the recognition of Certificates of Succession.

Under Turkish law, the final judgment has the effect of ensuring that a court decision finally resolves a dispute and that the dispute is not subject to re-examination before superior courts. A judgment can be finalized in a material and a formal sense. In the formal sense, a formal judgment means that all legal remedies against the decision are exhausted or lapsed. To put it in other words, a decision finalized in a formal sense cannot be nullified. Finalization in a formal sense is not related to the substance of the judgment; it does not mean that the dispute between the parties has ended, but rather indicates the end of a pending case.[49] On the other hand, the finalization in the material sense, indicates that the substance of the decision has a binding effect.[50]

Pursuant to art. 50 of the PILA, whether the decision has been finalized is examined according to the law of the country where the decision was made. According to the dominant view in Turkish doctrine, the condition of finalization requires that the decision shall be finalized both in a material and in a formal sense according to the law in which it was rendered. [51] On the other hand, the opposing view considers sufficient for the foreign court decision to be recognized that it is

[49] Şanlı et al. (2021), p. 642.

[50] Çelikel and Erdem (2021), pp. 712–713; Şanlı et al. (2021), pp. 642–643.

[51] Şanlı et al. (2021), p. 643; Nomer (2021), p. 508; Nomer (2018), p. 224; Çelikel and Erdem (2021), p. 792; Şanlı (1990), p. 291; Bilkay (2021), pp. 922–923; Ruhi (2014), p. 23.

finalized in a formal sense only according to the law of the country where it was given.[52] This view argues that a contrary opinion would render the recognition of foreign decisions in the *ex parte* proceedings as ineffective, since they are never finalized in a material sense.[53] It is also argued that the fact that a decision has not been finalized in the material sense should not be interpreted as a disadvantage for the Turkish legal system, as the contrary can be proven by filing a lawsuit in Turkey.[54]

Under Turkish law the decisions granting Certificates of Succession are not finalized in the material sense, and they may at any time be contested. For example, if there is an assertion that there are other legal heirs along with the heirs named in the Certificate of Succession, the decision may be contested. As a matter of fact, it is obligatory under Turkish law to indicate within the Certificate of Succession that all known heirs of the deceased and the respective shares of each heir are valid until the contrary is proven.[55] Hence, according to the dominant view of the doctrine, which requires both the formal and material finalization of a foreign decision for the recognition, a Certificate of Succession granted by a foreign court does not satisfy the preconditions under art. 50 of the PILA and cannot be recognized.[56] This opinion has been confirmed by that Court of Cassation which stated that it is not possible for the Certificates of Succession to be recognized, since they are not finalized judgments. [57] On the other hand, the opposing opinion, to which this author subscribed as well, is that the since the finalization in a formal sense is sufficient, a Certificate of Succession granted by a foreign authority fulfills the precondition of finalization (while other conditions still have to be examined).

The Decision Given by a State Court

According to art. 50 of the PILA, to seek recognition, the existence of a foreign court decision is required. This condition may cause problems regarding the recognition of the Certificate of Succession issued by foreign authorities other than courts. As art. 50 of the PILA requires there to be a foreign court decision, decisions issued by administrative bodies such as municipalities, governorships or notaries cannot be

[52]For authors who support this view, see: Özkan and Tütüncübaşı (2020), p. 184 ff.; Demir-Gökyayla (2006), p. 562; Güngör (1997), p. 180; Sargın and Erten (2014), p. 79; Ertaş (1998), p. 391; Doğan (2022), p. 123; Sakmar (1982), p. 57; Şit (2011) p. 68 ff.

[53]Özkan and Tütüncübaşı (2020), p. 184.

[54]Özkan and Tütüncübaşı (2020), p. 186.

[55]Pürselim (2020), p. 4.

[56]Çelikel and Erdem (2021), p. 801; Şanlı et al. (2021), p. 641, dn. 405; Akıncı (2020), p. 143.

[57]For decisions in this direction, see: 14th Civil Chamber of the Court of Cassation Case no. 2015/4915 Decision no. 2015/3473 Date. 30.03.2015; 14th Civil Chamber of the Court of Cassation Case no. 2016/14569 Decision no. 2016/10281 Date. 12.12.2016; 7th Civil Chamber of the Court of Cassation Case no. 2012/7173 Decision no. 2013/366 Date. 23.01.2013 (www.legalbank.net).

enforced in Turkey pursuant to the PILA,[58] unless there is an international agreement to that effect. Hence, the Certificates of Succession given by foreign notaries, for instance, do not qualify for recognition in Turkey, but they may qualify as an official document.[59] Thus, although it is currently not possible to recognize a Certificate of Succession issued by a foreign authority other than a court, such a document can be still relied on as evidence before Turkish courts.[60]

Considering these two prerequisites, a Certificate of Succession that cannot be finalized under Turkish law and/or has not been issued by a foreign court shall not be recognized in Turkey. Therefore, a foreigner who is an heir to an estate in Turkey will need to request a Certificate of Succession from a court in Turkey despite there being a decision from a foreign authority. Nevertheless, in this case, there is also the risk for such a foreigner not being able to find a competent court in Turkey. Bearing in mind the abovementioned doctrinal discussion if the rules of jurisdiction in art. 40 of the PILA are applied, the risk of not being able to establish a competent court in Turkey increases. For this reason, considering that the problems in the recognition of foreign Certificates of Succession might lead foreigners to apply to a Turkish court for the issuance of a Certificate of Succession, it is even more important to consider the rule under art. 43 of the PILA as the grounds for jurisdiction in the proceedings for issuance of the Certificates of Succession.

4.2.2 Main Conditions of Recognition

In the case of a Certificate of Succession obtained as a result of a contested proceeding, the foreign court decision will constitute a final judgment (*res judicata*) in a material sense, therefore, unlike the Certificate of Succession obtained as a result of the non-contentious proceeding, it will carry the precondition of finalization. However, pursuant to art. 54, par. 1, subpar. (b) of the PILA, it is necessary to verify if the foreign court decision was not given in a matter that falls under the exclusive jurisdiction of Turkish courts. The foreign judgments, given on matters which the Turkish courts have exclusive jurisdiction to resolve, cannot be recognized. If there is a determination in the Certificate of Succession given by a foreign court, regarding the immovables in Turkey, this part of the Certificate cannot be recognized due to the exclusive jurisdiction of the Turkish courts in this matter. This however, is not unanimously supported in the doctrine.

Although the exclusive jurisdiction forms an impediment to recognition pursuant to art. 54, par. 1, subpar. (b) of the PILA, what is captured under the scope of this provision remains uncertain because matters falling within the exclusive jurisdiction of Turkish courts are not listed as such. Therefore, in order to understand whether a rule is within the scope of exclusive jurisdiction, an interpretation has to be made on

[58] Şanlı et al. (2021), pp. 634–635; Pürselim (2020), p. 13.

[59] Ekşi (2013), p. 113.

[60] Akıncı (2020), p. 143; Demir-Gökyayla (2006), p. 559.

the basis of the purpose and the wording of the respective rule.[61] For a jurisdictional rule to be deemed as granting exclusive jurisdiction to the Turkish courts, it has to concern the matter reserved for the Turkish courts only.[62] As it is unanimously accepted in Turkish law, Turkish courts have exclusive jurisdiction in cases regarding rights *in rem* over immovable property located in Turkey.[63] The Court of Cassation accepts the same principle and decides that part of the Certificate of Succession about the rights *in rem* over immovables in Turkey falls within the exclusive jurisdiction of Turkish Courts.[64] Therefore, the recognition of the Certificates of Succession issued by a foreign court, which includes rights *in rem* on immovables located in Turkey, will not be recognized.[65] An alternative view which opposes the opinion that Turkish courts are exclusively authorized to issue the Certificate of Succession regarding immovable properties in Turkey, since it is argued that there is no exclusive jurisdiction rule that would prevent the recognition or enforcement of foreign court decisions regarding succession.[66] Some state that the international jurisdiction of Turkish courts, in terms of issuing the Certificate of Succession, is not exclusive without the distinction of movable or immovable property.[67] Thus, since Turkish courts do not have exclusive jurisdiction regarding movable properties included in the estate, this part of the Certificate of Succession

---

[61] Çelikel and Erdem (2021), p. 609; Şanlı et al. (2021), p. 660.

[62] Çelikel and Erdem (2021), p. 750.

[63] Çelikel and Erdem (2021), p. 750; Şanlı et al. (2021), p. 661; Pürselim (2020), p. 15; Ekşi (2014), p. 137.

[64] For the judgments of the Court of Cassation which state that in order for the decision to be enforceable, it must have been given on a subject that does not fall under the exclusive jurisdiction of Turkish courts, and that decisions on real rights on immovables are within the exclusive jurisdiction of Turkish courts, see: 2nd Civil Chamber of the Court of Cassation Case no. 2002/8254, Decision no. 2002/9339, Date. 12.07.2002: *"The plaintiffs requested the recognition of the Certificate of Succession issued in accordance with the French Civil Code by the French notary public. Article 43 of the Law numbered 2675 on International Private and Procedural Law; admissibility of a foreign judgment as conclusive evidence or final judgment depends on the court's determination that the foreign judgment fulfills the conditions of enforcement. In article 34 of the same Law, it is stated that only the decisions that have been finalized can be enforced. The Certificate of Succession that is requested to be recognized does not qualify as a finalized court decision and cannot be recognized in a way that indicates the transfer of real estate under the exclusive jurisdiction of the Turkish Courts."* For decisions in this direction, see: 2nd Civil Chamber of the Court of Cassation Case no. 1990/6373, Decision no. 1990/6410; 2nd Civil Chamber of the Court of Cassation Case no. 1986/808, Decision. no. 1986/1284 Date. 10.02.1986; Court of Cassation Grand Assembly of Civil Chambers Case no. 2001/2-922, Decision no. 2001/746 Date. 24.10.2001; Court of Cassation Grand Assembly of Civil Chambers Case no. 2001/2-922, Decision no. 2001/746, Date. 24.10.2001; 8th Civil Chamber of the Court of Cassation Case no. 2013/23629, Decision no. 2014/18556, Date. 17.10.2014.

[65] For authors who hold this view, see: Nomer (2021), p. 552 dn. 316; Ekşi (2014), p. 137; Ekşi (2013), p. 28; Özkan and Tütüncübaşı (2020), p. 199; Pürselim (2020), pp. 190–191; Şanlı (1990), pp. 298, 302.

[66] Demir-Gökyayla (2006), p. 575; Nomer (2003), p. 577; Demir-Gökyayla (2006), p. 575; Nomer (2003), p. 577; Tanrıbilir (2018), pp. 137–138.

[67] Tanrıbilir (2018), p. 138.

given by a foreign court can be recognized in accordance with both opinions. It is submitted here that the rule of jurisdiction regarding succession in art. 43 of the PILA is not defined as exclusive jurisdiction. However, if there are immovable properties in Turkey belonging to the estate, the Turkish courts should be considered as having exclusive jurisdiction. Therefore, since the Turkish courts have exclusive jurisdiction in terms of immovables included in the estate in Turkey, only the Certificates of Succession in respect to the movables can be recognized.

5 Conclusion

The Certificates of Succession are important legal documents based on which the heirs may exercise their rights over the estate. The difference exists in Turkish law between the Certificates of Succession which are issued in the contentious and those issues in the non-contentious proceedings, the latter being at the focus of this paper. The above discussion reveals three important areas in which Certificates of Succession may poste difficulties before Turkish authorities in cases with a foreign element.

The first is the issue of international jurisdiction. In a succession matter with a foreign element, if there is an item of the estate located in Turkey, the heirs need a Certificate of Succession to be able to dispose of this estate. In the authors' opinion, the court having international jurisdiction should be determined in accordance with art. 43 of the PILA to issue a Certificates of Succession both in the non-contentious and contentious proceedings. Otherwise, a foreigner who will request a Certificate of Succession may not be able to find a competent court in Turkey.

The second issue is the determination of applicable law. When deciding in succession maters, including issuing of the Certificate of Succession in cases with a foreign element, the respective shares of those who made a request will be determined according to the national law of the deceased in accordance with art. 20, par. 1 of the PILA. However, if the deceased has immovable property in Turkey, Turkish law will be applied in relation to the succession of this property.

Third and final issue concerns the legal effects in Turkey of the Certificate of Succession issued abroad. Decisions made by foreign administrative authorities will not be recognized due to the express provision of the PILA limiting recognition to court decisions. Thus only, the Certificate of Succession which has been issued by the competent state court is eligible for recognition under art. 50 of the PILA. Further condition under the same provisions is that the decision has to be finalized, which, according to the dominant view of the doctrine, entails finalization in both the material and the substantive sense. However, even if the Certificate of Succession brought before a Turkish court with a request to be recognized, is obtained through the contested proceedings, and constitutes a final judgment in a material sense, it may still be denied recognition fully or in part. There is a condition for recognition that Turkish courts do not have exclusive jurisdiction in the matter, hence, foreign judgments given on issues that the Turkish courts have exclusive jurisdiction to resolve may not be recognized in Turkey. Since Turkish courts have exclusive jurisdiction over rights *in rem* in immovables located in Turkey, recognition of the Certificate of Succession will be refused in part in which it concerns the immovable assets in Turkey.

References

Acun-Mekengeç M (2017) Türk Hukuku'nda Teminat Gösterme Yükümlülüğü (*Obligation of Posting a Guarantee in Turkish Law*). Public Priv Int Law Bull 37(2):1–33

Akıncı Z (2020) Milletlerarası Özel Hukuk (*Private International Law*). Vedat Kitapçılık, İstanbul

Altınkaya M (2020) Medeni Usul Hukuku Açısından Mirasçılık Belgesine İlişkin Talep (*Request For Certificate of Succession In Terms of Civil Procedure Law*). İstanbul Üniversitesi Hukuk Fakültesi Özel Hukuk Yüksek Lisans Tezleri Dizisi, On İki Levha Yayıncılık, İstanbul

Antalya G, Sağlam İ (2015) Miras Hukuku (*Inheritance Law*). Legal Yayıncılık, İstanbul

Baran-Çelik N (2019) Türkiye'de Yabancılık Unsuru İçeren Mirasçılık Belgelerinin Düzenlenmesi (*Issuing of Certificate of Succession Involving Foreign Elements In Turkey*). Dicle Üniversitesi Hukuk Fakültesi Dergisi 24(41):439–511

Bilkay M (2021) Miras Hukukuna İlişkin Dava ve İslerde Türk Mahkemelerinin Milletlerarası Yetkisi (*International Jurisdiction of Turkish Courts in Cases and Affairs Related to Inheritance Law*). Public Priv Int Law Bull 41(2):905–929

Can H, Tuna E (2019) Milletlerarası Usul Hukuku (*International Procedural Law*). Adalet Yayınları, Ankara

Çelikel A, Erdem B (2021) Milletlerarası Özel Hukuk (*Private International Law*). Beta, İstanbul

Demir-Gökyayla C (2006) Yabancı Mahkemelerden Alınan Mirasçılık Belgesinin Türkiye'de Hüküm ve Sonuç Doğurması (*The Effect and Consequences of Certificates of Succession Issued by Foreign Courts in Turkey*). Prof. Dr. Fikren Eren Armağanı: 599-581. Yetkin Yayınları, Ankara

Doğan V (2022) Milletlerarası Özel Hukuk (*Private International Law*). Savaş Yayınları, Ankara

Dursun A (2020) Türk Hukukunda Mirasçılık Belgesi ve Uygulama Sorunları (*Heritage Certificate and Application Problems in Turkish Law*). Uluslararası Avrasya Araştırmalar Dergisi 5(10): 192–212

Ekşi N (2013) Yargıtay Kararları Işığında Milletlerarası Miras Hukuku (*International Inheritance Law in Light of the Court of Cassation Decisions*). Beta Yayınevi, İstanbul

Ekşi N (2014) Comparison of Articles 20 and 43 of the Turkish private international law and procedural law ('PILA') with the EU succession regulation'. In: Beaumont P, Yüksel B (eds) Turkish and EU private international law: a comparison. XII Levha, pp 117–152

Ertaş S (1998) Yabancı İlamların Tanınması ve Tenfizi (*Recognition and Enforcement of Foreign Judgments*). Kudret Ayiter Armağanı, Ankara

Güngör G (1997) Milletlerarası Özel Hukukta İflas (*Bankruptcy in Private International Law*). Ankara Hukuk Fakültesi Yayınları, Ankara

Güngör G (2021) Türk Milletlerarası Özel Hukuku (*Turkish Private International Law*). Yetkin Yayınları, İstanbul

Kocaağa K (2005) Mirasçılık Belgesi (*Certificate of Succession*). Gazi Üniversitesi Hukuk Fakültesi Dergisi 1–2:83–105

Kocayusufpasaoğlu N (1987) Miras Hukuku (*Inheritance Law*). Filiz Kitabevi, İstanbul

Nomer E (2003) Yabancı Mahkeme İlamlarının Tenfizinde Mahkemenin Yetkisi ve Kamu Düzeni (*Court's Jurisdiction in the Recognition of Foreign Court Judgments and Public Policy*). Gülören Tekinalp'e Armağan:565–577

Nomer E (2018) Milletlerarası Usul Hukuku (*International Procedural Law*). Beta, Istanbul

Nomer E (2021) Devletler Hususi Hukuku (*Private International Law*). Beta, Istanbul

Özkan I, Tütüncübaşı U (2020) Uluslararası Usul Hukuku (*International Procedural Law*). Vedat Kitapçılık, İstanbul

Pürselim HS (2020) Uygulanacak Hukuk, Yetkili Mahkeme ve Tanıma Davası Kapsamında Mirasçılık Belgesinin İncelenmesi (*Examination of Certificate of Succession with Respect to Applicable Law, International Jurisdiction and Action for Recognition*). Kadir Has Üniversitesi Hukuk Fakültesi Dergisi 9(1):179–197

Ruhi AC (2014) Mirasçılık Belgesi ve Yabancı Bir Ülke Mahkemesinden Alınan Mirasçılık Belgesinin Türkiye'de Tanınması (*Certificate of Succession and Recognition of the Certificate Issued by a Foreign Country Court*). Terazi Hukuk Dergisi 9(92):14–28

Sakmar A (1982) Yabancı İlamların Türkiye'deki Sonuçları (*Effects of Foreign Judgments in Turkey*). İstanbul Fethi Derneği, İstanbul

Şanlı C (1990) Yabancı Veraset İlamlarının Türk Mahkemelerinde Tanınması veya Delil Olarak Kullanılması (*Court of Cassation Decisions regarding the Recognition of Foreign Certificates of Succession*). Prof. Dr. İlhan E. Postalcıoğlu'na Armağan:291–307

Şanlı C, Esen E, Ataman-Figanmeşe İ (2021) Milletlerarası Özel Hukuk (*Private International Law*). Beta, Ankara

Sargın F, Erten R (2014) MÖHUK Hükümleri Dairesinde Tanımanın Hukuki Niteliği, Usulü ve Karşılaşılan Bazı Sorunlar: Yeni Bir Düzenleme Yapma Gereği (*The Legal Nature of, and Procedure for, Recognition Under the Turkish Private International Law and Procedural Law Act (PILA) and Some Problems Encountered: The Need For New Regulation*). Legal Uluslararası Ticaret ve Tahkim Hukuku Dergisi 3(2):37–136

Serozan R, Engin B (2021) Miras Hukuku ve Uygulama Çalışmaları (*Inheritance Law and Application Exercises*). Seçkin Yayıncılık, Ankara

Şit B (2011) Yabancı Mahkeme Kararlarının Tanınması ve Tenfizinde Kesinleşme Şartı (*Finality Requirement in Recognition and Enforcement of Foreign Court Decisions*). Gazi Üniversitesi Hukuk Fakültesi Dergisi 15(1):61–74

Süral C (2016/2017) Matters of succession under Turkish Private International Law. In: Yearbook of Private International Law, vol 18, pp 371–391

Tanrıbilir FB (2018) MOHUK ve Mirasa İlişkin Bağlama Kurallarının Uygulanmasında Öne Çıkan Hususlar (*Main Issues in the Application of the Conflicts of Laws Rules relating to Inheritance and the (Turkish Private International Law and Procedural Law Act) PILA*). Feriha Bilge Tanrıbilir Gülce Gümüşlü Tunçağıl 10. Yılında Milletlerarası Özel Hukuk ve Usul Hukuku Hakkında Kanun (*The Act on Private International Law and Procedural Law in it 10th Anniversary*): 125–148

Tarman ZD (2021) Milletlerarası Özel Hukuk Pratik Çalışma Kitabı (*Private International Law Problem Solving Questions*). Vedat Kitapçılık, İstanbul

Tekinalp G (2020) Milletlerarası Özel Hukuk Bağlama ve Usul Hukuku Kuralları (*Private International Law Conflicts of Laws and Procedure Rules*). Vedat Kitapçılık, İstanbul

Division of Property Between Spouses in Lithuania: From Substantive to Private International Law

Kristina Pranevičienė and Agnė Limantė

1 Introduction

Modern law is complicated and multidimensional, and applying it presents significant challenges to courts, litigants, and their lawyers. The principle of sovereignty empowers any state to regulate a wide range of internal matters when adopting legislation. All natural persons and legal entities in the territory of a state must obey the legal order established by it. However, the possibilities and powers of the legal regulation of the state end within its borders—other sovereigns are already exercising their legal regulation.[1] When a case involves persons, property or activities in multiple states, one must not forget that the laws of several states may interact and courts in different states might have jurisdiction. Spouses are sometimes free to choose courts or the applicable law, but most of the time, there are mandatory regulations or laws that must be followed.

In a case of a cross-border couple break-up, these challenges become particularly apparent. Different EU instruments and private international law of several states might have to be employed in a divorce case where the parties seek to dissolve the marital ties, define parental responsibilities, settle maintenance and matrimonial property issues. As a result, the list of questions to be assessed as preliminary questions is fairly long. For instance, when dividing the matrimonial property in a cross-border case, firstly one has to check whether the spouses are of different or same nationality; secondly, their (shared or separate) habitual residence will have to

[1] Mikelėnas et al. (2009), p. 151.

K. Pranevičienė
Vilnius University, Faculty of Law, Vilnius, Lithuania

A. Limantė (✉)
Law Institute of the Lithuanian Centre for Social Sciences, Vilnius, Lithuania

I. Kunda et al. (eds.), *Balkan Yearbook of European and International Law 2022*,
Balkan Yearbook of European and International Law 2022,
https://doi.org/10.1007/978-3-031-29432-7_3

be identified; then, it might be relevant to establish the country where their marriage was registered and to take into account the country of their first habitual residence after the marriage. It will also be important to know whether the spouses have reached an agreement regarding the law applicable to their matrimonial property regime and, if they did—if such an agreement is valid. After that, the one has to proceed determining which court has jurisdiction and which law applies to the couple's matrimonial property regime. Lastly, the possible consequences of the court's judgment will have to be evaluated, assessing whether it would be recognised and enforceable abroad, especially in the countries where the property is located.

In the EU states, the cross-border cases on the division of matrimonial property follow two different tracks. One track is observed when a Member State in which the parties apply to a court participates in the enhanced cooperation and applies the Matrimonial Property Regulation[2] and the Regulation on Property Consequences of a Registered Partnership[3] (the Twin Regulations). In such a situation, these EU instruments come first to define jurisdiction and applicable law. A different path is followed in states that do not participate in the enhanced cooperation and where private international law of that particular state will be consulted.

Lithuania is one of the EU countries which were reluctant to join the Twin Regulations and the country is not participating in the enhanced cooperation yet. The main argument against joining the enhanced cooperation was political concern that under the Twin Regulations a state that does not recognise same-sex marriages or registered partnerships between same-sex couples would have to recognise such unions if they were concluded in other Member States.

As Lithuania does not participate in the Twin Regulations and neither other EU instrument nor the Lugano Convention[4] regulates the division of joint property of the spouses, Lithuanian courts apply the private international law of the Republic of Lithuania and bilateral agreements[5] (where existent). This article presents the national legal regulation and, through the analysis of the recent Lithuanian case law, exemplifies the challenging application of private international law rules in complicated cross-border cases noting that the accession to the Twin Regulations

[2]Council Regulation (EU) 2016/1103 of 24 June 2016 implementing enhanced cooperation in the area of jurisdiction, applicable law and the recognition and enforcement of decisions in matters of matrimonial property regimes, OJ L 183, 8.7.2016, pp. 1–29.

[3]Council Regulation (EU) 2016/1104 of 24 June 2016 implementing enhanced cooperation in the area of jurisdiction, applicable law and the recognition and enforcement of decisions in matters of the property consequences of registered partnerships, OJ L 183, 8.7.2016, pp. 30–56.

[4]See Article 1 (2) of the Lugano Convention which establishes that the Convention does not apply, *inter alia*, to property rights in matrimonial matters. Convention on jurisdiction and the enforcement of judgments in civil and commercial matters (Lugano Convention) of 16 September 1988.

[5]In April 2022 (the date of finalising this paper), Lithuania has bilateral agreements in the field of international legal cooperation in civil and family matters with the following countries which are not the members of the EU: Azerbaijan, Belarus, Moldova, Kazakhstan, Russia, Ukraine and Uzbekistan.

would bring advantages to many couples at least in cases related to the European Union Member States which participate in the enhanced cooperation.[6]

2 Family Law in Lithuania

The general framework of family law in Lithuania is built on the understanding that family is a valuable part of society. Family is based on the principles of monogamy, the voluntary nature of the marriage, the equality of the spouses (cohabitating persons) and the protection of the rights and interests of the child. Legal regulation of family relationship covers the relationship between spouses (cohabitating persons), as well as the relationship between parents and children.[7] Lithuanian Constitution does not directly establish other forms of family except from marriage but also it does not forbid registered partnership. To the date of this article, the Lithuanian law recognises as families only spouses or cohabitating persons of different sexes.[8] Cohabitating same sex persons can expect the protection of their property rights under the legal norms regulating general joint activity (Article 6.969 CC) but not the recognition of their marriage or partnership registered abroad under national family law.

In Lithuania, two main sources of family law are the Constitution of the Republic of Lithuania and the Civil Code. While the Constitution sets the main principles, the Civil Code (CC) regulates family law in detail. Lithuanian CC is divided into 6 books, one of which—Book Three—is entirely dedicated to family law matters.[9] The provisions of the Book Three of the CC define the general principles of the legal regulation of family relations and govern the grounds and procedures of entering into marriage, validity and dissolution of marriage, property and non-property personal rights of spouses, establishment of maternity and paternity, mutual rights and responsibilities between children, parents and other family members. It also sets the basic provisions on adoption, guardianship, curatorship, and the procedures for registering acts of civil status.

The CC establishes two types of formal relationships between couples: marriage and registered partnership. However, partnerships may not be registered officially due to the lack of the implementing law. Even though in the recent years the need of registered partnerships was one of the most predominant topics of political and public debate, the political unity to adopt the Partnership Law was not yet achieved. The most heated discussions start when it comes to the same sex partnerships. So far,

[6]Belgium, Bulgaria, Cyprus, Czech Republic, Germany, Greece, Spain, France, Croatia, Italy, Luxembourg, Malta, Netherlands, Austria, Portugal, Slovenia, Spain, Finland and Sweden.

[7]Constitutional Court Ruling of 28 September 2011, Nr. 21/2008.

[8]On the concept of "family" in Lithuania, see further Sagatys (2010); Ambrazevičiūtė et al. (2012); Mizaras (2012).

[9]For its commentary (in Lithuanian) see Mikelėnas et al. (2002).

same-sex relationships in Lithuania have gained no legal recognition—same-sex marriages remain constitutionally banned,[10] and partnerships between same-sex couples also may not be registered (prohibited by CC[11]). As a result, the analysis in this paper refers only to spouses of different sexes.

3 Matrimonial Property Regimes in Lithuanian Law

Articles 3.81–3.129 CC regulate the property relations between the spouses.[12] Part of those provisions directly addresses the regime of matrimonial property.

Under Article 3.81 CC, the property of the spouses could either be regulated under the statutory or the contractual legal regime. The statutory legal regime is applied in cases where no marriage agreement was concluded between the spouses. In such a case, the principle of common joint ownership is applied. The contractual legal regime, on the opposite, is created when a marriage agreement is concluded. In Lithuanian law, there is also an understanding of "family property" which falls under the special regime and cannot be changed by the parties' agreement. Such mandatory rules are necessary in order to protect children or the financially weaker spouse.

3.1 Family Property

Following Article 3.84 CC, family property (whether owned by one or by both spouses) includes (i) the house/apartment where the family lives and (ii) movable property intended for the use in the household, including furniture. The family property also includes the right to use the family dwelling.

Regarding assets that fall under the family property regime, certain restrictions apply. For example, the spouse who is the owner of the real estate considered to be a family property, may transfer it, mortgage it or otherwise encumber the rights to it only with the written consent of the other spouse. Where the spouses have minor

---

[10] See Article 38 of the Constitution of the Republic of Lithuania, stating that "Marriage shall be concluded upon the free mutual consent of man and woman." In addition, under Article 3.7 of the Civil Code of the Republic of Lithuania, marriage is a voluntary agreement between a man and a woman to create legal family. Article 3.12 prohibits marriage of persons of the same sex.

[11] Under Article 3.229 CC (in Chapter "Living together without marriage"), "the norms of this chapter establish the property relations between a man and a woman who, having registered their partnership in accordance with the procedure established by law, have been living together for at least one year without registering a marriage (cohabitants) for the purpose of establishing a family relationship".

[12] As noted above, special law regarding registered partnerships was not adopted so far, thus special rules on governing the property relationship between partners (Articles 3.230 – 3.235 CC) have not entered into force. Political debates on the adoption of the Partnership Law are ongoing in Lithuania.

children for such transactions permission from the court should be acquired. Moreover, there are limitations for the creditorial claims against the family property (Article 3.85 CC).[13]

3.2 *Statutory Legal Regime*

The statutory legal regime (applied where no marriage agreement was concluded) is based on the principle of common joint ownership. Unless proved otherwise, property is presumed to be of joint ownership (equal parts). Under the statutory matrimonial property regime, co-owned property of spouses is managed and disposed of jointly and in mutual agreement of spouses. Both spouses' consent is needed, for example, to take a loan, mortgage the property, to sell real estate owned by the family.

Under Article 3.88 CC, common joint ownership of the spouses applies for the following property:

(i) property acquired after the marriage in the name of one or both of the spouses;
(ii) income and fruits received from the property personally owned by one of the spouses;
(iii) income received from the joint activity of the spouses, as well as income received from the activity of one of the spouses (except for the funds required for that spouse's professional occupation);
(iv) the company and the income received from it or another type of business provided the spouses started such business activities after the marriage. Where the business was owned by one of the spouses before the marriage, the common joint ownership includes the income received from such business as well as an increase in its value;
(v) income received from the employment or intellectual activities, dividends, pensions, benefits or other payments received by both spouses or one of them after the marriage (except for payments received for specific purposes such as damages for moral or corporal injury, allowances or other benefits paid specifically to only one of the spouses, etc.).

In case of the statutory property regime, the following is considered to be the personal property of a spouse (Article 3.89 CC):

(i) property acquired separately by each spouse before the marriage;
(ii) property received by a spouse by succession or as a gift during the marriage (unless the will or donation agreement indicates that the property is given to common joint ownership of the spouses);

[13] See also Kudinavičiūtė-Michailovienė (2009).

(iii) a spouse's personal belongings (footwear, clothing, instruments required for the spouse's professional occupation);
(iv) the rights to intellectual or industrial property, excluding the income received from those rights;
(v) funds and items required for the personal business of one of the spouses, excluding those used in the business conducted jointly by both spouses;
(vi) damages and compensation payments received by one of the spouses for non-pecuniary damage or personal injury, benefits received for specific purposes and other benefits related specifically to only one of the spouses, non-transferable rights;
(vii) property that was acquired with personal funds or proceeds from the sale of personal property with the express intention of the spouse to acquire it as personal property.[14]

It should be noted, however, that under Article 3.90 CC, the court may declare a personal property of one of the spouses to be common joint ownership of the spouses if it is established that during the marriage the property was fundamentally improved with the joint funds of the spouses or with the funds of or due to the work of the other spouse (capital investments, reconstruction, etc.). Moreover, where a spouse used both his/ her personal funds and the funds owned jointly with the other spouse to acquire a property for his/her personal needs, the court may also declare such property to be a joint property where the value of the joint funds used exceeded the value of the personal funds of the spouse used for acquisition.

In this regard, the Supreme Court of Lithuania (*Lietuvos Aukščiausiasis Teismas*) has recognised that assets' value, especially real estate, may fluctuate. The courts have to take into account only the change in the value of the property, which is determined by its improvement itself, and not for other reasons (such as changes in the market price), and such an assessment must be made taking into account the value of the property that was before improvement and its change after the improvements were made.[15] Moreover, the Supreme Court has repeatedly stated that, in order to deny the presumption of joint ownership, it is not sufficient to determine that the property was acquired at the expense of one of the spouses.[16] Even the property acquired during marriage from personal funds is recognised as one spouse's personal property only if it is proved by permissible means that the will of the spouse to acquire the property in personal rather than joint ownership was clearly expressed at the time of acquisition. Legal regulation requiring a clear expression of the will of the spouse using his or her funds to acquire property in personal property means nothing more than a presumption of joint ownership prevailing in the property relationship of the spouses, so if such a will had not been expressly stated and the

[14] See further Vitkevičius (2006).
[15] Supreme Court, Ruling of 8 May 2015, No. 3K-3-259-378/2015.
[16] Supreme Court, Ruling of October 27, 2021, No. e3K-3-266-403/2021.

spouses do not agree on property rights, such property is the joint property of the spouses.[17]

Article 3.123 CC lists the conditions under which the assets of the spouses may be divided into unequal parts. Depending on the interests of the minor children, the state of health of one spouse or his or her financial situation or other important circumstances, the court may deviate from the principle of equal shares of the spouses' joint property and award a larger share of the property to one spouse.[18] The Supreme Court has also repeatedly stated that the abovementioned criteria must also be taken into account when deciding on the general method of division of property (Article 3.123(1) CC).[19] Furthermore, an important criterion for derogating from the principle of equal share of matrimonial property is the recognition that one of the spouses' personal funds (acquired by one of the spouses before marriage) were used in the creation of joint property of the spouses.[20] Article 3.98(2) CC stipulates that the spouse is entitled to compensation in cases where the personal funds of the spouse have been used to acquire property that is the joint property of the spouses. It is necessary to determine to what extent such deviation is necessary to protect the interests of spouse consequently, the criteria for determining the spouses' share of property must be sufficiently clear.[21]

3.3 *Contractual Legal Regime*

The contractual legal regime of marital property is created when a marriage agreement is concluded. It is regulated by Articles 3.101–3.108 CC. The marriage agreement might be concluded before the marriage or at any time during the marriage. Notary approval is required for the marriage agreement, and it should be registered in the special State register of marriage contracts.

In the marriage contract, spouses may stipulate that:

(i) the property acquired both before and during the marriage shall be the personal property of each spouse;
(ii) personal property acquired by a spouse before the marriage shall become common joint ownership of the spouses after the marriage;

[17] Supreme Court, Ruling of 16 November, 2005 No. 3K-3-529/2005; Supreme Court, Ruling of 11 April, 2012, No. 3K-3-52/2012; Supreme Court, Ruling of 21 February, 2019, No. 3K-3-55-916/2019.

[18] See further Keserauskas et al. (2002), pp. 244–245.

[19] Supreme Court, Ruling of 27 October, 2021, No. e3K-3-266-403/2021.

[20] Supreme Court, Ruling of 15 February, 2006, No. 3K-3-126/2006; Ruling of 20, June, 2007, No. 3K-3-220/2007; Ruling of 16 December, 2011, No. 3K-3-517/2011; Ruling of 21 February 2021, No. 3K-3-55-916/2019.

[21] Supreme Court, Ruling of 10 April, No. 3K-3-251/2006; Ruling of 3 November, 2009, No. 3K-3-479/2009, Ruling of 18 May, 2017, No. 3K-3-243-969/2017.

(iii) property acquired during the marriage shall be owned on the basis of common divided (partial) ownership. In such cases, rules on common divided (partial) property shall be applied (Articles 4.72–4.85 CC).

The spouses may select that one of the listed matrimonial legal regimes shall be applied to their entire property or only to its certain part or to specified items only. A matrimonial legal regime could be set for both: existing and (or) future property.

In addition, a marriage contract may contain the rights and duties related to the disposal of property, mutual maintenance, participation in the provision for family needs and covering expenses, the procedure for dividing property in case of divorce, as well as other matters related to the spouses' mutual property relations. As confirmed by the case law, the marriage agreement may not limit the application of imperative norms, ignore the requirement of fair dealing, good morals, public order, or be concluded to avoid liabilities.[22]

3.4 Property Relations in Case of Cohabitating Couples

It should be noted that despite the lack of formal rules, informal partnerships—cohabitation without any registration formalities—gained recognition in the case law. In general, unmarried cohabitants are not treated as spouses, so the presumption of community of property does not apply to property acquired by such persons. The property relations of unmarried cohabitants are not governed by family law, and disputes arising out of such relations are therefore to be settled in accordance with the general rules of property law.[23] In the jurisprudence of the Supreme Court of Lithuania, it has been repeatedly held that in case of unmarried persons living together (especially if their living together is not episodic but lasts for a longer time) and having a life similar to that of a married couple,[24] their property relations are seen as 'joint activity agreement' ('joint venture')/partnership.[25] Article 6.969 (4) of CC imperatively establishes that the joint activity (partnership) agreement must be in writing and, in cases provided by law, in notarial form, and if the requirements of the form of the contract are not complied with, the contract becomes invalid. However, under Lithuanian case law, the agreement between unmarried

[22] See e.g. Supreme Court, Ruling of 13 June 2018, No. 3K-3-229-378/2018.

[23] Supreme Court, Ruling of 9 June 2022, No. e3K-3-159-916/2022.

[24] This can be proved by all possible evidence, for example, by referring to witnesses (neighbours, relatives, friends, etc.), written evidence (e.g. letters, delivery of receipts, invoices for goods or services addressed to cohabitants' common place of residence, photographs), etc.

[25] Supreme Court, ruling of 28 March 2011, No. 3K-3-134; Supreme Court, ruling of 3 October 2005, No. 3K-3-410, and later cases, e.g. Supreme Court, Ruling of 9 June 2022, No. e3K-3-159-916/2022.

persons living together may not necessarily be in writing and it can be proved by any means of proof (witnesses, photographs, other documents, etc.).[26]

Due to such case law, property and assets acquired by cohabitees may be recognised by a court as being their joint ownership. However, this is the fact to be proved before the court. The fact that a party is bound by such an unwritten joint venture agreement does not mean that all the assets acquired by any of its parties will be regarded as joint ownership or that the parties may not acquire a particular asset to personal ownership. This is a considerable difference from property relations in the case of marriage.[27]

4 The Law Applicable to the Couple's Property in Cross-Border Cases According to Lithuanian Rules

The private international law rules in Lithuania are established in the Civil Code. They are codified in Book One of the CC and include rules on jurisdiction and law applicable to the matrimonial property regimes and division of the matrimonial property.

Several features of Lithuanian private international law should be noted. Firstly, when talking particularly about the matrimonial property, these rules are designed to ensure that there is a link between the situation of the spouses and the law that will apply to their matrimonial property regime. Therefore, the connecting factors of nationality, habitual residence, and location of the property (*lex rei sitae*) typically appear in Lithuanian law, similar to the national laws of many European states. Secondly, since in cases of cross-border marriages or marriages that have an international element (for instance, due to the property located abroad), the cross-border recognition of agreements and court judgements is often needed, the national

[26]The Supreme Court has pointed out that the requirement that unmarried cohabitants (cohabitants), when acquiring property jointly, should only agree with each other in writing is not in accordance with the principles of fairness and reasonableness (Art. 1.5 CC). Thus, notwithstanding the imperative nature of Article 6.969(4) CC, which provides for the mandatory written form of a joint venture agreement, the case-law treats the relationship between unmarried persons as a contractual relationship of a joint venture/partnership, irrespective of whether the unmarried persons have entered into such a written agreement. An unwritten agreement on a contractual relationship of joint activity (partnership) with a view to the creation of a community of property may be proved by circumstances such as the cohabitation of the parties (in particular, if it is not episodic, but lasts for a long time and is permanent and stable), the management of the household together, the creation of common property by means of personal funds and/or by own work, etc. Cohabitation, joint management of the household, the creation of joint property by unmarried persons (cohabitants) with their own means and by their own joint labour may be proved by all available evidence (Supreme Court, Ruling of 11 April 2019, No. e3K-3-133-421/2019). See also Kudinavičiūtė-Michailovienė (2008).

[27]See further: Limantė and Chochrin (2019), pp. 407–426; Petrylaitė (2014); Ravluševičius (2017), p. 2293; Tamošiūnienė and Kudinavičiūtė-Michailovienė (2013).

private international law rules and their coherence with the private international law of related states (especially the states where the enforcement will be needed) become very important. In this regard, the Lithuanian private international law and case law reveal that both—the legislator and the judiciary—take these concerns into account.

4.1 *Default Rules When the Choice of Law Was Not Made*

The CC establishes a cascade of connecting factors to be applied to establish applicable law in cross-border cases. This cascade can be summarised as follows: the law of common habitual residence—the law of common nationality—*lex loci celebrationis*. In particular, Article 1.28 (1) CC as the main rule provides that the legal status of the spouses' property is determined by the law of the country of their habitual residence (*lex domicilii*). This rule is applied when both spouses live in the same country before they decide to divorce and takes precedence over the other two factors. However, Article 1.28 (1) CC also foresees the situations when spouses have their habitual residences in different countries. In such a situation, the law of common nationality applies (for instance, in a case of two Lithuanian nationals where one is resident in Lithuania and the other in the United States, the Lithuanian law as the law of the country of common nationality applies). Article 1.28 (1) CC also takes into account the possibility of a situation where both spouses are nationals of different states and have never had a common habitual residence. In such a case, the Lithuanian law provides that the law of the state where the marriage was concluded applies (*lex loci celebrationis*). It has to be noted that this rule can only be applied if spouses have no common habitual residence and no common nationality. For instance, if a wife is a Lithuanian national and a husband is an Indian national, and after the marriage which took place in Lithuania, they both continue to live in their home countries, Lithuanian law (as the law of the state where they got married) would apply to determine the legal status of spouses' property.

A very peculiar case where Article 1.28 CC was applied by Lithuanian courts in 2017.[28] Both parties were Irish nationals, the wife (the applicant) lived in Lithuania, and the husband (the defendant) was domiciled in the Dominican Republic. The spouses owned real estate in Lithuania. The parties' civil marriage was contracted in the Dominican Republic, and the church marriage was registered in the USA. The marriage has not been dissolved, although the spouses have been living apart since 2009. The wife asked the court to divide the matrimonial property as she believed that the defendant was managing the matrimonial property at a loss. The case file reveals that the defendant had filed for divorce in Thailand (last common habitual residence); however, under Thai law, assets located abroad are not divided. The Lithuanian court highlighted that under Lithuanian laws, claims regarding rights *in rem* are subject to the exclusive jurisdiction of the courts of Lithuania. The court also

[28] Vilnius Regional Court, Ruling of 17 January 2017, No. 2A-535-580/2017.

noted that in the procedural documents, the parties expressed their will to apply the laws of the Republic of Lithuania when dividing the assets located in Lithuania. As both spouses also indicated in the procedural documents that their addresses were in Lithuania, the property to be divided was located in Lithuania, the court concluded that there were grounds to refer to Article 1.28 (1) of CC and to apply the law of Lithuania. The court emphasised that although the parties had more than one place of residence, the determination of their habitual residence is a matter of proof. In order to guarantee the parties' right to a fair trial, the place of residence indicated in the parties' pleadings was relied on to assess this aspect without making additional proof of residence for the purpose of the proceedings. Such a position, according to the court, was in accordance with the will of the parties since neither party had requested the application of foreign law. The court concluded that the choice of the Lithuanian law reflected the choice of the parties and the location of the immovable property, as well as the place of residence of the parties indicated in the procedural documents. Therefore, Lithuanian law was applied.

The situation is different where a bilateral agreement concluded between Lithuania and another country exists in the field concerned. In such a case, the provisions of an international bilateral agreement take precedence over Article 1.28 CC. This was considered by the Supreme Court of Lithuania in one of its cases.[29] The plaintiffs were spouses (husband and wife), both Polish nationals, living in Poland. During the marriage, the Polish couple purchased the premises, and the husband (issuing a wide scope power of attorney) authorised the defendant, a Lithuanian citizen, to manage this property. The defendant sold the premises to his mother-in-law. When the spouses learned about this, they filed a lawsuit for improper management of property against the defendant. They argued that the power of attorney did not comply with the will of the wife and that the premises were sold without her consent and authorization. After the ruling of the first instance court and the appeal court, the case reached the Supreme Court, which noted that the real estate in dispute was in the territory of Lithuania; therefore, the law of Lithuania (and not Poland) was applicable to determine its legal status. Such ruling was based on the Lithuanian-Polish bilateral agreement on legal aid,[30] which stipulates that the matrimonial property regime of the spouses shall be governed by the law of the Contracting Party in whose territory the property is situated (*lex rei sitae*). The Supreme Court concluded that the written consent of the plaintiff was required for concluding the disputed real estate sale-purchase contract, and in the absence of wife's written consent, the contract should be declared invalid as contrary to imperative norms of Lithuanian law.

[29] Order of the Supreme Court of Lithuania of 8 November 2010 in civil case No. 3K-3-432/2010.

[30] Article 26 of the Agreement between the Republic of Lithuania and the Republic of Poland on Legal Assistance and Legal Relations in Civil, Family, Labour and Criminal Matters of 26 January 1993.

4.2 Conflict of Law Rules and Party Autonomy

In addition to the default rules, the Civil Code also guarantees party autonomy allowing the spouses to choose the law that will govern the legal status of property acquired during their marriage. Article 1.28 (2) CC stipulates that the legal status of the spouses' contractual property regime is determined by the law of the country chosen by the agreement between the spouses. It should be noted, however, that the choice of law is limited to the law of the states with whom the spouses have a certain connecting link. In particular, the spouses may choose the law of the state: (i) in which they are or will be domiciled; or (ii) in which their marriage took place; or (iii) of one of the spouses' nationality. These options are alternative, but they may also apply cumulatively if the selected connecting factors overlap.

As to the form of the choice of law agreement,[31] an agreement reached between spouses on the applicable law is only valid if it complies with the law of the state which law was chosen and of the state in which an agreement was concluded. For instance, if the spouses choose Latvian law but conclude an agreement in Lithuania, they must comply not only with the law of Lithuania but also with the law of Latvia (the law which is chosen as the applicable law).

Two situations could be observed in this case. Firstly, the spouses may decide to conclude a marriage agreement (prenuptial or postnuptial agreement)[32] and include in it the provisions on the choice of applicable law. In such a situation, under Lithuanian law, the notary form is obligatory for the whole agreement, as a matrimonial property agreement is only valid if concluded before the notary registered in the Register of Marriage Agreements. Secondly, the choice of law agreement might be concluded separately. In such a case, the requirements are more flexible: in theory, the agreement on the choice of law can be made orally (in practice, this means that spouses can choose the applicable law by expressing such wish before the court proceedings), by conclusive actions during the court proceedings (recognising certain law as applicable by concrete actions, e.g. if the defendant does not object to the claim of the plaintiff that a law of a certain state should be applied) or in a written form (simple or approved by a notary). This was clarified by the Supreme Court of Lithuania, which ruled that the choice of the applicable law must be sufficiently clear in terms of the contract or may be determined by the facts of the case.[33] The Supreme Court had also ruled that in order to determine the applicable law, the court should first check whether there is an express agreement between parties as to the applicable

[31] Choice of law agreement might be concluded as a separate instrument or be included as a provision in the marriage (prenuptial or postnuptial) contract.

[32] Notary approval is required for the marriage agreement and it should be registered in the special State register—"Register of Marriage Agreements". Marriage agreements concluded in a foreign country may also be registered in the Register of Marriage Agreements. This possibility is available to persons whose marriage agreement contains a Lithuanian personal identification code of at least one of the parties to this agreement.

[33] Supreme Court, Ruling of 8 November 2010, No. 3K-3-432/2010.

law or whether such an agreement could be implied. Only in the absence of the parties' choice, the court must determine the applicable law *ex officio*.[34]

The agreement reached by the spouses must correspond to their true will and should not contradict the imperative norms of law and public order.[35] Moreover, the contract between spouses may not violate the principle of equality and should not be very unfavourable to one of the spouses.[36] Otherwise, it might be declared invalid under the general grounds for invalidity of contracts. The Supreme Court has also clarified that a marriage contract may be declared invalid in whole or in part if the grounds for invalidity of the term of the marriage contract listed in Article 3.105 CC are established or the grounds for invalidity of contracts specified in the Book I of CC are established.[37]

The private international law also foresees the effects of law chosen by the spouses in respect of third parties. In particular, Article 1.28 (3) CC stipulates that the applicable law chosen by the agreement may be invoked against third parties only if the third parties knew or reasonably ought to have known this fact. One might argue that if an agreement on applicable law was incorporated in the marriage agreement, notarised and registered in the register of marriage agreements, third persons had a reasonable possibility to learn about it. However, an obligation to third parties to check the public registers would be rather an unreasonable burden for them, and such a burden cannot be justified solely in the interests of the spouses. The spouses have an obligation to inform their creditors about their agreement on the law, which would be applicable to the legal status of their matrimonial property. In such cases, a letter or message transmitted by post, e-mail or other means of communication should be considered appropriate and sufficient information for the third parties. Even the oral form of such notification is appropriate if the spouses can reliably prove that the creditor (or another third party) has received such information in a language he or she understands. Otherwise, the spouses bear the consequences of not informing their creditors.

The reason for the creditors to have the information about the law which would be applicable to the legal status of spouses' (debtors) matrimonial property is justified by the need for the creditors to self-assess the risks of the division of the matrimonial property in the case of divorce. There may be cases when spouses manipulate the choice of applicable law to protect their property and default on debts. Therefore, debt obligations may be breached, and the interests of the creditors may suffer.

Particular rules concerning immovable property are established in Article 1.28 (4) CC. It stipulates that the applicable law chosen by the agreement between spouses may be used to settle a dispute concerning right *in rem* in the immovable property only if the requirements for the public registration of that property and

[34] Supreme Court, Ruling of 30 May 2013, No. 3K-7-159/2013.

[35] Article 3.83 (2) CC regulates that terms of a marriage contract that are contrary to imperative legal norms, good moral or public order are null and void.

[36] Article 3.108 (2) CC. Supreme Court, Ruling of 10 May 2013, No. 3K-3-191/2013.

[37] Article 3.108 (1) CC.

rights *in rem* in the state in which the property is situated have been complied with. This obliges to register the immovable property under the law of the *lex rei sitae*. In 1996, the Real Property Register Act[38] was passed. This law, *inter alia*, regulates the registration of land, buildings and other immovable property, property rights to immovable property, and restrictions on these rights in the Real Property Register. The property located in Lithuania should be registered in this register. However, if the spouses acquire any immovable property located in another country, the requirements for public registration in that country must be complied with.

Lastly, it should be mentioned that Article 1.28 (5) CC establishes that an agreement between the spouses to change the legal status of their marital property shall be governed by the law of the state of the habitual residence of the spouses at the time of the change. This is a special legal norm, and it is applicable only in cases when spouses change the marital agreement or sign a new marital agreement but do not discuss the law which is applicable to their marital agreement. If the spouses resided in different states at the time of the change of legal status of their property, the law of the state of their last common habitual residence is applicable or, in the absence thereof, the law which governs the property relations of the spouses. This means that if the spouses had a marital agreement which indicated that all the property that they acquire during their marriage is their common joint property and later they changed such marital agreement indicating that all the property acquired by each spouse in his or her own name will be treated as his or her personal property, but the spouses do not discuss the law which is applicable to such agreement, Article 1.28 (5) CC must be applied. For instance, if an Estonian couple living in Lithuania previously having signed a prenuptial contract in Estonia decides to sign a new marital agreement in Lithuania but does not discuss which law is applicable to this agreement, the Lithuanian law as the law of their common habitual residence will apply.

A conclusion can be made that the spouses choosing to reach an agreement on the law which would be applicable to the legal status of their matrimonial property must not only follow their true will, the requirements of the law of the place where such an agreement is concluded (*lex contractus*) but also to consider in which state such an agreement will have to be implemented and enforced. In other words, the couple have to foresee in which country they might get divorced. The spouses should also take into account whether the judgment on the division of their matrimonial property might have to be enforced in a foreign state. In such cases, it is necessary to evaluate whether the choice of law does not violate the mandatory legal norms and public policy of that state. In addition, it might be important to inform interested third parties about such an agreement.

[38]Real Property Register of the Republic of Lithuania Act, Valstybės žinios, 1996-10-16, Nr. 100-2261.

5 Jurisdiction in Matrimonial Property Cases According to Lithuanian Law

5.1 *Subject-Matter and Territorial Jurisdiction and Procedure*

Article 25 of the Lithuanian Code of Civil Procedure (CCP)[39] establishes the rule that all civil cases in Lithuania are heard by district and regional courts as courts of first instance in accordance with the CCP. The court system of the Republic of Lithuania is made up of courts of general jurisdiction and courts of special jurisdiction. The Supreme Court of Lithuania (*Lietuvos Aukščiausiasis Teismas*), the Court of Appeal of Lithuania (*Lietuvos apeliacinis teismas*), the regional courts (*apygardų teismai*) and the district courts (*apylinkių teismai*) are courts of general jurisdiction dealing with civil and criminal cases. District courts also hear cases of administrative offenses coming within their jurisdiction by law. The regional courts, the Court of Appeal, the Supreme Court of Lithuania have the Civil Division and the Criminal Division. The Supreme Administrative Court of Lithuania (*Lietuvos vyriausiasis administracinis teismas*) and regional administrative court (*Regionų apygardos administracinis teismas*) are courts of special jurisdiction.[40]

All disputes arising from family legal relations (including those in matrimonial property cases) regardless of the amount of the dispute are firstly heard in the district courts.[41]

Article 153 CCP stipulates that the court hearings shall be held orally, inviting the parties to the proceedings, unless otherwise provided in the CCP. As the legislator established the rule that in divorce proceedings (in which the matrimonial property is divided), the court takes measures to reconcile the spouses and has the power to set a time limit for the spouses to reconcile[42] the preparation for the hearing in every family case take place by holding a preparatory hearing.[43]

The Lithuanian legislator has also established the simplified procedure (*Ypatingoji teisena*) for divorce and division of matrimonial property in cases when there is a mutual consent of the divorcing spouses (Article 3.51 CC) or by the request of one of the divorcing spouses (Article 3.55 CC). An application for divorce by mutual consent of both spouses is submitted to the district court of the place of residence of one of the spouses.[44] An application for divorce under the request of one of the spouses is submitted to the district court of the applicant's place

[39] Valstybės žinios, 2002-04-06, Nr. 36-1340.

[40] See further about Lithuanian judicial system in the official Lithuanian judicial system website: https://www.teismai.lt/en/courts/judicial-system/.

[41] See Articles 26, 27 and 28 CCP.

[42] See Article 384 (3) CCP.

[43] See Article 228 (1) CCP.

[44] See Article 538 (2) CCP.

of residence.[45] An application for divorce in the interests of the spouse who is incapacitated to work in the area of divorce may be submitted by such spouse's guardian (appointed by the court), the public prosecutor or the guardianship authority.[46] In the abovementioned cases the hearing is simplified because during the oral proceedings the course of the court hearing is not recorded and sometimes the court even can examine the case in the written procedure if a judge recognises that such examination of the case will not prejudice the stability of family relationships and the interests of children and spouses.[47] When passing a judgment to dissolve a marriage by the mutual consent of both spouses, the court shall confirm the contract as to the consequences of the divorce submitted by the spouses if this contract meets the requirements of the laws.[48] When passing a judgment to dissolve a marriage on the application of one of the spouses, the court must also decide the questions of the residence of the minor children of the spouses, the establishment of participation in their upbringing and the communication and maintenance of the minor children with the separated parent, and the maintenance of the spouse, except in cases where the property is divided by a joint agreement of the spouses, certified by a notary, or a court decision on the division of joint property has entered into force.[49] The marriage is considered to be dissolved from the date of the effect[50] of court's decision to dissolve it. The court must send this decision to the civil registry office that registered the marriage by electronic means no later than the next working day after the court decision to dissolve the marriage takes effect, so that the civil registry office can register the divorce in accordance with the procedure established by the Law on the Registration of Civil Status Acts.[51] The simplified procedure also gives a lot of benefit for spouses as they save time and money—the applications submitted by mutual consent of both spouses or under one of the spouses request[52] shall be

[45] See Article 538 (3) CCP.

[46] See Article 538 (4) CCP.

[47] See Article 540 (1) CCP.

[48] See Article 541 (1) CCP.

[49] See Article 541 (2) CCP.

[50] The judgements of the court of the first instance that have not been appealed against shall become effective after the time-limit for appeal has elapsed. The judgement which has been appealed shall become effective, unless it has been reversed, after the case has been heard on appeal, and the ruling or a new judgement of the court of the appeal instance shall come into effect as of the day of the adoption thereof. In case the judgement or ruling is not subject to appeal in the instances specified in the CCP, they shall come into effect on the day of the adoption thereof (see Article 279 (1) CCP).

[51] TAR, 2015-12-14, Nr. 19697.

[52] Only in cases and under the conditions that are listed in Articles 3.51 (1) and 3.55 CC.

Article 3.51 (1) CC establishes that a marriage may be dissolved by mutual consent of the spouses if all the following conditions are met: (1) more than one year has elapsed since the marriage; (2) both spouses have entered into an agreement on the consequences of the divorce (division of property, maintenance of children, etc.); (3) both spouses are fully active in this area.

Article 3.55 (1) CC establishes that a marriage may be dissolved at the request of one of the spouses before the district court of the applicant's place of residence under at least one of the following conditions: (1) the spouses have been living apart for more than one year; (2) one of the

heard by a court no later than thirty days from the date of their receipt[53] and in such cases the spouses are exempted from stamp duty[54] which in case of a dispute can exceed thousands depending of the amount of the claim which in matrimonial property disputes can be rather high.[55]

Also, in every family case a party dissatisfied with the outcome of the case has the right to appeal to the district court within the term of thirty days counting from the date of delivery of the judgment of the court of first instance.[56] In very exceptional cases the time limit for lodging an appeal may be extended if the court finds that this time limit has been missed for important reasons.[57]

A party dissatisfied with the outcome of the case in the appeal has also the right to apply to the Supreme Court (Court of Cassation) for cassation procedure within the term of three months from the date of entry into force of the appealed decision[58] but only in cases when there are grounds for cassation.[59] An appeal in cassation may be filed by the persons participating in the case.[60] The cassation appeal must be prepared and sign by the attorney at law.[61] The decision of the Supreme Court is final, not subject to any further appeal in national judicial system and takes effect from the date of its adoption.[62] Also, the interpretations set out in the order of the Court of Cassation shall be binding to the courts hearing the case once again (if the

spouses has been recognised as legally incapacitated in this field or limited in capacity by a court decision adopted after the marriage; (3) one of the spouses has been declared missing by the court; (4) one of the spouses has been serving a term of imprisonment for over a year for the commission of a non-premeditated crime.

[53] See Article 540 (2) CCP.

[54] See Article 83 (1)(12) CCP.

[55] See Article 80 (1)(1) CCP.

[56] See Articles 301 (1), 301 (3), 307 (1) CCP.

[57] A separate complaint (*atskirasis skundas*) may be lodged against a court decision rejecting an application to renew a missed time limit for lodging an appeal. If the appellate court upholds such a separate complaint and renews the time-limit for lodging an appeal, the Chairman of the Civil Division of the appellate instance court shall remit the appeal to the panel of judges of that court or return it to the court of first instance. When the case is remitted to a panel of judges of the Court of Appeal, the court of appeal shall comply with the requirements laid down in Article 317 (1) CCP. Where, in accordance with Article 317 (2) CCP, the case is referred to a court of appeal and that court finds that the time-limit for lodging an appeal has expired, it may: (1) on its own initiative (ex officio) renew the time-limit for lodging an appeal if it is clear from the material available that the time-limit was missed for important reasons; (2) propose to the person participating in the case to submit an application for renewal of the term for filing an appeal. An application for renewal of the missed time limit for lodging an appeal may not be made more than three months after the date of the judgment (Article 307 CCP).

[58] See Article 345 (1) CCP.

[59] See Article 346 CCP.

[60] See Article 342 CCP.

[61] See Article 347 (3) CCP.

[62] See Article 362 (1) CCP.

case is returned for re-examination) and as precedents for all the courts of lower instances and the Supreme Court itself.

5.2 International Jurisdiction

As noted above, since Lithuania has not acceded to the EU Matrimonial Property Regulation, Lithuanian courts have no EU instrument to be applied for determining jurisdiction, applicable law and the recognition and enforcement of decisions in matters of matrimonial property regimes. Such matters also do not fall within the scope of the Lugano Convention. Therefore, when deciding on the jurisdiction in matrimonial property cases, Lithuanian courts apply international (bilateral) agreements (where existent), or national private international law on international jurisdiction established by the CCP.

In family cases, there are usually several claims (such as divorce and division of matrimonial property, determination of paternity, the child's place of residence, contact rights with the child, and the award of maintenance). Therefore, upon the receipt of the claim, the court must first determine the international (foreign) element for each of the requirements, and the state concerned and establish whether it has international jurisdiction. In the case of several claims, the court must decide on the jurisdiction of each of them separately. This might sometimes result in an inconvenient scenario for the litigants as the jurisdiction for related matters might lie within the jurisdiction of courts located in different countries. Under Lithuanian case law, the jurisdiction for one of the issues filed with the claim does not automatically presuppose the possibility for the courts of the Republic of Lithuania to hear other issues in the same claim.[63]

Under Article 784 (1) CCP, Lithuanian courts have jurisdiction in family cases if at least one of the spouses is a citizen of the Republic of Lithuania or a stateless person who has a habitual residence in Lithuania. Moreover, if both spouses have their habitual residence in the Republic of Lithuania, their family cases shall be heard exclusively by the courts of the Republic of Lithuania.[64] If both spouses are foreigners but have common habitual residence in Lithuania, Lithuanian courts will also have jurisdiction.[65] In addition, Article 786 CCP establishes that Lithuanian courts have exclusive jurisdiction to hear cases concerning legal relations *in rem* related to the immovable property located in Lithuania. Naturally, these rules are only applicable if the case is not related to another EU state[66] and there is no

[63] Supreme Court, Ruling of 20 October 2016, No. e3K-3-426/2016, para 13.

[64] Article 784 (2) CCP.

[65] Article 784 (3) CCP.

[66] If this is the case, the Regulation Brussels II bis or other EU instruments are applicable.

international agreement[67] that should be applied. Therefore, in situations where Lithuanian national private international law applies, there are two cases—under Article 784 (1) and Article 786 CCP—when Lithuanian courts have exclusive jurisdiction to hear a family dispute. These provisions are very important as failure to observe them might lead to non-recognition of a foreign court judgement.[68] If a court, that is requested to recognise foreign judgement, determines that the case falls within the exclusive competence of the courts of the Republic of Lithuania or a third country,[69] this ground alone would be sufficient for the court to refuse recognition and enforcement of the foreign judgment.

In one case before the Court of Appeal of Lithuania,[70] the applicant applied to the court for recognition and enforcement of the British Bury St. Edmunds Family Court decisions in order he could register his personal ownership of the apartment in the Lithuanian Real Property Register. Even though the interested person (ex-wife) upheld the applicant's position, the Court of Appeal refused recognition and enforcement. The court referred to the consistently formed case law[71] and refused recognition due to violation of the exclusive jurisdiction rules.

It is important to note that this rule works and *vice versa*: the Lithuanian courts take into account whether the judgement adopted in Lithuania would be recognised in the country of enforcement. In this regard, the Supreme Court had clearly stated that the rule of Article 786 CCP means that in the absence of international agreements or EU legal acts allowing to do so, the courts of the Republic of Lithuania may

---

[67] For instance, 1996 Hague Convention on Jurisdiction, Applicable Law, Recognition and Enforcement and Cooperation in Respect of Parental Responsibility and Measures for the Protection of Children.

[68] Article 810 (1) of CCP declares that judgments of foreign courts shall be recognised on the basis of international agreements. In the absence of an international agreement, recognition of foreign judgments shall be refused if: (1) the judgment has not entered into force under the law of the state in which it was given; (2) in accordance with the law of the Republic of Lithuania or the provisions of an international agreement, the case falls within the exclusive competence of the courts of the Republic of Lithuania or a third country; (3) the party who did not take part in the proceedings was not duly notified of the initiation of civil proceedings and no procedural defines was available during the proceedings and, in cases where the party was incapacitated or restricted in a particular area, adequate representation; (4) the judgment of the foreign court the recognition of which is requested is not compatible with the judgment of the court of the Republic of Lithuania made in a case between the same parties; (5) the decision is in conflict with the public order established in the Constitution of the Republic of Lithuania; (6) in making a decision, the court of a foreign state has resolved issues regarding the legal capacity of a citizen of the Republic of Lithuania, legal representation, family property or inheritance legal relations and this is contrary to private international law of the Republic of Lithuania, unless Lithuanian courts have made the same decision.

[69] Article 810 (1)(2) CCP.

[70] Supreme Court, Ruling of 14 October 2021, No. e2T-105-798/2021.

[71] See i.e. Lithuanian Court of Appeal, Ruling of 12 August 2021, No. e2T-74-407/2021; Lithuanian Court of Appeal, Ruling of 12 May 2020, No. e2T-38-370/2020; Lithuanian Court of Appeal, Ruling of 13 May 2014, No. 2T-46/2014; Lithuanian Court of Appeal, Ruling of 6 August 2012, No. 2T-66/2012.

not rule on rights *in rem* to immovable property located in other states.[72] A good example illustrating such a situation was analysed by the Supreme Court.[73] The case concerned spouses (Lithuanian nationals) residing in Switzerland. The couple applied to the court in Lithuania for divorce and division of their matrimonial property some of which were located in Lithuania and some in Switzerland, and other related issues. Having analysed the situation, the Supreme Court noted that when deciding on the jurisdiction to hear a claim for the division of immovable property located in the Swiss Confederation, special attention should be paid to the principles of reciprocity and respect that are established in international law. Under Swiss law,[74] the Swiss courts have exclusive jurisdiction in matters relating to immovable property situated in Switzerland. The Supreme Court observed that in accordance with such regulation and the established rule that the right of a state to decide on immovable property in its territory is exclusive and related to its sovereignty, the courts of Lithuania may not decide on property rights to immovable property in the Swiss Confederation. The court underlined that the Lithuanian court's judgment would not be recognised and enforced in Switzerland.

In another recent case decided by the Supreme Court of Lithuania, the question of future enforceability of a judgement was also one of the main questions considered by the court.[75] In this case, the spouses had their habitual residence in Norway, and they owned movable and immovable property there. However, as both spouses were Lithuanian citizens, they decided to apply for divorce in Lithuania. Considering the strong link of the spouses to Norway, the place of matrimonial property and the fact that there was no international agreement with Norway that could be applied, the court ruled that it did not have jurisdiction to decide on immovable property and movable property in Norway. The court noted that a Lithuanian court's decision on the division of movable property would not be recognised in Norway, which, as the country of habitual residence, has jurisdiction to decide on the couple's matrimonial property in Norway.

To sum up, one must take into account that Lithuanian courts have exclusive jurisdiction to hear cases concerning legal relations in rem related to the immovable property located in Lithuania. This includes also disputes between spouses. Foreign court judgement will not be recognised and enforced in Lithuania if the spouses ignore this rule. The same rule vice versa means that Lithuanian court, hearing an international divorce case, have to check whether any other foreign court has exclusive jurisdiction to hear the same case.

---

[72] Supreme Court, Ruling of 2 October 2015, No. 3K-3-515-687/2015.

[73] Supreme Court, Ruling of 22 February 2018, No. e3K-3-73-378/2018.

[74] Article 97 of the Swiss Federal Act on Private International Law.

[75] Supreme Court, Ruling of 3 June 2020, No. e3K-3-309-916/2020.

6 Would the Application of the Matrimonial Property Regulation Bring Positive Changes to Lithuanian Practice?

In the light of the legal framework and case law discussed above, as well as taking into account international treaties and other international obligations, it can be seen that, as long as Lithuania has not joined the Twin Regulations, national courts can practically never rule on the immovable property located abroad, as there is a risk of non-recognition of the judgment. Such problems can arise even in the case of the division of movable matrimonial property located in another country. However, as it is evident from an increasing number cases, spouses often acquire movable and immovable property in several countries. As a result, couples have to face inconvenient consequences: in order to separate and divide their matrimonial property they have to undergo court proceedings in several countries with often different laws to be applied (in case they did not choose the applicable law).

Similarly, even when divorcing by mutual consent, the spouses have no possibility to agree on the division of assets located outside Lithuania. Such an agreement on the division of matrimonial property abroad would not be certified by notaries or approved by national courts, as resulting court decisions would face recognition and enforcement problems. This poses a number of practical problems for individuals.

The situation would change at least with regard to the 18 EU Member States participating in the enhanced cooperation should Lithuania join the Twin Regulations.[76] If that were the case, national courts would be able to resolve all family property issues in a single case, even when the property is located in different EU Member States.[77] Moreover, the rules on applicable law for matrimonial property would be unified and interpreted autonomously.[78] The Twin Regulations enable individuals to resolve their cases efficiently before the courts of a single EU Member State, in particular by empowering a single court to resolve the division of property located in different countries by applying the law of a single country. The Twin Regulations also do not prevent the parties from settling their dispute amicably out of court, for example, by applying to a notary or mediator in the EU Member State of their choice.

From the legal perspective, the participation of Lithuania in the Twin Regulations is feasible. In Lithuanian law, the rules on applicable law in family property cases are similar to those laid down in the Twin Regulations, which leads to the conclusion that there should be no major problems with the application of the Regulations.

---

[76] According to Article 328(1) TFEU, the enhanced cooperation is to be open to all Member States, subject to compliance with conditions of participation laid down by the authorising decision and the acts already adopted within that framework. See further: Kavoliūnaitė-Ragauskienė (2022), pp. 25–37.

[77] See Kunda and Limantė (2022), pp. 71–101; Frimston (2019); Franzina (2018), p. 159.

[78] See, e.g., Pogorelčnik Vogrinc (2022), pp. 101–128; Lagarde (2019).

However, this again brings the question of regulation of registered partnerships—something Lithuanian politicians find hard to agree on.

7 Concluding Remarks

The division of matrimonial property between spouses in Lithuania is scrupulously regulated both at the domestic and private international law level. However, one has to admit that the private international law rules were developed in times when the number of cross-border couples was limited, and it was not common for spouses to own property in several countries. The situation has changed in the last few decades, and cases with foreign elements arise increasingly often. Consequently, in family cases Lithuanian courts often have to deal with the complex and uneasy questions of international jurisdiction and the application of foreign law.

In the opinion of the authors of this paper, such a situation calls for reconsidering Lithuania's position regarding joining the enhanced cooperation in the area of jurisdiction, applicable law and the recognition and enforcement of decisions in matters of family property regimes. Though it would not simplify all the cross-border cases, the rules with at least 18 other EU Member States would be unified and simplified. This would bring legal certainty and more clarity and practical solutions to a considerable number of families that otherwise might face a need to litigate twice or even more times to have their matrimonial property rights settled.

Legal Instruments and Case-Law

Council Regulation (EU) 2016/1103 of 24 June 2016 implementing enhanced cooperation in the area of jurisdiction, applicable law and the recognition and enforcement of decisions in matters of matrimonial property regimes, OJ L 183, 8.7.2016, p. 1–29.

Council Regulation (EU) 2016/1104 of 24 June 2016 implementing enhanced cooperation in the area of jurisdiction, applicable law and the recognition and enforcement of decisions in matters of the property consequences of registered partnerships, OJ L 183, 8.7.2016, p. 30–56

Convention on jurisdiction and the enforcement of judgments in civil and commercial matters (Lugano Convention) of 16 September 1988

Agreement between the Republic of Lithuania and the Republic of Poland on Legal Assistance and Legal Relations in Civil, Family, Labour and Criminal Matters of 26 January 1993

Constitution of the Republic of Lithuania. Lietuvos aidas, 1992-11-10, Nr. 220-0

Civil Code of the Republic of Lithuania. Valstybės žinios, 2000-09-06, Nr. 74-2262

Code of Civil Procedure of the Republic of Lithuania. Valstybės žinios, 2002-04-06, Nr. 36-1340

Law on the Real Property Register of the Republic of Lithuania, Valstybės žinios, 1996-10-16, Nr. 100-2261
Law on the Registration of Civil Status Acts, TAR, 2015-12-14, Nr. 19697
Constitutional Court Ruling of 28 September 2011, Nr. 21/2008
Supreme Court, Ruling of 3 October 2005, No. 3K-3-410/2005
Supreme Court, Ruling of 10 April, No. 3K-3-251/2006
Supreme Court, Ruling of 16 November, 2005 No. 3K-3-529/2005
Supreme Court, Ruling of 15 February, 2006, No. 3K-3-126/2006
Supreme Court, Ruling of 20, June, 2007, No. 3K-3-220/2007
Supreme Court, Ruling of 3 November, 2009, No. 3K-3-479/2009
Supreme Court, Ruling of 18 May, 2017, No. 3K-3-243-969/2017Supreme Court, Ruling of 8 November 2010, No. 3K-3-432/2010Supreme Court, Ruling of 28 March 2011, No. 3K-3-134/2011
Supreme Court, Ruling of 16 December, 2011, No. 3K-3-517/2011
Supreme Court, Ruling of 11 April, 2012, No. 3K-3-52/2012
Supreme Court, Ruling of 10 May 2013, No. 3K-3-191/2013
Supreme Court, Ruling of 30 May 2013, No. 3K-7-159/2013
Supreme Court, Ruling of 8 May 2015, No. 3K-3-259-378/2015
Supreme Court, Ruling of 2 October 2015, No. 3K-3-515-687/2015
Supreme Court, Ruling of 20 October 2016, No. e3K-3-426/2016
Supreme Court, Ruling of 18 May, 2017, No. 3K-3-243-969/2017
Supreme Court, Ruling of 22 February 2018, No. e3K-3-73-378/2018
Supreme Court, Ruling of 13 June 2018, No. 3K-3-229-378/2018
Supreme Court, Ruling of 21 February, 2019, No. 3K-3-55-916/2019
Supreme Court, Ruling of 11 April 2019, No. e3K-3-133-421/2019
Supreme Court, Ruling of 3 June 2020, No. e3K-3-309-916/2020
Supreme Court, Ruling of 14 October 2021, No. e2T-105-798/2021
Supreme Court, Ruling of October 27, 2021, No. e3K-3-266-403/2021
Supreme Court, Ruling of 9 June 2022, No. e3K-3-159-916/2022
Lithuanian Court of Appeal, Ruling of 6 August 2012, No. 2T-66/2012
Lithuanian Court of Appeal, Ruling of 13 May 2014, No. 2T-46/2014
Lithuanian Court of Appeal, Ruling of 12 May 2020, No. e2T-38-370/2020
Lithuanian Court of Appeal, Ruling of 12 August 2021, No. e2T-74-407/2021
Vilnius Regional Court, Ruling of 17 January 2017, No. 2A-535-580/2017

References

Bibliography

Ambrazevičiūtė K, Kavoliūnaitė E, Mizaras V (2012) Šeimos kaip teisės kategorijos turinys Lietuvos Respublikos įstatymuose. Teisės problemos. 4(78):74–107
Franzina P (2018) Jurisdiction in matters related to property regimes under EU private international law (2017/2018). Yearb Priv Int Law 19:159

Frimston, R (2019) Jurisdiction: Articles 4-19. In: Bergquist U, Damascelli D, Frimston R, Lagarde P, Reinhartz B (eds) The EU regulations on matrimonial and patrimonial property. Oxford University Press, Oxford

Kavoliūnaitė-Ragauskienė E (2022) The twin regulations: development and adoption. In: Ruggeri L, Limantė A, Pogorelčnik Vogrinc N (eds) The regulation of matrimonial property and property of registered partnerships. Intersentia

Keserauskas Š et al (2002) Šeimos teisė. Lietuvos Respublikos civilinio kodekso komentaras. Trečioji knyga. Vilnius, Justitia

Kudinavičiūtė-Michailovienė I (2008) Bendro gyvenimo neįregistravus santuokos (sugyventi- niai) teisinio reglamentavimo problemos. Jurisprudencija 4(106)

Kudinavičiūtė-Michailovienė I (2009) Šeimos narių teisės į gyvenamąją patalpą įgyvendinimas ir gynimas. Socialinių mokslų studijos 3(3):193–212

Kunda I, Limantė A (2022) Jurisdictional provisions in the twin regulations. In: Ruggeri L, Limantė A, Pogorelčnik Vogrinc N (eds) The regulation of matrimonial property and property of registered partnerships. Intersentia

Lagarde P (2019) Applicable law: Articles 20-35. In: Bergquist U, Damascelli D, Frimston R, Lagarde P, Reinhartz B (eds) The EU regulations on matrimonial and patrimonial property. Oxford University Press, Oxford

Limantė A, Chochrin T (2019) "Lithuania". In: Ruggeri L, Kunda I, Winkler S (eds) Family property and succession in EU member states: national reports on the collected data. Sveučilište u Rijeci, Pravni fakultet/University of Rijeka, Faculty of Law, Rijeka, Croatia, 2019, ISBN 978-953-8034-25-1

Mikelėnas V et al (2002) LR civilinio kodekso komentaras. Trečioji knyga. Šeimos teisė. Vilnius, Justitia

Mikelėnas V et al (2009) Civilinė teisė. Bendroji dalis. Vilnius, Justitia

Mizaras V (2012) Teisė į šeimos gyvenimą: konstituciniai ir civiliniai teisiniai aspektai // Nepriklausomos Lietuvos teisė: praeitis, dabartis ir ateitis. Liber amicorum J. Prapiesčiui (mokslinių straipsnių rinkinys). Vilnius

Petrylaitė V (2014) Family and succession law in Lithuania. Kluwer Law International

Pogorelčnik Vogrinc N (2022) Applicable law in the twin regulations. In: Ruggeri L, Limantė A, Pogorelčnik Vogrinc N (eds) The regulation of matrimonial property and property of registered partnerships. Intersentia

Ravluševičius P (2017) "Lithuania". In: Basedow, J, Rühl G, Ferrari F, de Miguel Asensio P (eds) Encyclopedia of private international law. Edward Elgar

Sagatys G (2010) The concept of family in Lithuanian law. Jurisprudence. 1(119)

Tamošiūnienė E, Kudinavičiūtė-Michailovienė I (2013) Šeimos bylų nagrinėjimo ir teismo sprendimų vykdymo ypatumai. MRU

Vitkevičius P (2006) Šeimos narių turtiniai teisiniai santykiai. Vilnius, Justitia

Material Ambit of EU Regulations on Property Regimes of Cross-Border Couples: Which Family Formations Are Left to Croatian National Legislation?

Danijela Vrbljanac

1 Introduction

On 29 January 2019, two EU regulations on cross-border couples' property regimes started to apply, thus supplementing the existing mosaic of EU private international law instruments dealing with family and succession law. These are Council Regulation (EU) 2016/1103 of 24 June 2016 implementing enhanced cooperation in the area of jurisdiction, applicable law and the recognition and enforcement of decisions in matters of matrimonial property regimes[1] (hereinafter: Regulation 2016/1103) and Council Regulation (EU) 2016/1104 of 24 June 2016 implementing enhanced cooperation in the area of jurisdiction, applicable law and the recognition and enforcement of decisions in matters of the property consequences of registered partnerships[2] (hereinafter: Regulation 2016/1104), often referred to as the Twin Regulations. It is no coincidence that on the same day, the new Croatian PIL Act (*Zakon o međunarodnom privatnom pravu*)[3] entered into force and replaced the 1982 PIL Act (*Zakon o rješavanju sukoba zakona s propisima drugih zemalja u određenim odnosima*)[4] which Croatia continued to apply after the dissolution of the former Yugoslavia.

The material scopes of application of Regulation 2016/1103 and Regulation 2016/1104 are determined by the notions of marriage and registered partnership, respectively. Following the analysis of the respective terms, the conclusion on which

[1]Regulation 2016/1103, OJ L 183, 8.7.2016, pp. 1–29.

[2]Regulation 2016/1104, OJ L 183, 8.7.2016, pp. 30–56.

[3]Croatian PIL Act, NN 101/17.

[4]The 1982 PIL Act, NN 53/91, 88/01.

D. Vrbljanac (✉)
University of Rijeka, Faculty of Law, Rijeka, Croatia
e-mail: danijela.vrbljanac@uniri.hr

I. Kunda et al. (eds.), *Balkan Yearbook of European and International Law 2022*,
Balkan Yearbook of European and International Law 2022,
https://doi.org/10.1007/978-3-031-29432-7_4

family formations are not covered by the Twin Regulations ambit is reached. Against this backdrop, the author will scrutinise whether such family formations may be subjected to private international law provisions of the new Croatian PIL Act or another EU private international law instrument.

2 The Twin Regulations' Material Scope of Application

Articles 1(1) of the Twin Regulations determine the material scope of application of these instruments. The material scope is defined very briefly. Both of the Regulations state that they govern matrimonial property regime in case of Regulation 2016/1103 and property consequences of registered partnerships in case of the Regulation 2016/1104. Recitals 18 of both Regulations offer additional guidance in this respect by providing that material ambits cover all civil-law aspects of matrimonial property regimes or property consequences of registered partnerships, both the daily management of matrimonial property or property consequences of registered partnerships and the liquidation of the regime, in particular as a result of the couple's separation or the death of one of the spouses or partners.

Article 27 of the Twin Regulations may be used for further guidance in identifying matters which are covered by their material ambit. Article 27 is virtually identical in both Regulations and represents a provision on the scope of applicable law. However, its non-exhaustive list may be considered to enumerate matters falling into the material scope of Twin Regulations such as classification of property of either or both spouses or partners and responsibility of one spouse or partner for liabilities and debts of the other.

The limitation on the Twin Regulations' ambit is contained in Articles 1(2) of the Regulations. Some of the listed exclusions are matters which are left to national laws of Member States such as legal capacity of the spouses or partners and existence, validity or recognition of a marriage or registered partnership. Some other exclusions are the result of the fact that they are governed by another EU or international instrument. This is the case with maintenance regulated by the Maintenance Regulation[5] and the 2007 Hague Protocol,[6] as well as succession to the estate of a deceased spouse or partner regulated by the Succession Regulation.[7]

[5]Council Regulation (EC) No 4/2009 of 18 December 2008 on jurisdiction, applicable law, recognition and enforcement of decisions and cooperation in matters relating to maintenance obligations, OJ L 7, 10.1.2009, pp. 1–79.

[6]Hague Protocol of 23 November 2007 on the Law Applicable to Maintenance Obligations.

[7]Regulation (EU) No 650/2012 of the European Parliament and of the Council of 4 July 2012 on jurisdiction, applicable law, recognition and enforcement of decisions and acceptance and enforcement of authentic instruments in matters of succession and on the creation of a European Certificate of Succession, OJ L 201, 27.7.2012, pp. 107–134.

3 The Notion of Marriage and Registered Partnership in the Twin Regulations

Since the Twin Regulations' scopes of application encompass matrimonial property regime and property consequences of registered partnership, their material ambit will necessarily build upon the understanding of the terms "marriage" and "registered partnership".

Regulation 2016/1104 offers the definition of the registered partnership. It is defined in Art. 3(1)(a) as a "regime governing the shared life of two people which is provided for in law, the registration of which is mandatory under that law and which fulfils the legal formalities required by that law for its creation". The definition contains prerequisites which registered partnership must fulfil in order to be covered by the Regulation 2016/1104 ambit. First, the definition requires the existence of a shared life of two people which is provided by law. Therefore, polygamous relationships remain outside of its scope.[8] Second, the partnership must have an official nature in the form of registration. In Recital 16, the European legislator indicated that a distinction should be made between "couples whose union is institutionally sanctioned by the registration of their partnership with a public authority and couples in de facto cohabitation". Such *de facto* unions, should be distinguished from registered partnerships, "which have an official character that makes it possible to take account of their specific features and lay down rules on the subject in Union legislation". Third, for the registered partnership to fall into the Regulation 2016/1104 ambit, fulfilment of legal formalities required by the law under which the partnership is registered is required.[9]

The Regulation 2016/1103 does not provide the definition of the term marriage. The lack of the definition is a consequence of the fact that the concept of marriage is not unified on the EU level.[10] Marriage represents a traditional institution of family law recognised in all EU Member States. However, its regulation differs across the EU based on various elements, such as rights and obligations of spouses, possibility that a religious marriage produces civil consequences[11] and the possibility for same-sex couples to enter into marriage.[12] Even if one accepts that, in some aspects, EU

[8] Dutta (2018), p. 147.

[9] On these conditions Cazorla Gonzalez and Soto Moya (2022), pp. 44–45.

[10] Winkler (2021), p. 455.

[11] Antokolskaia (2010), p. 402.

[12] Laws and Families database, interactive database, provides various information on regulation of marriage and other formal and informal unions in EU Member States (not all Member States are included), including rights and obligations of spouses, partners or members of the union, as well as the fact whether marriage or other union may legally commence before the registry, public authority or religious authority. Laws and families. Available at: https://www.lawsandfamilies.eu/en/legal-project/interactive-database/. Accessed 14 Mar 2022.

On different understanding of marriage in civil and common law systems see Harding (2011), pp. 206–207.

Member States laws are evolving towards a unified understanding of marriage,[13] it is clear that, for the purpose of Regulation 2016/1103, there is no such unified concept of marriage. In Recital 17 of the Regulation 2016/1103, the European legislator stated that the definition of the term marriage is left to national legislation. However, it does not provide an unambiguous answer to which Member State national law is Recital 17 referring to for the definition of marriage.[14] The characterisation issue is of particular importance considering that not all Member States which participate in the enhanced cooperation regarding the Twin Regulations recognise same-sex marriages.[15] If a court of a Member State not recognising the same-sex marriage is seised with a property regime claim by one the spouses of a same-sex marriage, the question is raised which of the Twin Regulations will the seised court rely on. The *lex fori* approach undermines the uniform application of the Twin Regulations given that their material scope of application will differ before courts of different Member States. For that reason, characterisation of the term marriage according to the "State of the origin", i.e. the law of the state under which the couple regime was created or registered, was suggested as a more satisfactory solution, but at the same time, a less feasible one.[16] The predominant view in literature seems to point towards the *lex fori*.[17] Furthermore, the *lex fori* characterisation might be more acceptable from the perspective of the concerns certain Member States expressed during the legislative procedure of the Twin Regulations adoption, i.e. that they would be forced to recognise same-sex marriages and registered partnerships.[18] The unfortunate reluctance of these Member States which are currently not participating in the enhanced cooperation might be mitigated by the *lex fori* characterisation. The *lex fori* approach allocates more control to the state authorities seised with the property regime claim in terms of characterisation of the couple's union and may be, in the future, an advantage encouraging Member States to join the enhanced cooperation.

Another issue which the *lex fori* characterisation raises is the fact that it may be understood in two distinguished ways: as a reference to substantive law and a reference to national law, including private international law rules.[19] According to one part of the doctrine, the reference to the *lex fori* means reference to the substantive rules of the court seised. Such interpretation stems from Recitals

[13] See opinion of Advocate General Wathelet delivered on 11 January 2018, Case C-673/16, *Coman*, EU:C:2018:2, paras 56–67.

[14] Kunda (2019), p. 29; Rudolf (2019), pp. 134–135.

[15] For more information on which Member States provide the possibility of same-sex marriage, same-sex partnership or neither of these options, see Dougan (2022), pp. 219–220.

[16] Dutta (2018), pp. 150–151.

[17] Joubert (2017), p. 7; Dutta (2018), p. 149; Coester-Waltjen (2018), p. 198; Rodriguez Benot (2020), p. 18.

[18] Outcome of the Council Meeting, Brussels, 3 and 4 December 2015, p. 5. Available at: https://www.consilium.europa.eu/media/23027/st14937en15_v5.pdf. Accessed 30 May 2022. See Dougan (2022), p. 222.

[19] Rudolf (2019), pp. 134–135.

17 and 21 as well as Article 9 of the Regulation 2016/1103.[20] Under this approach, if the case regarding property regime of same-sex spouses is brought before the court of a participating Member State which recognises same-sex marriage, the court would apply Regulation 2016/1103. A more problematic situation occurs if the same case is brought before the court of the Member State which only allows registration of partnership to same-sex couples. The other part of doctrine advocates for understanding the *lex fori* characterisation as a reference to national law, including its private international law rules. It is argued that the term marriage may have a broader meaning in cross-border context compared to purely national situations.[21] According to the latter approach, when seised with a claim regarding property regime of same-sex spouses, the court of a participating Member State which recognises same-sex marriage, will not necessarily resort to Regulation 2016/1103. Similarly, if the same claim reaches the court of the Member State which only allows registration of partnership to same-sex couples, the court may, if its private international law rules provide so, apply Regulation 2016/1103. For instance, even though Germany provides for the possibility of same-sex marriage, under Art. 17b(4) of the Introductory Act to the Civil Code (*Einführungsgesetz zum Bürgerlichen Gesetzbuche*), same-sex marriage is, in some aspects, treated for the purpose of the private international law as registered partnership.[22] Under this second approach, there are additional options. The court could characterise the same-sex marriage in accordance with law applicable under national private international law rules or it could inspect if the same-sex couple union may be recognised in any form.[23] The extensive interpretation of the *lex fori* characterisation, so that it includes not only substantive provisions, but also private international law ruled of the forum, seems to be a preferred approach.[24]

4 Marriage and Registered Partnership in Croatian Law

In the Republic of Croatia, marriage is reserved only for opposite-sex couples since it is defined as a life union of a woman and a man in Croatian Constitution and Family Act (*Obiteljski zakon*).[25] Same-sex couples have the option of registering their partnership under Act on Life Partnership of Persons of the Same Sex (*Zakon o*

[20] Coester-Waltjen (2018), p. 198.

[21] Bonomi (2017), p. 131 *et seq*, particularly 132.

[22] Dutta (2018), p. 152.

[23] Dutta (2018), pp. 150–151.

[24] Bonomi (2017), p. 132; Dutta (2018), pp. 152–153.

[25] Art. 62(2) of the Croatian Constitution (NN 56/1990, 135/1997, 113/2000, 28/2001, 76/2010, 5/2014). This definition is the result of the national referendum held on 1 December 2014. See Decision of the Constitutional Court SuP-O-1/2014 of 14 January 2014, available at: https://narodne-novine.nn.hr/clanci/sluzbeni/2014_01_5_93.html. Accessed 18 Feb 2022. Croatian Family Act (NN 103/2015, 98/2019, 47/2020) contains a definition consistent with the one from the Constitution in Art. 12 which prescribes that a marriage is a life union of a man and a woman

životnom partnerstvu osoba istog spola, hereinafter: Life Partnership Act).[26] Under Croatian legislation, registered partnership, or more precisely, life partnership, as the Life Partnership Act refers to it, may only be entered into by same-sex couples.

Life partnership is defined as a family life union of two persons of the same sex concluded before the competent authority.[27] Life partnership under the Life Partnership Act requires shared life of a couple and mandatory registration.[28] Therefore it fulfils the conditions set out in the definition of the registered partnership in Regulation 2016/1104. When a court of a participating Member State is seised with the proceedings regarding property relations of a same-sex couple which registered their life partnership in Croatia, that partnership should fall into the ambit of the Regulation 2016/1104.

Since Croatia does not recognise same-sex marriages, the issue that occurs is the question which of the Twin Regulations should the Croatian court apply when confronted with a claim regarding matrimonial property regime of same-sex spouses. Croatian legislator anticipated the problem which may arise due to differences among states in regulating same-sex marriages. Croatian PIL Act contains a provision similar to the mentioned Article 17b(4) of the German Introductory Act to the Civil Code. Pursuant to Art. 32(2) of the Croatian PIL Act, same-sex marriage concluded in a foreign country is recognised as a life partnership if it is entered into in accordance with the law of the State in which it is concluded. Therefore, if the Croatian court is seised with the claim concerning the matrimonial property of same-sex spouses, the issue will be resolved through private international law provisions of the *lex fori* and the court will apply Regulation 2016/1104. Application of Regulation 2016/1103 before the Croatian court will only be reserved for opposite-sex marriages. If, on the other hand, Croatian court is confronted with the claim regarding the property of an opposite-sex registered partnership, autonomous definition of this family formation in Regulation 2016/1104 requires that the Croatian court applies Regulation 2016/1104, even though the Croatian legislation does not provide an option of registration to different-sex couples.

Certain authors refer to Art. 32(2) of the Croatian PIL Act as having "downgrading" effect since the same-sex marriage is reduced to registered partnership.[29] In the context of private international law, provisions are generally aimed at finding the seat of the relationship[30] and thus detecting the legal system most closely connected to the relationship. For this reason, it is questionable whether the term "downgrading" is appropriate. Unless they embody the favourability principle in terms of the substantive outcome of the proceedings, the private international law

regulated by law. The same definition was present even prior to the amendments of 2014, in the 2003 Family Act (NN 116/2003) in Art. 5.

[26] Act on Life Partnership of Persons of the Same Sex, NN, 92/2014, 98/2019.

[27] Art. 2 of the Life Partnership Act.

[28] Part I of the Life Partnership Act.

[29] Dougan (2022), p. 228.

[30] Lipstein (1981), p. 22.

provisions are outcome-neutral. Admittedly, the approach of redefining the couple's relationship demonstrates some disadvantages such as non-conformity with the legitimate expectations of the same-sex spouses and the fact that Regulation 2016/1103 is not uniformly applied in all participating Member States.[31] On the other hand, there is an advantage to that approach. The law applicable pursuant to Regulation 2016/1104, in the absence of choice of law, is the law of the State under whose law the registered partnership was created.[32] If the respective provision is applied to matrimonial property of same-sex spouses by operation of Art. 32(2) of the Croatian PIL Act, the parties interest may be safeguarded to a greater extent, in comparison to the situation in which applicable law is determined under Regulation 2016/1103. This is because, in the absence of choice, the law applicable will be the law of the state where the registered partnership was created, i.e. in the case of same-sex marriages, where the marriage was celebrated. Otherwise, if the Regulation 2016/1103 would be applicable, it might lead to application of the law of a state which does not recognise same-sex marriages.[33]

5 Other Family Formations in EU Private International Law

Family formation which remain outside of the scope of the Twin Regulations are *de facto* unions, i.e. unions of couples which are not registered, regardless of whether they consist of same-sex or opposite-sex persons.[34] Even partnerships which are formalised through mandatory conclusion of an agreement, but are not registered, are not included in the ambit of the Regulation 2016/1104.[35] It derives from the autonomous definition in Art. 3(1)(a) and Recital 16 of the Regulation 2016/1104 that such *de facto* unions are not covered by the ambit of the Regulation 2016/1104. It is arguable whether *de facto* partnerships which under laws of certain Member States are equalized with marriage in terms of their property regime effect may be subjected to Regulation 2016/1103.[36] A certain part of the doctrine advocates for such solution.[37] In defining whether *de facto* partnerships should be covered by the Regulation 2016/1103, again the *lex fori* characterisation should be employed based on Recital 17 of the Regulation 2016/1103. As already stated, the *lex fori*

[31] Marino (2017), p. 268.

[32] Art. 26(1) of the Regulation 2016/1104.

[33] See Art. 26 of the Regulation 2016/1103.

[34] In terms of substantive law, there are significant differences in regulating these unions and their property effects across the EU. Winkler (2019), p. 453.

[35] Dutta (2018), p. 154.

[36] Rudolf (2019), p. 134.

[37] Dutta (2018), p. 156.

characterisation should be understood as a reference to both substantive provisions and private international law provisions of the forum.

Before reaching a conclusion that *de facto* partnership which cannot be included into the Twin Regulations' ambit are a matter of national private international law rules, the ambit of other relevant EU private international law sources should be inspected. On the EU level, jurisdiction for civil and commercial matters is governed by the Regulation (EU) No 1215/2012 of the European Parliament and of the Council of 12 December 2012 on jurisdiction and the recognition and enforcement of judgments in civil and commercial matters (hereinafter: the Brussels I bis Regulation),[38] whereas applicable law, depending on whether the claim is characterised as a contractual or a non-contractual one is regulated by Regulation (EC) No 593/2008 of the European Parliament and of the Council of 17 June 2008 on the law applicable to contractual obligations (hereinafter: the Rome I Regulation)[39] or Regulation (EC) No 864/2007 of the European Parliament and of the Council of 11 July 2007 on the law applicable to non-contractual obligations (hereinafter: the Rome II Regulation),[40] respectively.

Art. 1(2)(a) of the Brussels I bis Regulation prescribes that rights in property arising out of a matrimonial relationship or out of a relationship deemed by the law applicable to such relationship to have comparable effects to marriage, are excluded from its material scope of application. Rights in property arising out of the relationships, which do not have a comparable effect to marriage, are covered by this instrument. The CJEU had the opportunity of interpreting this exclusion in *Weil v. Gulacsi.*[41] Ms Weil and Mr Gulacsi were unregistered partners who lived together from 2002 to 2006. Upon the application of Ms. Weil, the Municipal Court, Szekszard, Hungary, ordered Mr Gulacsi to pay Ms Weil the sum of approximately EUR 2 060 based on their property relationship. After the unsuccessful attempt of enforcing the judgment in Hungary, Ms. Weil became aware that Mr. Gulasci had been living in the United Kingdom where he had regular income. She lodged an application, on 22 November 2017, before the Szekszard District Court Hungary for issuing the certificate referred to in Art. 53 of the Brussels I bis Regulation with the aim of enforcing the judgment in United Kingdom. In the course of that proceedings, the Hungarian court sought clarification from the CJEU on whether the case at issue falls into the material scope of application of the Brussels I bis Regulation.

The CJEU established that according to Art. 66 of the Brussels I bis Regulation, the respective case falls outside of the Brussels I bis Regulation scope *ratione temporis* since the proceedings in which the judgment was rendered were commenced prior to 10 January 2015. It was not, therefore, necessary for the CJEU to conduct analysis on whether the case falls into the Brussels I bis material scope of application. The CJEU then proceeded to analyse whether it may be considered to

[38] Brussels I bis Regulation, OJ L 351, 20.12.2012, pp. 1–32.

[39] Rome I Regulation, OJ L 177, 4.7.2008, pp. 6–16.

[40] Rome II Regulation, OJ L 199, 31.7.2007, pp. 40–49.

[41] Judgment of 6 June 2019, *Weil v. Gulacsi*, C-361/18, EU:C:2019:473.

fall into the material scope of application of the Brussels I bis predecessor, i.e. the Council Regulation (EC) No 44/2001 of 22 December 2000 on jurisdiction and the recognition and enforcement of judgments in civil and commercial matters (hereinafter: the Brussels I Regulation),[42] which was the instrument in force at the time the proceedings were commenced in Hungary. Pursuant to Art. 1(2)(a) of the Brussels I Regulation, rights in property arising out of a matrimonial relationship are excluded from the scope of that Regulation. With the enactment of the Brussels I bis Regulation, this exclusion was extended to cover relationship which, under applicable law, have comparable effects to marriage. In the light of these amendments, the CJEU concluded that the case at issue falls into the ambit of the Brussels I Regulation. Otherwise, the extension of the exclusion in the Brussels I bis Regulation would be deprived of significance. Had *Weil* fallen into the temporal scope of application of the Brussels I bis Regulation, the conclusion on whether it is covered by the material ambit of application might have been different. The provision relevant for determining *ratione materiae* scope would be Art. 1(2)(a) of the Brussels I bis Regulation which excludes from its scope property arising out of relationships deemed by the law applicable to have comparable effects to marriage.

The equivalent exclusion may be found in Art. 1(2)(c) of the Rome I Regulation and Art. 1(2)(b) of the Rome II Regulation. These exclusions, along with the one from the Brussels I bis Regulation, may be traced back to the legislative procedure of enacting the Rome II Regulation. The term "non-contractual obligations arising out of matrimonial property regimes and successions" was amended to "non-contractual obligations arising or likely to arise out of matrimonial property regimes, property regimes of relationships deemed by the law applicable to such relationships as having comparable effects to marriage and successions" with the explanation that the exclusion should clearly demonstrate that not only marital property regime questions are excluded, but also property regime questions in connection with similar relationships in law (e.g. extra-marital cohabitation).[43] The exclusion was later included into the Rome I Regulation and the Brussels I bis Regulation to ensure consistency.[44] The wording of the provision suggests that the assessment whether a particular family relationship has comparable effects to marriage should be governed by *lex causae*.[45] However, recital 8 of the Rome I Regulation and Recital 10 of the Rome II Regulation state that the reference to relationships having comparable effects to marriage and other family relationships should be interpreted in accordance with the law of the Member State in which the court is seised. These recitals are in direct collision with provisions of Art. 1(2)(c) of the Rome I Regulation and

[42] Brussels I Regulation, OJ L 12, 16.1.2001, pp. 1–23.

[43] See Report of 27.6.2005 on the proposal for a regulation of the European Parliament and of the Council on the law applicable to non-contractual obligations ("Rome II") (COM(2003)0427 – C5-0338/2003 – 2003/0168(COD)), first reading in European parliament. Available at: https://www.europarl.europa.eu/doceo/document/A-6-2005-0211_EN.html. Accessed 12 Apr 2022.

[44] See, with regards to respective exclusion in the Rome I Regulation, McParland (2015), pp. 209 and 211.

[45] See Plender and Wilderspin (2009), pp. 479–480.

Art. 1(2)(b) of the Rome II Regulation. The issue is far from being a merely theoretical one. *Gray v Hurley*,[46] the case before the England and Wales High Court, dealt with the issue of jurisdiction for discussing division of couple's property. One of the parties argued that Art. 1(2)(a) of the Brussels I bis Regulation has to be understood as a reference to substantive law of the deciding court, i.e. English law which does not deem their relationship to have comparable effects to marriage. The other party contended that under Art. 1(2)(a), English private international law rules should be considered which point towards the laws of New Zealand, under which their relationship has comparable effects to marriage. The judge did not expressly opt for one of the options but it seems he employed the *lex fori* characterisation as a way of escaping the application of a controversial English conflict of laws rule according to which the law of husband's domicile governs the mutual property rights of the spouses.[47]

A part of the literature, relying on Recitals 8 and 10 of Rome I and Rome II, respectively, sides with the interpretation of Brussels I bis, Rome I and Rome II exclusions according to which the seised court should determine whether a particular family relationship has comparable effects to marriage in accordance with the *lex fori*.[48] Even if the intention of the European Union legislator was to subject the comparability assessment to the *lex fori*, one cannot disregard the fact that the wording of the provisions is pointing towards the *lex causae*. In the situation in which the recital is not consistent with the operative provision, the recital cannot be used as a ground for derogation from the provision.[49] This is why the explanation of the "paradox" according to which legal attributes of family relationships are fixed by the law which is applicable to them, whereas the *lex fori* determines whether they have comparable effects to marriage and other family relationship,[50] is a more feasible one.

6 Other Family Formations in Croatian Law

Apart from marriage and same-sex registered partnerships (or life partnerships to use the terminology of the Life Partnership Act), Croatian law recognises extramarital union (for partners of the opposite sex) and informal life partnership (for partners of the same sex). A third remaining category of family formations which may be

[46] Gray v Hurley [2019] EWHC 1636 (QB) (25 June 2019).

[47] Gray v Hurley [2019] EWHC 1636 (QB) (25 June 2019), paras 108–115.

[48] Lüttringhaus (2020), p. 37. Bach (2011), p. 45.

[49] See for instance judgment of 19 November 1988, *Nilsson and Others*, C-162/97, EU:C:1998:554, para 54. See also Humphreys et al. (2015), pp. 2–4 and Klimas and Vaičiukaite (2008), pp. 83–85.

[50] Garcimartín Alférez (2007), p. 81.

distinguished are other *de facto* unions (of either opposite-sex or same-sex partners).[51]

According to Art. 11(1) of the Family Act, extramarital union is a life union of an unmarried woman and an unmarried man lasting at least 3 years or a shorter period if a common child was born or it was continued with conclusion of the marriage. Informal life partnership is, according to Art. 3(1) of the Life Partnership Act, a same-sex equivalent to extramarital union. It is defined as a family life union of two persons of the same sex, who have not entered into a life partnership before the competent authority, if the union lasts at least three years and has met the preconditions for the validity of the life partnership. Finally, other de *facto* unions are family formations consisting of either opposite-sex or same-sex couples which do not meet the conditions for extramarital union and informal life partnership and are not protected in the realms of family law.

The distinction of family formations in substantive law is reflected in Croatian PIL provisions. Croatian PIL Act regulates international jurisdiction for extramarital union and informal life partnership in Art. 49 which prescribes that international jurisdiction for property relations arising out of extramarital union is governed by the Regulation 2016/1103, whereas international jurisdiction for property relations arising out of informal life partnership is regulated by the Regulation 2016/1104.[52] Applicable law for these types of family formations is governed in Art. 40 which follows the same logic: applicable law for property relations of extramarital partners and informal life partners should be determined in accordance with Regulations 2016/1103 and 2016/1104, respectively. In this manner, both for issues of international jurisdiction and applicable law, the Croatian legislator opted for the approach of extending the application of the Twin Regulations provisions to cases which would not be covered by the Twin Regulations itself, since, they fall outside of their scope. Croatian PIL doctrine refers to these provisions as extending reference provisions (Croat. *proširujuće upućujuće odredbe*), based on the nomotechnical approach of the legislator in regulating the relations between the national and a supranational source of law.[53] This category of provisions has a constitutive effect, in the sense that the legislator refers to the application of the particular instrument for a case which would fall outside of the ambit of that instrument without the national provision with the extending effect.[54]

---

[51] For more on family formations in Croatia and their regulation, please see Bukovac Puvača et al. (2019), pp. 68–92.

[52] See paragraphs 2 and 4 of Art. 49 of the Croatian PIL Act.

[53] Kunda (2020), p. 33.

[54] Hoško refers to these provisions as constitutive, autonomous provisions. See Hoško (2019), pp. 24–27.

There are other instances in Croatian PIL Act of extending reference provisions. For more see: Kunda (2020), pp. 30–31. For instance, Italian legislator used the same approach when extending the application of the Brussels Convention to defendants domiciled outside of the EU in Art. 3(2) of the Italian PIL Act. See Einhorn et al. (2017), p. 2209. Another example is Belgian PIL Act which

It is undisputed that for extramarital unions and informal life partnerships which fulfil conditions from Art. 11(1) of the Family Act and Art. 3(1) of the Life Partnership Act, the Croatian court would determine its jurisdiction based on Art. 49 of the Croatian PIL Act and applicable law based on Art. 40. However, it is questionable whether family formations, which do not meet the conditions under Family Act and Life Partnership Act would be covered by the provisions of Arts. 40 and 49 of the Croatian PIL Act. In other words, should the terms extramarital union and informal life partnership in Croatian PIL Act be understood in the *lex fori* sense, as the substantive law defines them? Or should they convey a broader meaning? The previous 1982 PIL Act provided for a conflict of laws rule for property relations of an extramarital union in Art. 39, which was widely known as a pioneering rule, first of its kind to regulate property regimes of these types of family formations in PIL history.[55] The interpretation according to which extramarital union should be characterised in accordance with the *lex fori* was widely accepted.[56] Such interpretation relied on Art. 9 of the 1982 PIL Act which was a characterisation provision according to which "the law of a foreign state will be applied in accordance with its meaning and notions".[57] Art. 9 was understood as referring to a second stage of a step-by-step characterisation. In the first step characterisation was carried out under domestic law, and in the second one under foreign law, if foreign law was applicable.[58] In the new PIL Act, the provision equivalent to Art. 9 is Art. 8(2) which states that "the law of a foreign state is applied in the way it is interpreted in that state". It might be derived that, by maintaining a virtually same provision on the second step of the characterisation, the Croatian legislator kept the step-by-step characterisation. This interpretation is corroborated by the fact that in the Explanatory memorandum to the Proposal of the PIL Act, it was stated that Theses for the New PIL Act, which were published in 2001 by a part of the Croatian PIL scholarship, served to the working group as a basis for drafting

extends the application of the Rome I Regulation even for matters excluded from its material scope of application. See Francq (2017) p. 1914.

[55] Šarčević (2004), pp. 368–369.

Art. 39 of the 1982 PIL Act:

1. The law governing the property relations of persons who live in cohabitation without form of marriage is the law of the state of which they are citizens.
2. If the persons referred to in paragraph 1 of this Article do not have the same nationality the law of the state where they have common domicile is to be applied.
3. The law governing the contractual property relations between persons who live in cohabitation without form of marriage is the law governing their property relations at the time the contract is concluded.

Translation of the 1982 PIL Act from Matić (1983), p. 223.

[56] Knežević (1991), p. 133.

[57] Translation of the 1982 PIL Act from Matić (1983), p. 228.

[58] Šarčević (1985), pp. 287–288.

the proposal for the new PIL Act.[59] In the Thesis on characterisation, it was suggested that step-by-step characterisation should be maintained.[60] Therefore, if the family formation fulfils conditions for being characterised as an extramarital union or life partnership under Croatian law as the *lex fori*, they should be covered by Arts. 40 and 49 of the Croatian PIL Act. The *ratio* of the Croatian legislator was subjecting to the Twin Regulations, the family formations which have equivalent effects to marriage.[61]

As it was previously established, before turning to assessment whether a particular family formation may be characterised as an extramarital union of informal life partnership for the purpose of Arts. 40 and 49 of the Croatian PIL Act, the Croatian court should check whether the property claim of a particular family formation may fall into the ambit of the Brussels I bis Regulations and the Rome I or the Rome II Regulation. Such hierarchy derives from the principle of the supremacy of the EU law, in this particular case the supremacy of Brussels I bis, Rome I and Rome II provisions over Arts. 40 and 49 of the Croatian PIL Act. The exclusion in Arts. 1(2)(a) of the Brussels I bis Regulation, Art. 1(2)(c) of the Rome I Regulation and Art. 1(2)(b) of the Rome II Regulation should be understood as referring to the *lex causae* for the purpose of establishing whether a family formation has comparable effects to marriage. If under the *lex causae* the Croatian court reaches the conclusion that family formation does not have comparable effects to marriage, it should apply the Brussels I bis Regulation and the Rome I or the Rome II Regulations. If it reaches a contrary conclusion, that a family formation has comparable effects to marriage, it should assess whether it may be characterised as an extramarital union or informal life partnership for the purpose of Arts. 40 and 49 of the Croatian PIL Act. If this is the case, the Croatian court should apply the provisions of the relevant Twin Regulation. However, there is a possibility that under the *lex causae,* the family formation will have comparable effects to marriage and will therefore fall outside of the ambit of the Brussels I bis Regulation and the Rome I or the Rome II Regulation, and under Arts. 40 and 49 of the Croatian PIL Act the same family formation cannot be characterised as an extramarital union or informal life partnership, because, for instance it does not last at least 3 years. For such category of family formations, the

[59] Assessment of the Situation and Basic Issues Regulated by the Act on Private International Law and the Consequences of the Adoption of the Act, p. 1. Available at: https://esavjetovanja.gov.hr/Documents/Download?documentId=3789. Accessed 15 Jun 2022.

[60] Sajko et al. (2001), p. 272.

[61] According to Art. 11(2) of the Family Act, the extramarital union produces the same personal and property effects as a marital union. See Lucić (2020), p. 156 *et seq*. Life partners generally have the same rights as spouses in Croatia and life partnership produces equivalent effect to those of a marriage. See also for instance Art. 37(4) and Art. 79 of the Life Partnership Act. Informal life partnership produces personal and property effects equivalent to those of a life partnership in the area of personal rights, relations related to children and property relations of life partners, whereas with respect to areas such as succession, tax system, pension insurance, social welfare system, mandatory health insurance and health protection, rights and obligations from employment relations, access to public and market services and public legal position, it creates effects comparable to those of an extramarital union. See Art. 4(1) and (2) of the Life Partnership Act.

Croatian court should apply a jurisdictional and conflict of laws rule applicable for civil and commercial matters. Art. 46(1) of the Croatian PIL Act indicates that jurisdiction for civil and commercial matters should be determined based on provisions of the Brussels I bis Regulation.[62] Art. 46(2) extends the application of the Brussels I bis provisions even to cases involving a defendant which does not have his or her domicile in the EU.[63] Art. 46 does not verbatim extend application of the Brussels I bis provisions to cases which fall outside of its material scope of application. However, such interpretation may derive from the fact that there is no other provision on jurisdiction for civil and commercial matters and that Croatian legislator generally opted for the approach of extending the application of EU instruments to all cases. That means that, even though, in the previous step, the property claim concerning particular family formation was excluded from the ambit of the Brussels I bis Regulation, its provisions may be applied by operation of Art. 46 of the Croatian PIL Act. The same principle is valid for determining applicable law. Arts. 25 and 26 of the Croatian PIL Act which indicate that the Rome I Regulation and the Rome II Regulation govern the applicable law for the contractual and non-contractual obligations, also extend the application of their provisions to cases excluded from their material scope of application.

7 Conclusion

The interrelation of the Twin Regulations, Arts. 40 and 49 of the Croatian PIL Act and exclusions from the Brussels I bis, the Rome I and the Rome II Regulations' scopes of application regarding rights in property arising out of a matrimonial or comparable relationship results in a particularly complex system for determining which of the instruments should be applied before the Croatian court in a cross-border dispute on couple's property. First, if such claim falls into the ambit of one of the Twin Regulations, rules of the respective Twin Regulation should be applied. While the Regulation 2016/1104 provides for an autonomous interpretation of the term registered partnership, the Regulation 2016/1103 refers to national legislations for the definition of the term marriage, thus generating uncertainty regarding the applicable instrument before the courts of the participating Member States which do not recognise same-sex marriages. Art. 32(2) of the Croatian PIL Act solves this issue by providing that Croatian court should recognise the same-sex marriage celebrated abroad as registered partnership. Second, if neither of the Twin Regulations is applicable, the Croatian court should check if the couple's property claim is

[62] This type of provisions in Croatian PIL Act which merely indicate which instrument needs to be applied are of purely educative character. Župan (2018), p. 2.

[63] As a general rule, the Brussels I bis Regulation does not apply to defendants domiciled outside of the EU. However, there are exceptions to such rule: Arts. 18(1), 21(2), 24, 25 and 26 (according to CJEU judgment of 13 July 2000, *Group Josi*, C-412/98, EU:C:2000:399, para. 44).

covered by the Brussels I bis Regulation and the Rome I Regulation or the Rome II Regulation. These instruments apply under the condition that the case concerns right in property arising out of relationship which, under law applicable to such relationship, does not have comparable effects to marriage. It is suggested that the comparability assessment should be carried out in accordance with the *lex causae*. If a family formation does have comparable effects to marriage, it is excluded from the Brussels I bis Regulation, the Rome I Regulation and the Rome II Regulation. The Croatian court should then proceed with the assessment whether Arts. 40 and 49 of the Croatian PIL are applicable to such family formations, i.e. whether the family formation may be characterised as extramarital union or informal life partnership under Croatian law as the *lex fori*. If this is the case, then one of the Twin Regulations will be applied by operation of Arts. 40 or 49 of the Croatian PIL Act. If this is not the case, the family formation cannot be characterised as an extramarital union or informal life partnership and the Croatian court should apply Art. 46 of the Croatian PIL Act which extends the application of the Brussels I bis Regulation to cases that fall outside of its scope of application. As for applicable law, the Croatian court should apply either Art. 25 or Art. 26 of the Croatian PIL Act, which refer to the Rome I Regulation and the Rome II Regulation, depending on whether the claim should be characterised as a contractual or a non-contractual one.

Legal Instruments

Council Regulation (EU) 2016/1103 of 24 June 2016 implementing enhanced cooperation in the area of jurisdiction, applicable law and the recognition and enforcement of decisions in matters of matrimonial property regimes, OJ L 183, 8.7.2016, pp. 1–29

Council Regulation (EU) 2016/1104 of 24 June 2016 implementing enhanced cooperation in the area of jurisdiction, applicable law and the recognition and enforcement of decisions in matters of the property consequences of registered partnerships, OJ L 183, 8.7.2016, pp. 30–56

Regulation (EU) No 650/2012 of the European Parliament and of the Council of 4 July 2012 on jurisdiction, applicable law, recognition and enforcement of decisions and acceptance and enforcement of authentic instruments in matters of succession and on the creation of a European Certificate of Succession, OJ L 201, 27.7.2012, pp. 107–134

Regulation (EU) No 1215/2012 of the European Parliament and of the Council of 12 December 2012 on jurisdiction and the recognition and enforcement of judgments in civil and commercial matters, OJ L 351, 20.12.2012, pp. 1–32

Council Regulation (EC) No 4/2009 of 18 December 2008 on jurisdiction, applicable law, recognition and enforcement of decisions and cooperation in matters relating to maintenance obligations, OJ L 7, 10.1.2009, pp. 1–79

Regulation (EC) No 593/2008 of the European Parliament and of the Council of 17 June 2008 on the law applicable to contractual obligations, OJ L 177, 4.7.2008, pp. 6–16

Regulation (EC) No 864/2007 of the European Parliament and of the Council of 11 July 2007 on the law applicable to non-contractual obligations, OJ L 199, 31.7.2007, pp. 40–49

Council Regulation (EC) No 44/2001 of 22 December 2000 on jurisdiction and the recognition and enforcement of judgments in civil and commercial matters, OJ L 12, 16.1.2001, pp. 1–23

Constitution of the Republic of Croatia, NN 56/1990, 135/1997, 113/2000, 28/2001, 76/2010, 5/2014

Croatian PIL Act (*Zakon o međunarodnom privatnom pravu*), NN 101/2017

The 1982 PIL Act (*Zakon o rješavanju sukoba zakona s propisima drugih zemalja u određenim odnosima*), NN 53/1991, 88/2001

Family Act (*Obiteljski zakon*), NN 103/2015, 98/2019, 47/2020

The 2003 Family Act, NN 116/2003

Act on Life Partnership of Persons of the Same Sex, NN, 92/2014, 98/2019

Judgments

CJEU judgment of 6 June 2019, Weil v. Gulacsi, C-361/18, EU:C:2019:473

CJEU judgment of 19 November 1988, Nilsson and Others, C-162/97, EU:C:1998:554

Judgment of the England and Wales High Court Gray v Hurley [2019] EWHC 1636 (QB) (25 June 2019)

Decision of the Constitutional Court of the Republic of Croatia SuP-O-1/2014 of 14 January 2014. Available at: https://narodne-novine.nn.hr/clanci/sluzbeni/2014_01_5_93.html. Accessed 18 Feb 2022

Opinion of Advocate General Wathelet delivered on 11 January 2018, Case C-673/16, Coman, EU:C:2018:2

Other Sources

Laws and families. Available at: https://www.lawsandfamilies.eu/en/legal-project/interactive-database/. Accessed 14 Mar 2022

Outcome of the Council Meeting, Brussels, 3 and 4 December 2015. Available at: https://www.consilium.europa.eu/media/23027/st14937en15_v5.pdf. Accessed 30 May 2022

Report of 27.6.2005 on the proposal for a regulation of the European Parliament and of the Council on the law applicable to non-contractual obligations ("Rome II") (COM(2003)0427 – C5-0338/2003 – 2003/0168(COD)), first reading in

European parliament. Available at: https://www.europarl.europa.eu/doceo/document/A-6-2005-0211_EN.html. Accessed 12 Apr 2022

Assessment of the Situation and Basic Issues Regulated by the Act on Private International Law and the Consequences of the Adoption of the Act. Available at: https://esavjetovanja.gov.hr/Documents/Download?documentId=3789. Accessed 15 Jun 2022

References

Bibliography

Antokolskaia M (2010) Harmonisation of substantive family law in Europe: myths and reality. Child Family Law Q 22(4):397–421

Bach I (2011) Article 1. In: Huber P (ed) Rome II Regulation, pocket commentary. Sellier, European Law Publishers, Munich, pp 28–58

Bonomi A (2017) Fragen des Allgemeinen Teils: Qualifikation, Vorfrage, Renvoi und ordre public. In: Dutta A, Weber J (eds) Die Europäischen Güterrechtsverordnungen. Verlag C.H. Beck, Munich, pp 123–143

Bukovac Puvača M, Kunda I, Winkler S, Vrbljanac D (2019) Croatia. In: Ruggeri L, Kunda I, Winkler S (eds) Family property and succession in EU Member States, National Reports on the Collected Data. Faculty of Law in Rijeka, Rijeka, pp 68–92. Available at: https://www.euro-family.eu/documenti/news/psefs_e_book_compressed.pdf. Accessed 12 Apr 2022

Cazorla Gonzalez MJ, Soto Moya M (2022) Main concepts and scope of application of the twin regulations. In: Ruggeri L, Limante A, Pogorelčnik Vogrinc N (eds) The EU regulations on matrimonial property and property of registered partnerships. Intersentia, Cambridge, pp 41–70

Coester-Waltjen D (2018) Connecting factors to determine the law applicable to matrimonial property regimes. In: Bonomi A, Romano GP (eds) Yearbook of private international law, 2017/2018, vol XIX. Otto Schmidt, Cologne, pp 195–211

Dougan F (2022) Property relations of cross-border same-sex couples in the EU. In: Ruggeri L, Limante A, Pogorelčnik Vogrinc N (eds) The EU regulations on matrimonial property and property of registered partnerships. Intersentia, Cambridge, pp 219–244

Dutta A (2018) Beyond husband and wife. In: Bonomi A, Romano GP (eds) Yearbook of private international law, 2017/2018, vol XIX. Otto Schmidt, Cologne, pp 146–158

Einhorn T, Bonomi A, Ballarino T (2017) Italy. In: Basedow J, Rühl G, Ferrari F, de Miguel AP (eds) Encyclopedia of private international law, vol 3. Edward Elgar, Cheltenham, pp 2207–2219

Francq S (2017) Belgium. In: Basedow J, Rühl G, Ferrari F, de Miguel AP (eds) Encyclopedia of private international law, vol 3. Edward Elgar, Cheltenham, pp 1906–1918

Garcimartín Alférez FJ (2007) The Rome II regulation: on the way towards a European private international law code. Eur Legal Forum 3:77–91

Harding M (2011) The harmonisation of private international law in Europe: taking the character out of family law. J Priv Int Law 7(1):203–230

Hoško T (2019) Novo uređenje međunarodnog privatnog prava u RH – Zakon o međunarodnom privatnom pravu. Zakonitost 1(1):19–31

Humphreys L, Santos C, di Caro L, Boella G, van der Torre L, Robaldo L (2015) Mapping Recitals to Normative Provisions in EU Legislation to Assist Legal Interpretation. Available at: https://iris.unito.it/retrieve/handle/2318/1639625/337609/jurix-recitals-CameraReady.pdf. Accessed 12 Apr 2022

Joubert N (2017) La dernière pierre (provisoire ?) à l'édifice du droit international privé européen en matière familiale, Les règlements du 24 juin 2016 sur les régimes matrimoniaux et les effets patrimoniaux des partenariats enregistré. Revue critique de droit international privé 1(1):1–26
Klimas T, Vaičiukaite J (2008) The law of recitals in European community legislation. ILSA J Int Comp Law 15(1):61–93
Knežević G (1991) Član 39. In: Dika M, Knežević G, Stojanović S (eds) Komentar Zakona o međunarodnom privatnom i procesnom pravu. Beograd, Nomos
Kunda I (2019) Novi međunarodnoprivatnopravi okvir imovine bračnih i registriranih partnera u Europskoj uniji: polje primjene i nadležnost. Hrvatska pravna revija, Mar 2019:27–36
Kunda I (2020) Upućivanje na propise Europske unije i međunarodne konvencije u Zakonu o međunarodnom privatnom pravu. In: Barbić J, Sikirić H (eds) Međunarodno privatno pravo – Interakcija međunarodnih, europskih i domaćih propisa. Hrvatska akademija znanosti i umjetnosti, Zagreb, pp 21–48
Lipstein K (1981) Principles of the conflict of laws, national and international. Martinus Nijhoff Publishers, The Hague, Boston, London
Lucić N (2020) Izvanbračna zajednica i pravna sigurnost. Narodne novine, Zagreb
Lüttringhaus JD (2020) Article 1. In: Ferrari F (ed) Concise commentary on the Rome I regulation, 2nd edn. Cambridge University Press, Cambridge, pp 20–55
Marino S (2017) Strengthening the European civil judicial cooperation: the patrimonial effects of family relationships. Cuadernos de Derecho Transnacional 9(1):265–284
Matić Ž (1983) The Yugoslav act concerning private international law. Netherlands Int Law Rev 30(2):220–239
McParland M (2015) The Rome I regulation on the law applicable to contractual obligations. Oxford University Press, Oxford
Plender R, Wilderspin M (2009) The European private international law of obligations, 3rd edn. Sweet and Maxwell, London
Rodriguez Benot A (2020) Article 1. In: Viarengo I, Franzina P (eds) The EU regulations on the property regimes of international couples, a commentary. Edward Elgar, Cheltenham, pp 17–28
Rudolf C (2019) European property regimes regulations – choice of law and the applicable law in the absence of choice by the parties. LeXonomica 11(2):127–150
Sajko K, Sikirić H, Bouček V, Babić D, Tepeš N (2001) Izvori hrvatskog i europskog međunarodnog privatnog prava, sa sudskom i arbitražnom praksom i tezama za Zakon o međunarodnom privatnom pravu. Informator, Zagreb
Šarčević P (1985) The new Yugoslav private international law act. Am J Comp Law 38(2):283–296
Šarčević P (2004) Private international law aspects of legally regulated forms of non-marital cohabitation and registered partnership. In: Essays in private international and comparative law. Faculty of Law in Rijeka, Rijeka, pp 365–378
Winkler S (2019) Imovinski odnosi u obitelji: Nacionalna pravna rješenja i europski trendovi. Godišnjak Akademije pravnih znanosti 10(1):447–467
Winkler S (2021) Obiteljski odnosi. In: Mišćenić E (ed) Europsko privatno pravo, Posebni dio. Školska Knjiga, Zagreb, pp 442–485
Župan M (2018) Novi Zakon o međunarodnom privatnom pravu. Hrvatska pravna revija, Mar-Apr 2018:1–12

Property Regime for De Facto Couples in Croatia: International Jurisdiction and Applicable Law

Ines Medić

1 Introduction

Family is one of the building bricks of every society. Without procreation supported by a strong family ties there would be no society as we know it. Traditionally, such ties have been based predominantly on marriage. However, other forms of families developed over time as it is not so easy to legally restrain life. As a result, there are different types of family legal constructions in the Western world nowadays. Despite significant variation among states in regulating informal cohabitation of heterosexual couples (*de facto* cohabitation), this form of couples' formation seems to be the most prominent among the alternatives to marriage.[1] In most of the countries in Europe it is considered socially acceptable, while the question remains as to the approach towards the legal protection of personal and property relations of cohabitants. The homosexual formations, including informal cohabitation between persons of same sex, are on the other hand, recognised with more variations among the states.

First global trend towards more open family relationships dates back to 1979, when Netherlands introduced a sex-neutral concept of "joint household" into housing legislation,[2] opening the door to unmarried cohabiting couples irrespective of their sex. This route, though mainly with regard to *de facto* cohabitation, was soon followed by some other European countries.[3]

[1] Even more so, according to some indicators number of *de facto* cohabitations is on the rise. See: Boele-Woelki et al. (2015), pp. 331–350.

[2] Wintermute (2020), p. 133.

[3] Jakovac-Lozić (2004), pp. 9–10.

I. Medić (✉)
University of Split, Faculty of Law, Split, Croatia
e-mail: ines.medic@pravst.hr

I. Kunda et al. (eds.), *Balkan Yearbook of European and International Law 2022*, Balkan Yearbook of European and International Law 2022, https://doi.org/10.1007/978-3-031-29432-7_5

Explicit legal recognition of informal cohabitation of homosexual couples (*de facto* life partnership) began in 1987 in Sweden, when informal relationships of the same-sex couples were given a similar legal status to those of opposite sex.[4] However, this affirmative development was put to test between 1981 and 1996 due to HIV epidemic which in many proceedings showed the discrimination based on sexual orientation.[5] This trend was soon overturned, by the European Court for Human Rights (hereinafter: the ECtHR) judgment in *Karner v. Austria*,[6] based on Art. 14 (non-discrimination based on sexual orientation) of the European Convention on Human Rights (hereinafter: the ECHR). Some years later, a similar approach was adopted by the Inter-American Court for Human Rights, as well.[7]

In the meantime, in prescribing legal basis for informal partnerships different legal systems have emerged,[8] varying between legal ignorance and (almost) equating it with marriage. Within the European judicial area three approaches prevail: legal systems which do not have any statutory provisions concerning informal relationships; legal systems which have enacted a special registration system which requires an entry in a public register and legal systems with statutory regulations which take the individual circumstances of the relationship as the starting point for legal consequences.[9]

This paper addresses development of legislation in Croatia concerning *de facto* couples, on substantial and private international law level, with the emphasis on the latter. Most importantly, it is focused on new legislative framework for such couples, enacted in Croatia in 2017 in the form of the Private International Law Act (hereinafter: the 2017 PILA).[10] Given the particular methodology which relies on referencing to expand the scope of application of the EU legal instruments in the filed, this paper provides insight into the operational aspects of the new rules to discover their strong and weak points.

2 Development of Legislation on *De Facto* Couples in Croatia

2.1 Legislative Developments on Substantial Level

Despite certain traditionalisms in the Croatian society, the avant-garde is long- and well-established in Croatian family law and private international law. The same

[4] Scherpe (2013), p. 83.

[5] Wintermute (2020), p. 134.

[6] Application no. 40016/98 *Karner v. Austria.*

[7] Wintermute (2020), p. 136.

[8] Alinčić (2005), p. 1181.

[9] Aeschlimann (2005), p. 244.

[10] Official Gazzette, 10/2017.

progressive wave which started in the late 1970s in the Netherlands emerged also in Croatia (at that time, the Socialist Republic of Croatia, a federal unit within the former Yugoslavia)[11] yet limited to heterosexual cohabitations. Interestingly enough, case-law preceded the actual legislation on *de facto* cohabitations. Certain property rights of *de facto* cohabitants were recognised in the Croatian case-law following the Instruction of the then Federal Supreme Court No. SC 42/54,[12] dated 4 March 1954. This protection was based on constitutional grounds, i.e. the Federal Constitution of 1946,[13] "which treated the institution of marriage and family equally, proclaiming that both are entitled to the special protection of society".[14]

Two decades later, in 1978, the Marriage and Family Relations Act[15] was adopted which, for the first time, explicitly recognized cohabitations, but only between heterosexual *de facto* cohabitants.[16] This Act provided cohabitants with property and maintenance rights identical to those provided to the spouses. With regard to property in particular, Art. 293 provided that property acquired by the work of both *de facto* cohabitants in life community which lasted for a long time was considered their joint property. Division of this property was subject to the same rules as the property of spouses.

With the change of political system, legal protection of *de facto* cohabitation expanded even further. Following the declaration of its independence in 1991, Croatia proclaimed *de facto* cohabitation (along with marriage and family) as a Constitutionally protected category.[17] Apart from property and maintenance rights, Croatian contemporary family legislation[18] stretches the protection also to the same inheritance rights in the same vein as for the spouses. By now, the rights of heterosexual *de facto* cohabitants expanded to the point of full equality with marriage in the Croatian Family Act currently in force (hereinafter: the FA).[19]

Legal protection of homosexual partners was introduced later, more precisely, in 2003 with the enactment of the Same-Sex Unions Act.[20] According to Art. 2 of this Act, the same-sex union was defined as "a life community of two persons of the same-sex (hereinafter: partners) who are not married, or in cohabitation or other same-sex life community, and which lasted no less than three years and is based on

[11] Part of the former Yugoslavia.

[12] Stevanov (1978), pp. 84 ff.

[13] Official Gazzette of the Federal People's Republic of Yugoslavia 4/1946.

[14] Šarčević (1981), pp. 84 ff.

[15] Official Gazzette of the Socialist Republic of Croatia 11/78. Amendments, Official Gazzette 27/1978, 45/1989, 59/1990, 25/1994.

[16] Alinčić and Bakarić-Mihanović (1980), p. 364; Korać Graovac (2015), pp. 802–804.

[17] Art. 62, Croatian Constitution, Official Gazette 56/90, 135/97, 08/98, 113/00, 124/00, 28/01, 41/01, 55/01, 76/10, 85/10, 05/14.

[18] The 1999 Family Act, Official Gazette 162/1998 which was soon replaced with the 2003 Family Act, Official Gazette 116/2003, 17/2004, 107/2007, 57/2011, 61/2011, 25/2013, 75/2014, 5/2015, 103/2015.

[19] Official Gazette 103/15, 98/19.

[20] Official Gazette 116/03.

the principles of equality of partners, mutual respect and help, and emotional attachment between the partners". Partners had to be at least 18 years old to commence such a community, have capacity to act and must not have had been relatives in the direct line or in the lateral line up to the fourth degree. They enjoyed the same property and maintenance rights as the spouses.[21]

Given that the Same-Sex Unions Act did not provide for registration of those relationships, nor the right to adopt, or the rights relating to tax, health insurance, pensions, etc., in 2014 the Same-Sex Unions Act was replaced with the Life Partnership Act (hereinafter: the LPA),[22] which expanded the rights of such couples by equating the legal effects of homosexual life partnerships with marriage and heterosexual *de facto* cohabitation.[23]

This LPA defines two types of same-sex relationships, registered life partnership (as equal to marriage) and informal or *de facto* life partnership (as equal to heterosexual *de facto* cohabitation). According to Art. 3 para. 1 of the LPA, "an informal life partnership is a family life relationship between two persons of the same sex who have not concluded a life partnership before a competent body, provided the relationship has lasted no less than three years and from its beginning has met the requirements prescribed for the validity of a life partnership." With this new definition the accent is placed on "family life", which is a direct consequence of the ECtHR jurisprudence,[24] more precisely *P.B. and J.S. v. Austria,*[25] *Schalk and Kopf v. Austria*[26] and *Pajić v. Croatia.*[27] As it can be inferred from the *Pajić v. Croatia*, more than one Croatian competent authority (the Croatian Ministry of the Interior, the Administrative Court in Zagreb, as well as the Croatian Constitutional Court) struggled with the acknowledgement of informal life partnership as a form of family life, thus, this explicit acknowledgement is to be welcomed.

The criteria for the establishment of *de facto* life partnership are the same as for the conclusion of marriage, homosexual registered life partnership or heterosexual *de facto* cohabitation.[28] Accordingly, the legal effects of homosexual *de facto* life partnership, within the scope of family law, are nearly equal to those of homosexual registered life partnership or marriage or heterosexual *de facto* cohabitation.[29] Within the scope of family law the *de facto* life partners enjoy personal rights,

---

[21] Alinčić (2005), pp. 1182–1184.

[22] Official Gazette 92/14, 98/19.

[23] See: Petrašević et al. (2017), pp. 154–160.

[24] Jakovac-Lozić (2017), pp. 9–15.

[25] ECtHR, Application no. 18984/02 *P.B. and J.S. v. Austria.*

[26] ECtHR, Application no. 30141/04 *Schalk and Kopf v. Austria.*

[27] ECtHR, Application no. 68453/13 *Pajić v. Croatia.*

[28] See: Lucić (2020), pp. 134–155. Within other areas of law (succession law, social security law, law on pensions) which also give legal effects to *de facto* partnerships, requirements for the existence of *de facto* partnership vary.

[29] Lucić (2013), p. 12.

property rights and maintenance rights.[30] The main difference is that partners in a homosexual life partnership (both registered and *de facto*) are not recognised the adoption rights, however, the recognition of this right is currently a subject-matter of the national court proceedings.[31] On the other hand, in certain aspects, homosexual *de facto* partners enjoy even more rights than heterosexual *de facto* partners. Unlike heterosexual *de facto* partners, they enjoy maintenance rights during their partnership.[32]

The LPA also deals with public law aspects of the homosexual partnerships contracted abroad (Arts. 73 to 75 of the LPA). Thus, according to Art. 73 of the respective Act (in conjunction with Art. 70 of the Foreigners Act), homosexual partners living in *de facto* life partnership which lasts at least three years have the right to ask for temporary residence permit. In case they keep their family life undisclosed, this has to be given due attention in the course of the legal proceedings.

2.2 *Legislative Developments on Private International Law Level*

2.2.1 Starting with the Interlocal Conflict of Law Provisions...

The first legislation dealing exclusively with conflict of law rules at the territory of (today's) Croatia dates back to 1979.[33] It was the Resolution of Conflict of Laws and of the Jurisdiction in Status, Family and Succession Matters Act (hereinafter: the 1979 Interlocal Act),[34] dealing with interlocal conflict of laws within the former Yugoslavia.

Despite the fact that the case-law at the time and the legislation pertaining to family already accepted *de facto* cohabitations (of heterosexual couples) as a part of the family law corpus, provisions of the 1979 Interlocal Act did not contain corresponding provisions. There was no mention of *de facto* cohabitation (nor any other kind) nor the appropriate conflict of law rule.[35] According to its Art. 6, in the absence of other direct conflict of law rules the *lex fori* was applied. In cases of *de facto* cohabitation, this option was applied rather restrictively due to the *fraud à la loi* concern. Instead, the existing conflict of law rules pertaining to marriage and

[30] For more about property rights see: Winkler (2019), pp. 435–459.

[31] The Ministry for Demography, Family, Youth and Social Policy decree of 17 July 2020, rejecting the request of the same-sex registered partners to adopt, has been overturned by the Administrative Court in Zagreb on 21 April 2021, however, the appeal proceedings are still ongoing before the High Administrative Court.

[32] Lucić (2015), p. 13.

[33] Šarčević (1980), p. 177.

[34] Official Gazette of the former Socialist Federative Republic of Yugoslavia 9/1979.

[35] Šarčević (1980), p. 178.

marriage-related matters were applied by analogy.[36] However, given that this Act was dealing with interlocal conflict of laws only, the solutions for cross-border conflicts did not always produce the most appropriate results (i.e. in cases in which the connecting factor did not refer to any area within the former Yugoslavia).[37]

According to the respective rules of procedure, there was no special jurisdiction for *de facto* cohabitants. It was possible to use the general jurisdiction forum—the place of residence of the defendant or the court where the plaintiff resides.[38]

2.2.2 ... to Reach the Most Progressive Codification of PIL of Its Time

The enactment of the Resolution of Conflicts of Laws with the Provisions of Other Countries in Certain Matters Act (hereinafter: the 1982 PILA),[39] in 1982, undoubtedly represents the turning point. At the moment of its enactment it was considered to be the world's most modern codification of international conflicts and procedural law.[40] In 1991, after the Croatian declaration of independence, this Act continued to be applied as a part of Croatian law.[41]

The conflicts rules for international family law (Arts. 32-45 of the 1982 PILA) have been particularly influenced by the principles of equality between sexes and the well-being of the child, both of which had a dominant role in the former Yugoslav family law.[42]

In line with the provisions of substantive family law, and thanks to the late Professor Šarčević, the 1982 PILA was the first statutory texts in the history of private international law which contained a special conflict of law rule for property relations of persons living in *de facto* cohabitation.[43] Even without any explicit exceptions to that effect, it is safe to assume that the respective provisions of the 1982 PILA were not considered applicable to the homosexual partnerships at the time they entered into force. With the enactment of the LPA in 2014,[44] the homosexual partnerships were placed on an equal footing when it comes to substantive law with both, marriage and *de facto* cohabitations (of heterosexual couples). The lack of respective conflict rules for *de facto* homosexual partnerships created a

[36] Šarčević (1981), p. 333.

[37] Varady (1983), p. 107.

[38] Art. 51 of the Federal Civil Procedure Law (1976), Official Gazzette of the (former) Socialist Federative Republic of Yugoslavia 4/1977.

[39] Official Gazette of the former Socialist Federative Republic of Yugoslavia 43/1982. After the declaration of its independence, this Act was.

[40] Šarčević (1985), p. 283.

[41] Official Gazette, 53/1991.

[42] Šarčević (1985), p. 290.

[43] Šarčević (1981), p. 315.

[44] Official Gazzette, 92/14.

systemic legal gap in Croatian private international law. This *lacuna legis* could have been solved in different ways, including by means of an analogous application of the conflict of law rules provided for matrimonial matters or *de facto* cohabitations (of heterosexual couples). We are, nevertheless, unaware of any case-law to that effect, which may be due to the limited number of judgments by Croatian courts that are made publicly available and perhaps also the sensitivity of the topic which possibly dissuaded some parties from turning to the Croatian courts.

Law Applicable to *De Facto* Cohabitation (of Heterosexual Couples)

Based on the equal treatment of *de facto* cohabitations (of heterosexual couples) and marriages in substantial family law, the conflict of law rules for *de facto* cohabitations in the 1982 PILA were inspired (with some minor adjustments) by Art. 36, governing statutory property relationships between the spouses, and Art. 37, governing contractual property relationships between the spouses.

According to Art. 39, paras. 1 and 2 of the 1982 PILA, there were only two relevant connecting factors governing the statutory property relations of persons living in *de facto* cohabitation leading to two potentially applicable laws, the law of the state of which they are citizens (*lex patriae*) and the law of the common domicile of the parties (*lex domicilii communis*). The law applicable due to one of those connecting factors governed all property relations of cohabitants, including those relating to immovable property irrespective of its situs.[45] The advantage of such solution was the avoidance of the *depeçage* (applicability of different laws, one for movable and one for immovable property), but it did not come without challenges.[46] This approach could have easily backfired at the stage of recognition and enforcement, if the application of a foreign law to an immovable property was deemed incompatible with provisions of relevant substantial law of the country in which the recognition and enforcement was sought.

However, the legislator opted for a common nationality of de *facto* cohabitants as the primary connecting factor. Reasons for such choice were twofold. First, at that time, nationality was considered to be the basic connecting factor for all family relations. Second, the legislator's intention was to avoid cumulation of two or more national laws since their normative solutions could contradict each other, which would make them inapplicable.[47] Issues of lack of any nationality or of multiple nationalities of one or both parties were governed by Arts. 10-12 of the PILA 1982. According to this provision, in case of multiple nationalities precedence was always given to Croatian nationality (if applicable).

The law of the common domicile was laid down as the subsidiary connecting factor, applicable only in cases in which *de facto* cohabitants did not hold the

---

[45] Dika et al. (1991), p. 126.

[46] Matić (1978), pp. 26 ff.

[47] Lešić et al. (1983), p. 58.

common nationality. The choice of the common domicile of *de facto* cohabitants (unlike just "domicile" for spouses) reflected the legislator's view at the time that the existence of *de facto* cohabitation is not possible without actual community of life in a single household—the couple's domicile. In practice, this proved to be a burden for the competent authority since life community is a legal standard under Croatian law, whose constitutive elements are not detailed by the law. On a purely substantive law level, proving the existence of a life community was difficult not only due to its informal nature, but also owing to the inconsistencies between different Croatian statutes.[48] Still, "life community" remained *conditio sine qua non* until 2007, when the Croatian Supreme Court reasoned that living at the same household is not a precondition for the existence of the *de facto* cohabitation.[49]

This only exaggerated the complexity existing at the private international law level. Namely, the 1982 PILA contained a legal gap concerning the question as to the law applicable in the absence of common nationality and common domicile of *de facto* cohabitants. Since relevant moment for the operationalization of the connecting factor was the moment when the question is asked (according to Art. 36 para. 3 of the 1982 PILA, whose logic *per analogiam* applied to Art. 39 which was silent on this issue), determination of the *lex communis domicilii* as the only subsidiary connecting factor could not answer the question of the applicable law in cases in which petition for the resolution of property relations between *de facto* cohabitants was filed after the cessation of the life community. Academic writers unanimously suggested the recourse to Art. 2 od the 1982 PILA (dealing with *lacunae legis*)[50] and analogous application of *lex ultimi domicilii communis* (Art. 36, para. 3).[51] But this solution, however, was inappropriate in cases in which there was no actual life community in the same household. Since, according to Croatian law, *de facto* cohabitation was treated as equivalent to marriage, again, based on Art. 2 of the 1982 PILA, there was no obstacle to apply the last step of the cascade envisaged for matrimonial property relations—the *lex fori*.

According to Art. 39 para. 3 of the 1982 PILA, contractual property relations of the *de facto* cohabitants were governed by the law which was applicable for the statutory regime at the time the contract was concluded. This was the law of their common nationality or, subsidiarily, the law of their common domicile (Art. 39, paras. 1 and 2). The same law determined whether the parties were allowed to exercise their autonomy and choose other national law as applicable for their

[48] Lucić (2015), p. 101. Compare definitions in family law and succession law in Šarčević (2005a), p. 128 and Josipović (2005), p. 214.

[49] Rev 1121/2007-2, 22 November 2007.

[50] If there is no provision in this Act concerning the law to be applied in respect of one of the cases in art. 1 para. 1 of this Act, the provisions and principles of this Act, the principles of the legal order of Republic of Croatia and the principles of private international law are to be applied accordingly.

[51] Šarčević (1985), p. 291; Dika et al. (1991), pp. 133–134; Varadi et al. (2010), p. 317.

property relations. If the answer was yes, the law they agreed upon was the *lex contractus*.[52]

International Jurisdiction for *De Facto* Cohabitation (of Heterosexual Couples)

Unlike for the applicable law, the 1982 PILA did not explicitly address the international jurisdiction for *de facto* cohabitants. In the absence of a rule of special jurisdiction for property relations of *de facto* cohabitants, the existing heads of jurisdiction had to be applied. Accordingly, Croatian court was the competent authority if the respondent's domicile was on the territory of Croatia (general jurisdiction, Art. 46), or if the parties agreed in favour of jurisdiction of Croatian courts (prorogation of jurisdiction, Art. 49, or if the respondent tacitly submits to the jurisdiction of the Croatian courts (Art. 50), or if the property or the object sought in the lawsuit was situated on the territory of Croatia or the lawsuit concerned the respondent's obligation incurred during his or her stay on the territory of Croatia (Art. 54).

3 New Croatian PILA (2017)

Since the 1982 PILA did not keep track with the developments in the area of family law[53] and hence failed to address the *de facto* cohabitations both heterosexual and homosexual, its reform presented an opportunity to also deal with these issues. After many years of expectations among academic circles, and more than a decade after the concrete academic initiative and a proposed text,[54] the Private International Law Act[55] (hereinafter: the 2017 PILA) was finally enacted in in October 2017.

Following the significant change of legal scenery propelled by the intensity and nature of cross-border disputes, the new Act is based on innovative and at the same time well-established approach in European Union.[56] Almost all autonomous legislative solutions in areas covered by international legal instruments (international treaties and/or EU regulations) are abandoned in favour of unified approach towards all cross-border cases (intra-EU or other). This unified approach is reflected (among other things) in a number of provisions referring to current European Union regulations in an area of civil and commercial matters, and family and succession matters,

[52] According to the FA, parties cannot choose the applicable law. On the effects of this rule see: Šarčević (2005b), p. 186.

[53] The FA dates back to 2015 and the LPA dates back to 2014.

[54] Sajko (2001), pp. 259–340.

[55] Official Gazzette, 10/2017.

[56] More on this Act: Hoško (2019), pp. 19–31, Sikirić (2018), pp. 61–140, Župan (2018), pp. 1–12.

or to the Hague conventions whose application is extended beyond their intended scopes of application.[57] The idea behind the extension of international legal regimes beyond their original scope of application was to avoid dual legal regimes, one for cross-border cases captured by the scopes of the EU legal instruments and one for other cross-border cases, since running parallel regimes proved to be rather burdensome to implement in practice.[58] Actually, Croatian case law reveals that the omission of the court to identify cross-border element in a given case was not uncommon in the times before the accession to the European Union,[59] and also though situation has improved significantly may still occur especially in cases with prevalently national factual substratum, e.g. in a matrimonial property case in which a large part of property was situated in Croatia and there was only a foreign bank account.[60]

However, unification approach did not stop at this. In certain areas of law, the existing international regimes were extended also to areas which are not envisaged or are otherwise explicitly excluded from their scope of application. One of those areas are property relations of *de facto* partnerships. In accordance with substantial solutions contained in the FA and LPA, which do not discriminate between formal and *de facto* unions, in the 2017 PILA legal regimes envisaged for property relations of spouses (heterosexual only, under Croatian law) and registered partners (homosexual only, under Croatian law) cover also their informal counterparts.

3.1 Law Applicable to De Facto *Partnerships*

With regard to the applicable law, the 2017 PILA explicitly refers to property relations of not only the heterosexual *de facto* partnership (which were previously been referred to as *de facto* cohabitations) but also homosexual *de facto* partnerships. Additionally, the 2017 PILA lays down the rules on establishment and termination, personal relations and maintenance of both those types of *de facto* partnerships. While the issues of establishment and termination, and personal relations of *de facto* partnerships are regulated by the autonomous provisions of the 2017 PILA, with regard to property relations and maintenance the 2017 PILA[61] simply refers to relevant European Regulations—the Council Regulation (EU) 2016/1103[62] and

[57] For more about this approach see: Kunda (2020), pp. 21–48.

[58] Kunda (2020), pp. 21–48; Župan (2018), pp. 2–3.

[59] Puljko and Živić (2011), pp. 311–330.

[60] Poretti (2017), p. 60.

[61] Art. 40 para. 3 of the 2017 PILA and Art. 40 para. 2 in connection with Art. 35 of the 2017 PILA.

[62] Council Regulation (EU) 2016/1103 of 24 June 2016 implementing enhanced cooperation in the area of jurisdiction, applicable law and the recognition and enforcement of decisions in matters of matrimonial property regimes, OJ L 183/1, 8. 7. 2016.

the Council Regulation (EU) 2016/1104,[63] and to the 2007 Hague Maintenance Protocol.[64] Although such solution *prima faciae* may seem a good one, in reality it is far from ideal and brings about many challenges as will be shown in the below subchapters.

Before going into details of these provisions and their practical implications, it seems important to clarify that the 2017 PILA contains different conflict of laws provisions for the heterosexual *de facto* partnerships and for the homosexual *de facto* partnerships, reflecting the approach on the substantive level of Croatian law, the FA and the LPA respectively. The below text will refer to heterosexual *de facto* partnership and the homosexual *de facto* partnership where necessary to specifically refer to one or the other, while they will be jointly referred to as *de facto* partnerships.

3.1.1 Law Applicable to Establishment and Termination of *De Facto* Partnerships

According to Art. 38 applicable to heterosexual *de facto* partnership and Art. 39 para. 3 of the 2017 PILA applicable to homosexual *de facto* partnership, the law applicable for the establishment of *de facto* partnerships and for its termination is based on the same connecting factor. It is the law of the state with which the respective *de facto* partnership has or, if it ceased to exist, had the closest connection (*lex connexitatis*). Obviously, the determination of the applicable law for the establishment and termination of *de facto* heterosexual partnership is based on criterion of proximity. It is the informal nature of the relationship which calls for such solution, based on the idea that in case of dispute all the elements relevant for the determination of the existence or termination of *de facto* partnership will be situated in that state.

In case of applicability of Croatian family law, since personal elements relevant for the determination of existence of heterosexual *de facto* partnership are the same (with the exception of sex) as for the determination of homosexual *de facto* partnership,[65] it is to be expected that in determining the existence of homosexual *de facto* partnership competent court will be faced with the same challenges as with the determination of heterosexual *de facto* partnerships.[66] In order to determine the existence of the *de facto* partnership, court must be satisfied that there is a life community, appropriate sex, free personal status and at least three years duration

[63] Council Regulation (EU) 2016/1104 of 24 June 2016 implementing enhanced cooperation in the area of jurisdiction, applicable law and the recognition and enforcement of decisions in matters of the property consequences of registered partnership, OJ L 183/30, 8. 7. 2016.

[64] Hague Protocol of 27 November 2007 on the Law Applicable to Maintenance Obligations, OJ L 331, 16. 12. 2009.

[65] See: Art. 11 para 1 of the FA and Art. 4 para. 1 of the LPA.

[66] See: above note 49.

(with some exceptions).[67] As explained above, the case law confirmed that living at the same household (although desirable) is not a necessary precondition for the establishment of a *de facto* partnership. In the attempt to establish the existence of the *de facto* partnership under the Croatian family law, the court will also have to examine whether there is an emotional connection, sexual connection, common property, connection with relatives and friends, joint trips, etc.[68] However, determining the duration of the life community may prove to be the biggest challenge for the courts. In most cases it is very difficult, if not impossible, to determine the exact date of the beginning of life community. On top of that, legal precondition of fixed minimal time can lead to loss of legal protection for the weaker party in cases in which life community lasted shorter than the prescribed time, even if just a little bit.

3.1.2 Law Applicable to Personal Relations in *De Facto* Partnerships

The law applicable to personal relations in *de facto* partnerships is also determined by an autonomous provision, which derives from the parallel one for the marriages.[69] In fact, the connecting factors are determined by reference to the provision prescribing the law applicable to personal relations of spouses.[70] This is an apparent consequence of equalization of effects of marriage and *de facto* unions in Croatian substantive law. Thus, the law of the common habitual residence (*lex firmae habitationis communis*) is set as primary connecting factor, while the rest of the cascade comprises of, in the order of application, the last common habitual residence (*lex ultimae firmae habitationis commmunis*), the common nationality (*lex nationalis communis*) and, finally, Croatian law (*lex fori*).

3.1.3 Law Applicable to Property Relations in *De Facto* Partnerships

As already mentioned, according to Art. 40, para 3 of the 2017 PILA, law applicable to property relations in *de facto* partnerships is determined in line with Regulation (EU) 2016/1103 and Regulation (EU) 2016/1104 (jointly referred to as the Twin Regulations) for the heterosexual *de facto* partners and homosexual *de facto* partners, respectively. From the perspective of the EU legislator, "*de facto* life partnerships should be considered separately from registered partnerships" for the purposes of the application of the Regulation (EU) 2016/1104.[71] This may be explained by the attempt to accommodate the diversity among Member States since only some Member States make provisions for *de facto* partnerships in their national laws.

[67] See: Art. 11 para 1 of the FA and Art. 3 para. 1 of the LPA.

[68] For more information see: Lucić (2015), pp. 112.–120.

[69] Art. 40 para. 1 of the 2017 PILA.

[70] Art. 34 of the 2017 PILA.

[71] Rec. 16 of Regulation (EU) 2016/1104.

From the perspective of the Croatian legislator there seems to be no need for differentiation between registered and *de facto* partnerships for the private international law purposes. Since there is no obstacle for a Member State to extend the application of the Twin Regulations also to *de facto* partnerships,[72] Croatia did so with interesting implications for the partners.[73] One such implication is that in case Croatian courts would hear the case on property of a *de facto* couple, the applicable law in situation in which *de facto* partners made the choice of applicable law or failed to make that choice would differ for the heterosexual and homosexual *de facto* partnerships. This is the result of the operation of Art. 40 of the 2017 PILA which indirectly subjects the former to the rules in Regulation 2016/1103 and the latter to the rules in Regulation 2016/1104.

Prior to dealing with particular choice of law provisions, a brief comment on the characterization seems appropriate considering that principles of continuity in interpretation and of consistent interpretation of provisions of European Union law, require national courts of the Member States to apply the same provisions in the same way and independently from the national law concepts (autonomous interpretation). Thus, the notion of "habitual residence" should be interpreted according to its meaning in the respective instrument of European Union law, the Twin Regulations in particular, when dealing with property relations in *de facto* partnerships. In addition, the notions of the "matrimonial property regime" and "property consequences of registered partnerships" also need to be interpreted according to the each of the Twin Regulations[74] and legal characterization of the factual substratum should be based on that interpretation, instead of the pre-existing national concepts. This transition from a formalistic, dogmatic and positivist pattern to substantively oriented and pragmatic approach may require adjustment in approach for some courts in Croatia.

Parties' Choice of Applicable Law to Property Relations in *De Facto* Partnership

Following the provisions of the Twin Regulations as extended by the 2017 PILA, *de facto* partners (heterosexual and homosexual) are under Croatian private international law given the right, though limited, to choose the applicable law for their property relations.[75] The chosen law applies to all legal issues concerning the property regime. In addition, both Regulations preserve the principle of universality, thus chosen law also applies to all assets falling under the property regime.

[72] Župan (2016), p. 156.

[73] See: Art. 40 paras. 2 and 3 of the 2017 PILA.

[74] See: Kunda (2019), p. 30.

[75] Art. 22 of the Council Regulation (EU) 2016/1103 and Council Regulation (EU) 2016/1104. For general deliberations on party autonomy in couples' property matters see: Župan (2012), pp. 633–641.

According to Art. 22 of both Regulations as extended by the 2017 PILA, *de facto* partners or future *de facto* partners may choose Croatian law if at the time the agreement is concluded: at least one of them is either habitually resident in Croatia (*lex firmae habitationis*) or Croatian national (*lex patriae*). Additionally, homosexual *de facto* partners may also choose Croatian law if their partnership was created according to Croatian law. This option provides certainty in case the other potentially applicable laws do not envisage property effects of *de facto* partnerships.

Any change of the applicable law during their partnership shall have prospective effects only, unless agreed otherwise, in which case it shall not adversely affect the rights of third parties deriving from that law.[76] The principle of unity of applicable legislation and its twofold effect (on couple's relationship but also on the relationship that third parties may have with the couple) "balances the position of the third party by subordinating the enforceability of the law newly chosen by the parties to the knowledge possessed by the third party of the choice of law made by the couple".[77] The consequences occur not only when the third party has effective knowledge of the chosen law but also if the third party is negligent.

The Twin Regulations regulate both the choice-of-law agreement for the property relations and the property agreement itself.[78] The formal validity of both agreements depends on minimal requirements set in para. 1 of Arts. 23 and 25, respectively, (in writing, dated and signed by both parties)[79] and the possible additional formalities required by the law of a Member State of common habitual residence or habitual residence of either of the parties at the moment the agreement is concluded.[80] By reference to these provisions, with regard to the property agreement of the *de facto* partners, if the law applicable for the property consequences imposes additional requirements, those requirements shall apply as well.[81]

Where Croatian law should be applied to the validity of the property agreement, it has to be borne in mind that, according to both Art. 34 of the FA and Art. 53 of the LPA, *de facto* partners may contractually regulate their property relations with regard to acquired property. Thus, they are free to arrange their property relations in a way which departs from the statutory regime. But, according to Croatian law, this contractual freedom is limited, or more precisely, Croatian law explicitly prohibits the choice of foreign law as applicable to couple's property relations.[82] Given that strict interpretation of this rule would lead to nullity of the choice-of-law clause

---

[76] Art. 22 paras 2 and 3 of the Regulation (EU) 2016/1103 and Regulation (EU) 2016/1104.

[77] Ruggeri (2021), p. 265.

[78] Arts. 23 and 25 of the Twin Regulations.

[79] Including electronic communication which provides a durable record of the agreement. Consequently, a silent agreement on choice-of-law is not possible. Rudolf (2017), p. 276.

[80] Art. 23 paras. 2-4 and Art. 25 para 2 of the Twin Regulations.

[81] Art. 52 para. 3 of the Regulation (EU) 2016/1104.

[82] Art. 42 of the FA and Art. 53 para. 3 of the LPA. Justification lays in protection of the parties – in domestic cases *lex fori* is the law with which informal couples are most familiar and the law which (in most cases) has the closest connection with informal couples' property relations.

or the contract itself,[83] the issue remains which situations fall within its scope. While some authors submit that this limitation applies only to cases in which both partners are Croatian nationals,[84] others have held that this prohibition produces effects provided that the applicable law is Croatian.[85]

Where Croatian law is applicable to the formal validity of the *de facto* couples' property agreement, it is important to keep in mind that written form and the authentication of the parties' signatures by a notary are mandatory.[86] Since in cross-border cases provisions of European Union Regulations prevail, in some such cases the couple's property agreement or choice-of-law agreement concluded in Croatia would not have to be submitted for authentication of signatures by a notary. However, according to Arts. 23 and 25 of the Twin Regulations in connection with Art. 43, para. 3 of the FA and Art. 53, para. 2 of the LPA, if at the time the agreement is concluded both parties or only one of them is habitually resident in Croatia authentication of the parties' signatures by a notary would be mandatory.[87] Although not mandatory, it is possible under the Croatian law to conclude *de facto* partnership property agreement in the form of notarial act, which would provide parties with advice as to the legal consequences of their stipulations.[88]

The Law Applicable to Property Relations in *De Facto* Partnership in the Absence of Parties' Choice

In the absence of a choice-of-law agreement, Croatian court would decide that the Croatian law is applicable to the property consequences of the heterosexual *de facto* partnerships if: it was the law of the *de facto* partners' first common habitual residence (*lex primae firmae habitationis commmunis*) after the establishment of the partnership, or failing that, the law of the *de facto* partners' common nationality (*lex nationalis communis*) at the time of the establishment of the *de facto* partnership, or failing that, it is the law with which *de facto* partners jointly have the closest connection (*lex connexitatis*) at the time of the establishment of *de facto* partnership, taking into account all the circumstances.[89]

Habitual residence as a primary connecting factor may be challenging for Croatian courts for no less than three reasons. First, despite the fact that Art. 106, para. 2 of Croatian Civil Procedure Act[90] explicitly states that "petitions must be

---

[83] Hoblaj (2020), p. 99.

[84] See: Čulo and Radina (2011), p. 149, Belaj (2002), p. 194.

[85] Šarčević (2005b), p. 186.

[86] Art. 53 para. 2 of the LPA.

[87] Hoblaj (2020), p. 100.

[88] Hoblaj (2020), p. 99.

[89] Art. 26 para 1 of Regulation (EU) 2016/1103.

[90] Official Gazzette 53/91, 91/92, 58/93, 112/99, 88/01, 117/03, 88/05, 02/07, 84/08, 96/08, 123/08, 57/11, 148/11, 25/13, 89/14, 70/19, 80/22.

comprehensible and contain everything necessary to act upon them", usually they contain information about the residence of the parties but they do not contain all the elements relevant for establishing the habitual residence. Thus, the additional time and action is needed to organise the petition. Second, Art. 5 of the 2017 PILA explicitly lists the criteria for the determination of habitual residence and the question may arise whether to follow national criteria or CJEU case law regarding the determination of habitual residence under Regulation (EU) 2016/1104. Given that these 2017 PILA conflict rules are the result of the extended application of this Regulation, habitual residence in these cases should be determined according to notion of habitual residence within the meaning of that Regulation, including under the CJEU case-law. However, it is submitted that there would actually be no harm in relying on Art. 5 of the 2017 PILA instead, since the definition contained therein is generally in line with CJEU case-law and has an informative function above all. Third, the question could arise as to whether the first common habitual residence after the establishment of a *de facto* partnership has to be established within certain period of time or it is enough that it is established at any time before the beginning of proceedings. Although in the context of marriages some authors advocate in favour of restrictive approach,[91] and some in favour of a more liberal one,[92] it would be sensible to assume that in cases in which the first common habitual residence was not established within few months since the establishment of partnership, parties' legitimate expectations include application of the law of their common nationality. Besides, nationality is more stable factor which can be easily identified.[93]

Second connecting factor is the *de facto* partners' common nationality at the time their *de facto* partnership was established. Application of this connecting factor may also pose challenges to Croatian judiciary due to the provision of Art. 3 para. 1 of the 2017 PILA which, in case of dual nationality of a person, prescribes for exclusivity of the Croatian nationality. Such interpretation of dual nationality is under the scrutiny of the CJEU, and has important implications in cases within the scope of application of European Union law.[94] However, preambles of the Twin Regulations shine some clarity into the nuances of the "general principles of the Union". Namely, determination of nationality as a connecting factor is still left to national law, while the choice of national law as applicable law may not be subjected to the principle of exclusivity.[95] Along the same lines of reasoning and according to the explicit rule in Regulation (EU) 2016/1104, in case of common dual nationality and the absense of

[91] Dolžan (2019), p. 111, Rudolf (2018), p. 960.

[92] Damascelli (2018), p. 4.

[93] See: Podgorelčnik Vogrinc (2019), pp. 1081–1082.

[94] See: CJEU, C-369/90 *Micheletti and Others*, EU:C:1992:295; CJEU, C-168/08 *Hadadi*, EU: C:2009:474.

[95] Recital 50 of Regulation (EU) 2016/1103 and recital 49 of Regulation (EU) 2016/1104. Consequently, the solution in Regulation 650/2012 is no different. It actually follows the same line of reasoning—a person with multiple nationalities may choose the law of a State whose nationality he or she possesses at the time of making the choice or at the time of death (Art. 22). For the opposing view see: Podgorelčnik Vogrinc (2019), p. 1088.

choice of law, law with which the partners jointly have the closest connection at the time of the establishment of *de facto* partnership applies.[96]

Turning to the regime for homosexual *de facto* partnerships, in the absence of a choice-of-law agreement, Croatian law will be applicable to the property consequences of *such partnerships* if it is the law under which the *de facto* partnership was created.[97] Difficulties may appear with regard to the operationalization of this connecting factor—"the state under whose law the *de facto* partnership was created". Some are of the opinion that this connecting factor would be hard to apply to *de facto* partnerships since there is no formal registration and consequently no solid proof of the time and place of the establishment of the *de facto* partnership.[98] However, according to Arts. 38 and 39 para. 3 of the 2017 PILA 2017 applicable law for the establishment and termination of the *de facto* partnership is *lex connexitatis* (the law of the state with which the *de facto* partnership has or, if it ceased to exist, had the closest connection) which makes the determination of the state under whose law the *de facto* partnership was established slightly more complicated but not impossible.[99]

In line with parties' expectations, the Twin Regulations allow for a particular type of an escape clause.[100] In case of heterosexual *de facto* partnership it may be activated to replace the law of partners' first common habitual residence after the establishment of the partnership: if this replacement is proposed to the court by one of the parties, and if the applicant demonstrates that partners had their last habitual residence in another state and both relied on that other law for arranging or planning their property relations due to significantly longer residence in that state. In case of *de facto* partners it may be activated to replace the law of the state under whose law *de facto* partnership was created: if this replacement is proposed to court by one of the parties, if law of that other state attaches property consequences to *de facto* partners, and if the applicant demonstrates that cohabitants had their last habitual residence in another state and both relied on that other law for arranging or planning their property relations due to significantly longer residence in that state.

3.2 *Jurisdiction for* De Facto *Partnerships*

Based on the same reasons as regarding the applicable law, the Croatian legislator extended application of the Twin Regulations to the issue of jurisdiction for property relationships of *de facto* partners. Consequently, under Art. 49, paras. 2 and 4 of the 2017 PILA, international jurisdiction of Croatian courts, for property consequences of *de facto* partnerships is to be established on the same criteria as for the

[96] Art. 26 para. 1(c) of Regulation (EU) 2016/1103.

[97] Art. 26 para. 1 of Regulation (EU) 2016/1104.

[98] Kokić et al. (2019), p. 11.

[99] See: above Sect. 3.1.1.

[100] Art. 26 para. 2 of the Twin Regulations.

matrimonial property regimes and property consequences of registered partnerships, depending on whether *de facto* partnership is heterosexual or homosexual.

3.2.1 Concentration of Jurisdiction

Since the Twin Regulations aim at aligning jurisdiction regarding the couple's property with the jurisdiction regarding "the situation at the origin of the need to adjudicate on such property"[101] (e.g. death of one of the cohabitants or partners), according to Arts. 4 and 5, para. 1 of the Twin Regulations extended by the 2017 PILA, Croatian courts will have jurisdiction if there is the succession proceedings or proceedings concerning the establishment or termination of *de facto* partnership already pending before Croatian courts.[102]

However, in case of concentration of jurisdiction in the *forum hereditatis* application of national procedural rules may lead to partial concentration of jurisdiction since, in Croatia, public notaries are entrusted with deciding in succession matters while cases on couple's property are handled by the courts. Importantly, public notaries are entrusted to decide only in non-contentious succession matters[103] and their decision does not constitute proper legal ground to make an entry into the land registers. Thus, even in case of undisputed division of property, public notary's decision on succession with regard to couple's property will only constitute an *inter partes* title, thus, additional proceedings have to take place for the entry of the title into the land register.[104]

3.2.2 Prorogation of Jurisdiction

Only if there is no effect of the *vis attractiva* towards the existing proceedings, the jurisdiction of Croatian courts for property consequences of *de facto* partnerships is determined according to the cascading criteria, party autonomy being on the top in the hierarchy. According to Art. 7 para. 1 of the Twin Regulations, parties may agree on exclusive jurisdiction of Croatian courts in case of applicability of Croatian law, based either on Art. 22 (party autonomy) or on objective criteria contained in Art. 26[105] of both Regulations or the place of establishment of the homosexual *de facto* partnership. If parties missed the opportunity of conclude an explicit choice-of-court

---

[101] Kramberger Škerl (2021), pp. 720–721.

[102] Attraction of jurisdiction has precedence with regard to all other available jurisdictional criteria. *Vis attractiva* of *forum hereditatis* and forum dealing with the establishment or termination of *de facto* partnership simplifies situation in case of blurry lines between succession matters and matters concerning couple's property, provided that the same authority is competent to decide on both.

[103] Otherwise, they must refer the case to court.

[104] Poretti (2017), p. 63.

[105] More precisely Art. 26 para. 1 (a) or (b) for the heterosexual *de facto* partnerships, and Art. 26. para 1. for the homosexual *de facto* partnerships.

agreement (*prorogatio expressa*), there is still an available path for them to take and avoid otherwise competent courts. This path leads from where one of the parties brings the proceedings before the Croatian court although Croatian courts do not have jurisdiction. Provided that the defendant enters an appearance without contesting jurisdiction of Croatian court, Croatian court will assume jurisdiction (*prorogatio tacita*) and proceed with the case.[106] However, this is possible only if conditions prescribed for explicit prorogation are satisfied and, before assuming jurisdiction, court has ensured that the defendant is informed of their right to contest jurisdiction and of the consequences of entering or not entering an appearance.[107] If the party objects to jurisdiction, the court has to decline its jurisdiction.[108]

3.2.3 Jurisdiction in the Absence of Prorogation

If there is neither express nor tacit prorogation of jurisdiction, cascading criteria apply.[109] Accordingly, Croatian courts are competent if at the moment the court is seized: the couple's habitual residence is in Croatia (*forum firmae habitationis communis*), or failing that, if the couple's last habitual residence was in Croatia (*forum ultimae firmae habitationis communis*) under the condition that one of them is still residing in Croatia, or failing that, the respondent's habitual residence is in Croatia (*forum rei*), or failing that, the couple's common nationality is Croatian (*forum nationalis communis*). With regard to homosexual *de facto* partners, this cascade has an additional criterion according to which, in case all previous criteria fail to realise, Croatian court will be competent if the de facto partnership was established under Croatian law.

Considering synchrony of *forum* and *ius*, alternative jurisdiction, envisaged by Art. 9 of the Twin Regulations, is superfluous from the point of view of Croatian judiciary.

If, based on all previous criteria there is no ground for the assumption of jurisdiction of Croatian courts, Croatian courts shall have jurisdiction in so far as immovable property of one or both parties is located in Croatia (*forum rei sitae*), in which case Croatian court may rule only in respect of the immovable property in question.[110] When applied to *de facto* partnerships according to the extension of the scope of the Twin Regulations, subsidiary jurisdiction may brake the principle of unity of applicable law in favour of *depeçage* if a court in another country decides on a different applicable law.

---

[106] Art. 8. of the Twin Regulations.

[107] This is in line with jurisdictional provisions of Art 26 para. 2, regarding protective jurisdiction, in BU I bis.

[108] Kunda and Winkler (2020), pp. 109–110.

[109] Art. 6 of both Regulations.

[110] Art. 10 of both Regulations.

Finally, if there is no available forum in any other state or proceedings cannot reasonably be brought or conducted in any other state with which the case is closely connected, Croatian courts may, exceptionally, rule on the couple's property regime.

3.2.4 Jurisdiction for Counterclaims

There is also a jurisdictional rule for the counterclaims in Art. 12 of the Twin Regulations allowing the court hearing the claim to hear also the counterclaim. However, a problem may arise with regard to temporal scope of application of the Twin Regulations to the *de facto* partnerships, based on the references in the 2017 PILA. In case where the original proceedings predate the 2017 PILA and Regulations and the party wants to file a counterclaim there would be little or no available fora. According to the Twin Regulations, a counterclaim may be filed before the same court having jurisdiction over the claim if that jurisdiction is based on one of the criteria provided by the respective Regulation. Since, according to the 1982 PILA, jurisdiction could have been based on the *forum rei* and the *forum rei sitae*, the available fora in which to file the counterclaim would be extremely limited, which would results in limiting the right to access the court.[111] From that perspective, it is regrettable that the provision of Art. 27 of the Civil Procedure Act was deleted in the most recent amendment.[112] If still in force, it would offer a solution to this problem.

4 Conclusion

Legal recognition of effects of *de facto* partnerships in many European countries is still an area in development. Reasons may be found in the respect for the principle of individual freedom, according to which it would be unjustifiable not to respect the presumed will of partners to be kept outside the available legal matrimonial or registered partnership regime, or perhaps also in social and cultural setting specific to each state.[113]

---

[111] See: Elijaš et al. (2016), pp. 389–390, 393–394.

[112] See: Civil Procedure Act, Official Gazzette 53/91, 91/92, 58/93, 112/99, 88/01, 117/03, 88/05, 02/07, 84/08, 96/08, 123/08, 57/11, 148/11, 25/13, 89/14, 70/19, 80/22. Art. 27 of the CPA (before the amendment in force as of 19 July 2022): "A court in the Republic of Croatia will be deemed competent when its jurisdiction in a dispute with an international element is expressly determined by law or international treaty. If there is no express provision, in the law or international treaty, on the jurisdiction of the court in the Republic of Croatia for a certain type of dispute, the court in the Republic of Croatia is competent to judge that type of dispute even when its jurisdiction derives from the provisions of the law on local jurisdiction of the court in the Republic of Croatia."

[113] For more, see: Cazorla Gonzáles (2021), pp. 79–82.

However, exclusion of such relationships from the scope of family law (and other branches of law) may have negative consequences, first and foremost for the weaker party in that relationship.[114] Therefore, it is not surprising that the focus of many legislators has shifted "from status towards contract and relations",[115] i.e. from the external, formal nature of the relationship towards how people actually live.[116] *De facto* partnerships are at rise[117] and the number of laws recognizing their legal effects slowly rises as well.

In Croatia, legal recognition of heterosexual *de facto* partnership (termed as *de facto* cohabitation) has never been an issue. On the other hand, legal recognition of homosexual *de facto* partnerships (termed as life partnerships) is only a relatively recent development. As in some other European countries, it comes as a result of the efforts of non-governmental organizations and political parties.[118] Today, Croatian approach to legal recognition of the homosexual *de facto* partnerships may be described as intended to create treatment "functionally equivalent" to marriage,[119] meaning that the name of legal construct remains as the only difference. In line with substantive law, the 2017 PILA contains number of conflict-of-law rules regarding *de facto* partnerships, both heterosexual and homosexual.

Since number of *de facto* partnerships, both heterosexual and homosexual, is increasing, it is to be expected that the number of court cases concerning their property relations will be on the raise too. According to the 2017 PILA, jurisdiction and applicable law in those cases is to be determined according to the European Union rules for matrimonial property and property consequences of registered partnerships. There are obvious advantages of this approach, especially considering that the 2017 PILA employs the same scope-expanding technique with respect to other cross-border issues regulated by European Union regulations.

European Union regulations in the field of family property lean on previously adopted rules and tend to achieve synchrony of *forum* and *ius* which makes it easier for national authorities in exercising their function in cross-border cases. On the other hand, these goals may be hard to achieve for the reasons explained above, mainly due to essential differences between marriage and registered partnership on one hand, and *de facto* partnerships on the other. Sometimes the rules intended for one purpose do not fit another without encountering difficulties on the way. The challenges that this approach will impose over the Croatian courts and possibly other authorities, will have to be managed with the attention to both principles of private international law and family law as well as respect for human rights.

[114] E.g. denial of equal shares of assets, denial of inheritance, maintenance, welfare benefits, etc.

[115] Schwenzer (2001), p. 200.

[116] Aeschlimann (2005), p. 244.

[117] Župan (2016), p. 162.

[118] See: Scherpe (2013), p. 84.

[119] See: Scherpe (2013), pp. 85–85.

References

Aeschlimann S (2005) Financial compensation upon the ending of informal relationships – a comparison of different approaches to ensure the protection of the weaker party. In: Boele-Woelki K (ed) Common core and better law in European family law. Intersentia, Antwerp-Oxford, pp 243–281

Alinčić M (2005) Changes in regulations on marriage and other life unions. Zbornik Pravnog fakulteta u Zagrebu 55(5):1165–1199

Alinčić M, Bakarić-Mihanović A (1980) Family law. Pravni fakultet Zagreb, Zagreb

Belaj V (2002) Bračna stečevina po Obiteljskom zakonu. Zbornik Pravnog fakulteta u Zagrebu 23(1):179–200

Boele-Woelki K, Mol C, van Gelder E (eds) (2015) European family law in action, volume V: informal relationships. Intersentia, Cambridge-Antwerp-Portland

Cazorla Gonzáles MJ (2021) Agreements regarding the property relations of transnational couples and their effects under the application of the twin Regulations. Actualidad Juridica Iberoamericana 15:76–109

Čulo A, Radina A (2011) Valjanost bračnog ugovora. In: Rešetar B, Župan M (eds) Imovinskopravni aspekti razvoda braka – hrvatski, europski i međunarodni kontekst, pp 139–163

Damascelli D (2018) Applicable law, jurisdiction and recognition of decisions in matters relating to property regimes of spouses and partners in European and Italian private international law. Trusts Trustees 0:1–11

Dika M, Knežević G, Stojanović S (1991) Komentar zakona o međuarodnom privatnom i procesnom pravu. Nomos, Beograd

Dolžan J (2019) Uredba (EU) glede premoženjskopravnih razmerij za mednarodne pare – kolizijska pravila. Odvetnik 90(2):106–113

Elijaš D, Marković S, Trgovac S (2016) Pravo na pristup sudu kao aspekt prava na pravično suđenje, Zbornik Pravnog fakulteta Sveučilišta u Rijeci (1991), 37(1):385–421

Hoblaj H (2020) Javni bilježnici i usporedna primjena Uredbe br. 650/2012 o nasljeđivanju, Uredbe br. 2016/1103 o bračnoimovinskom režimu i Uredbe br. 2016/1104 o imovini registriranih partnerstava, Javni bilježnik XXIV(47):84–106

Hoško T (2019) Novo uređenje međunarodnog privatnog prava u Republici Hrvatskoj – Zakon o međunarodnom privatnom pravu. Zakonitost I/1:19–31

Jakovac-Lozić D (2004) Zakon o istospolnim zajednicama – izazov hrvatskog zakonodavstva u procesu približavanja Europskoj uniji. Zbornik Pravnog fakulteta u Splitu 41(1–2):3–42

Jakovac-Lozić D (2017) Hrvatska obitelj u procijepu između tradicionalna poimanja i međunarodnih očekivanja, Godišnjak akademije pravnih znanosti Hrvatske VIII(1):1–33

Josipović T (2005) Intestate succession. In: Croatia, family and succession law, international encyclopaedia of laws. Kluwer Law International, pp 210–219

Kokić T, Kunda I, Župan M (2019) Prekogranična pitanja bračnoimovinskih režima i režima imovine registriranih partnera, Pravosudna akademija, Zagreb. https://pak.hr/cke/obrazovni%20materijali/Prekograni%C4%8Dna%20pitanja%20bra%C4%8Dnoimovinskih%20re%C5%BEima%20i%20re%C5%BEima%20imovine%20registriranih%20partnera.pdf

Korać Graovac A (2015) Brak i obitelj kao vrijednost u hrvatskom pravnom sustavu. Bogoslovska smotra 85(3):799–811

Kramberger Škerl J (2021) International Jurisdiction under the EU Property Regimes Regulations – Bringing Coherence into Cross-Border Couples' Property Disputes, Zbornik Pravnog fakulteta Sveučilišta u Rijeci (1991), 42(3):717–735

Kunda I (2019) Novi međunarodnoprivatnopravni okvir imovine bračnih i registriranih partnera u Europskoj uniji: polje primjene i nadležnost. Hrvatska pravna revija 3:27–36

Kunda I (2020) Upućivanje na propise EU u Zakonu o međunarodnom privatnom pravu. In: Barbić J, Sikirić H (eds) Međunarodno privatno pravo – interakcija međunarodnih, europskih i domaćih propisa. HAZU, Zagreb, pp 21–48

Kunda I, Winkler S (2020) Prorogation of Jurisdiction. In: Cazorla Gonzáles MJ et al (eds) Property relations of cross border couples in the European Union. Edizioni Scientifiche Italiane, Napoli, pp 109–111

Lešić M, Polajnar-Pavčnik A, Wedam-Lukić D (1983) Mednarodno zasebno pravo. Zakon s komentarjem. Časopisni zavod Uradni list, Ljubljana

Lucić N (2013) Pravno uređenje braka i drugih oblika životnih zajednica, https://www.pravos.unios.hr/download/pravno-uredenje-braka-i-drugih-oblika-zivotnih-zajednica.docx

Lucić N (2015) Dokazivanje izvanbračne zajednice – odgovori na neujednačeno zakonodavstvo i sudsku praksu, Pravni vijesnik: časopis za pravne i društvene znanosti Pravnog fakulteta Sveučilišta J.J. Strossmayera u Osijeku 31(3–4):101–132

Lucić N (2020) Pravno uređenje izvanbračne zajednice u hrvatskom pravnom sustavu. Narodne novine, Zagreb

Matić Ž (1978) Bračnoimovinsko međunarodno privatno pravo. Prinosi za poredbeno proučavanje prava i međunarodno privatno pravo, Zagreb

Petrašević T, Duić D, Buljan E (2017) Prava istospolnih zajednica u Europskoj uniji s posebnim osvrtom na Republiku Hrvatsku. Strani pravni život 61(3):145–169

Podgorelčnik Vogrinc N (2019) Applicable law in matrimonial property regime disputes. Zbornik Pravnog fakulteta Sveučilišta u Rijeci (1991) 40(3):1075–1100

Poretti P (2017) Odlučivanje o imovinskim odnosima bračnih drugova u ostavinskim postupcima sukladno Uredbi 2016/1103 o bračnoimovinskom režimu. Javni bilježnik XXI/(44):57–71

Puljko V, Živić J (2011) Razvod braka s međunarodnim obilježjem u hrvatskoj sudskoj praksi. In: Rešetar B, Župan M (eds) Imovinskopravni aspekti razvoda braka – hrvatski, europski i međunarodni kontekst, Osijek

Rudolf C (2017) Kolizijske norme Uredbe Sveta (EU) 2016/1104 za premoženjskoprave posledice registriranih partnerskih skupnosti. In: Možina D (ed) Liber Amicorum Ada Polajnar Pavčnik. Raszežnosti zasebnega prava, Ljubljana, pp 256–279

Rudolf C (2018) Premoženjska razmerja med zakonci v mednarodnem zasebnem pravu. Podjetje in delo, XLIV(6–7):952–963

Ruggeri L (2021) Property and cross-border couples from the perspective of European regulation. Actualidad Juridica Iberoamericana 15:252–273

Sajko K et al (2001) Izvori hrvatskog i europskog međunarodnog privatnog prava – sa sudskom i arbitražnom praksom i tezama za zakon o međunarodnom privatnom pravu. Informator, Zagreb

Šarčević P (1980) Vanbračna zajednica i problem određivanje mjerodavnog prava kod interlokalnog sukoba zakona. Zbornik Pravnog fakulteta u Rijeci 1:177–190

Šarčević P (1981) Cohabitation without marriage: the Yugoslavian experience. Am J Comp Law 29(2):315–328

Šarčević P (1985) The new Yugoslav private international law act. Am J Comp Law 33(2):283–296

Šarčević P (2005a) Cohabitation without marriage. In: Croatia, family and succession law, international encyclopaedia of laws. Kluwer Law International, pp 126–131

Šarčević P (2005b) Property Rights in the Family. In: Croatia, family and succession law, international encyclopaedia of laws. Kluwer Law International, pp 177–190

Scherpe JM (2013) The legal recognition of same-sex couples in Europe and the role of the European Court of Human Rights. Equal Rights Rev 10:83–96

Schwenzer I (2001) Editorial: the evolution of family law – from status to contract and relation. Eur J Law Reform 3:199–202

Sikirić H (2018) Zakon o međunarodnom privatnom pravu, Aktualnosti hrvatskog zakonodavstva i pravne prakse. Organizator 25:61–140

Stevanov S (1978) Vanbračna porodica. Zbornik Pravnog fakulteta u Zagrebu 28(1–2):81–95

Varadi T, Bordaš B, Knežević G, Pavić V (2010) Međunarodno privatno pravo. JP Službeni glasnik, Beograd

Varady T (1983) Međunarodno privatno pravo. Forum, Novi Sad

Winkler S (2019) Imovinski odnosi u obitelji: nacionalna pravna rješenja i europski trendovi, Godišnjak akademije pravnih znanosti Hrvatske, X(1):447–467

Wintermute R (2020) Global trends in legal recognition of same-sex couples: cohabitaion rights, registered partnership, marriage and joint parenting. National Taiwan Univ Law Rev 15(2): 131–152

Župan M (2012) Izbor mjerodavnog prava u obiteljskim, statusnim i nasljednim stvarima, Zbornik Pravnog fakulteta Sveučilišta u Rijeci (1991) 33(2):629–666

Župan M (2016) Temeljna ljudska prava i prekogranične životne zajednice – registrirano partnerstvo u fokusu. In: Varady T et al (ed) Liber amicorum Gašo Knežević, Beograd, pp 142–166

Župan M (2018) Zakon o međunarodnom privatnom pravu. Hrvatska pravna revija 18(2):1–12

Mediation in Cross-Border Matrimonial Property Disputes and Property Disputes of Registered Partners: Greek Law and Policy

Vassiliki Koumpli

1 Introductory Remarks

1.1 General Observations

Mediation as a way of resolving disputes has been successfully applied in the Anglo-Saxon countries and the countries of the Far East for more than one century. In the last decade, mediation has been highly promoted also in the EU. Particularly with regard to cross-border family disputes, agreed, out-of-court, solutions are encouraged and gaining increasing importance. The *Jumeaux* (Twin) Regulations on property regimes of spouses[1] and registered partners[2] explicitly follow this trend, stating that "[t]he Regulation[s] should not prevent the parties from settling the case amicably out of court in a Member State of their choice where this is possible under the law of the Member State, even if the law applicable to the regime is not the law of that Member State" (recitals 39 and 38, respectively).

[1] Council Regulation (EU) 2016/1103, of 24 June 2016, implementing enhanced cooperation in the area of jurisdiction, applicable law and the recognition and enforcement of decisions in matters of matrimonial property regimes, OJ L 183, 8.7.2016, pp. 1–29.

[2] Council Regulation (EU) 2016/1104, of 24 June 2016, implementing enhanced cooperation in the area of jurisdiction, applicable law and the recognition and enforcement of decisions in matters of property consequences of registered partnerships, OJ L 183, 8.7.2016, pp. 30–56.

V. Koumpli (✉)
Hellenic Institute of International and Foreign Law, Athina, Greece

Koumpli Dispute Resolution, Athina, Greece
e-mail: vkoumpli@hiifl.gr; vkoumpli@koumpli.gr

I. Kunda et al. (eds.), *Balkan Yearbook of European and International Law 2022*,
Balkan Yearbook of European and International Law 2022,
https://doi.org/10.1007/978-3-031-29432-7_6

1.2 Concept and Main Features of Mediation

In the broad sense, the term 'mediation' refers to a voluntary, structured process whereby a third neutral, the mediator, facilitates the communication between the parties to a conflict and enables them to assume responsibility for finding a solution to their conflict. Mediation aims at developing an agreed solution between the parties, by contrast with litigation and arbitration, where the dispute is solved by a decision—court judgment or arbitration award.

It is the very nature of mediation to engage the parties in a voluntary process of finding an amicable resolution to their dispute. 'Voluntariness' is a basic and undisputed principle of mediation commonly used in mediation definitions. The principle of 'voluntariness' is not contrary to the requirements in some jurisdictions of mandatory information meetings on mediation. Even in jurisdictions where it is compulsory for the parties to a dispute to attempt mediation, it can be argued that this is compatible with the voluntary nature of mediation as long as the parties are not forced to actually settle their dispute in mediation.

Moreover, neutrality, independence, impartiality and fairness are crucial and indispensable elements of mediation and need to be safeguarded. Such features are closely linked, although they address different aspects of the mediation process. Mediation should be neutral in relation to the outcome of the process. The mediator needs to be independent as to the way in which he conducts mediation, whereas simultaneously he needs to be impartial towards the parties. At the same time, the mediation must be conducted fairly. The latter implies that the parties need to be given equal opportunity to participate in the mediation process and the mediation process needs to be adapted in each individual case to allow for balanced bargaining powers. For example, the parties' wish to use their mother tongue or a language with which they feel comfortable should be respected as far as possible.

It should be also ensured that appropriate safeguards are in place to support the confidentiality of mediation. Legislations—at both EU level and national level—have introduced rules ensuring that the mediator and others involved in the mediation may not be compelled to give evidence on communications related to the mediation in civil or commercial proceedings unless certain exceptions apply. In international family mediation, the parties need to be fully informed about the rules applicable to confidentiality in the different jurisdictions concerned. All communications in the course and in the context of mediation should, subject to the applicable law, be confidential, unless otherwise agreed by the parties. Confidentiality of communications related to the mediation helps to create the atmosphere of trust needed for the parties to engage in an open discussion on a whole range of possible solutions to their dispute. The parties may be less willing to consider different options if they fear that their proposals may be taken as a concession and held against them in legal proceedings.

1.3 Scope of the Chapter

Mediation has long been established as a suitable method for the resolution of family law disputes worldwide. To a great extent, this category of disputes touches sensitive issues involving not only the legal aspects of the matters at large but also other important elements, such as sentiments, emotions, social factors, responsibilities, personal duties and the mindset of the parties, as well as the inherent need for privacy. The divorce process, in particular, is a complex and multidimensional event, which also includes economic and social parameters requiring a good adjustment. In this context, mediation can ensure the best possible conditions: less tension, anger, loss of dignity and financial poverty. The resulting written agreement—being mutually acceptable and beneficial to the contracting parties—will help avoid conflicts and settle issues related not only to children but also to finances and property. At the same time, the steady expansion of international mobility of persons has led to an impressive increase of family disputes that display foreign elements.

Even though family mediation appears to constantly gain ground during the last decade in Greece, and despite the provisions of the twin Regulations, to date Greek legal doctrine has been reluctant to extensively analyse the applicable legal framework in particular focusing on mediation in cross-border family property disputes. In this framework, after this short introduction (1), the present chapter aims at providing a succinct illustration of the Greek policy on mediation (2), the legal issues arising (3) and the processual dimension of mediation (4) in cross-border property disputes of spouses and registered partners, ending with the resulting concluding remarks (5).

2 Greek Policy on Mediation in Cross-Border Family Property Disputes of Spouses and Partners

2.1 Underpinnings of Mediation Regulation in Cross-Border Family Property Disputes

2.1.1 The First Mediation Act

Cross-border family disputes have been traditionally resolved in Greece through recourse to litigation. In such a historical and regulatory environment, the Greek legislator introduced the legal institution of mediation in 2010 by enacting the first Mediation Act.[3] Its promulgation derived from the obligation of the legislature to implement Directive 2008/52/EC on certain aspects of mediation in civil and

[3]Law 3898/2010. Mediation in civil and commercial matters, Government Gazette A 211. An analysis of this regime in English can be found among others in Diamantopoulos and Koumpli (2014); Diamantopoulos and Koumpli (2015) and Koumpli (2017).

commercial matters.[4] Greece was among the first Member States to implement the EU Mediation Directive, adopting the monistic approach and establishing a uniform system for both domestic and cross-border mediation. Moreover, it delimitated its scope of application to private law disputes, which can be referred to mediation upon agreement of the parties provided that they have the right to dispose of the relative rights and obligations. In this sense, cross-border family property disputes are undoubtedly considered as "mediatable" under the Greek regime. Regulating in essence the core elements of the process, the first Mediation Act was accompanied by secondary legislation, which provided for specific details of its application.[5]

This initiative at EU level was a consequence of the increasing concern about court costs and workload as well as other obstacles to cross-border dispute resolution in the single market.[6] By establishing a core framework for cross-border mediation in Europe, which can also be applied to domestic disputes,[7] the Mediation Directive aims at promoting its use for all disputes concerning civil and commercial matters, *"ensuring a balanced relationship between mediation and judicial proceedings"*.[8] In order to avoid conceptual ambiguities, the Mediation Directive states that mediation shall be understood as *"a structured process, however named or referred to, whereby two or more parties to a dispute attempt by themselves, on a voluntary basis, to reach an agreement on the settlement of their dispute with the assistance of a mediator"*.[9] The key issues embodied in the Mediation Directive concern the voluntary[10] and confidential[11] character of the mediation process, its effect on limitation and prescription periods[12] and the enforceability of the agreements reached by the parties.[13]

The adoption of the first Mediation Act admittedly contributed to the creation of a strong ADR movement in Greece, as shown by the increased number of mediation

[4]Directive 2008/52/EC of the European Parliament and the Council of 21 May 2008 on certain aspects of mediation in civil and commercial matters, OJ L 136, 24.05.2008, pp. 3–8.

[5]Presidential Decree 123/2011. Determination of terms and conditions for the authorization and operation of training bodies for mediators in civil and commercial disputes, Government Gazette A 255; Decision of the Minister of Justice, Transparency and Human Rights Nr. 109088 οικ./12.12.2011. Procedure for recognition of mediators' accreditation – Adoption of Code of Conduct for Accredited Mediators and Determination of sanctions for infringements thereof, Government Gazette B 2824; Decision of the Minister of Justice, Transparency and Human Rights Nr. 1460/οικ./27.1.2012. Determination of mediator's fees, Government Gazette B 281; Decision of the Ministers of Finance and Justice, Transparency and Human Rights Nr. 85485 οικ./18.9.2012. Determination of administrative fees for mediation, Government Gazette B 2693.

[6]For a thorough analysis, see, instead of others, Esplugues (2014), p. 501 et seq.

[7]Recital 8 of Directive 2008/52/EC.

[8]Article 1 of Directive 2008/52/EC.

[9]Article 3(a) of Directive 2008/52/EC.

[10]Article 3(a) of Directive 2008/52/EC.

[11]Article 7 of Directive 2008/52/EC.

[12]Article 8 of Directive 2008/52/EC.

[13]Article 6 of Directive 2008/52/EC.

centres, trainings, publications and conferences. In practice, on the contrary, the application of mediation in civil and commercial matters remained extremely limited, despite its undisputed benefits. Such disconnect between the benefits of mediation and its current use, known as the 'Mediation Paradox',[14] could be explained through various factors, such as the fear before the unknown, the reluctance of lawyers or even features of the Greek judicial system. In fact, given the relatively low court costs, claimants have not been prevented from referring to court proceedings even when the possibilities of winning the case are limited. Similarly, significant delays in the administration of justice, at both the stage of hearing a case and the stage of execution of judgments, prevent defendants from agreeing to submit a dispute to mediation, particularly after this has arisen. In this context, for a long period of time mediation appeared to be preferable in cross-border commercial disputes where an arbitration clause already existed.

2.1.2 The Second Mediation Act

Almost eight years after the enactment of the first Mediation Act, a radical reform of the mediation regime took place with the enactment of the second Mediation Act,[15] which was published in January 2018 and replaced the former first Mediation Act as well as the secondary legislation accompanying this. The second Mediation Act repeated and enhanced the pre-existing legal framework whereas, at the same time, it introduced two significant innovations: (a) the establishment of the Central Mediation Committee and (b) a quasi-mandatory scheme consisting in the mandatory initial mediation session for limited categories of cases, including cross-border family law disputes. Such provisions, to the extent that they contained mandatory elements and, in effect, particularized the process, signaled a significant step towards institutionalization of mediation.[16]

This reform was not without criticism by a part of legal practitioners and the judiciary, which demonstrated the cultural hurdles mediation was still facing at that time. In this context, it is worth mentioning that Administrative Plenary Panel of *Areios Pagos*[17] issued opinion no. 34/2018 (with a marginal majority of 21–17 votes) holding that the mandatory mediation scheme introduced by the second Mediation Act was contrary to the Hellenic Constitution and the European

[14] See European Parliament – Directorate General for Internal Policies (2014) 'Rebooting' the Mediation Directive: Assessing the Limited Impact of its Implementation and Proposing Measures to Increase the Number of Mediations in the EU, http://www.europarl.europa.eu/RegData/etudes/etudes/join/2014/493042/IPOL-JURI_ET(2014)493042_EN.pdf.

[15] Law 4512/2018. Provisions on the implementation of the structural reforms of the economic adjustment program and other provisions, Government Gazette A 5.

[16] See Koumpli (2019).

[17] Areios Pagos is the Hellenic Supreme Civil Court.

Convention on Human Rights. The mediator's fee[18] and the mandatory attendance of the parties' lawyers at the mediation were considered to give rise to high costs and obstruct access to justice. Even though the opinion does not constitute a 'court judgment' and is not binding, it was, however, indicative of how the new mediation scheme was perceived at the moment. In this context and as a consequence of consecutive suspensions, the provisions of the second Mediation Act concerning the mandatory initial mediation session never applied.

2.2 *Current Regime of Mediation Regulation in Cross-Border Family Property Disputes*

2.2.1 The Third Mediation Act

Almost two years after the enactment of the second Mediation Act, the third Mediation Act[19] was published on 30 November 2019 and replaced all former legislation, constituting now the sole legal instrument regulating mediation in Greece. The third Mediation Act exhaustively deals with all issues pertaining to mediation in both cross-border and domestic civil and commercial disputes, including family law disputes. It contains detailed provisions on the regulation of the institution of mediation, the principles of the process (good faith, honesty, fairness, impartiality, confidentiality etc.), the enforceability of the mediated agreement, the qualifications of the mediator, the code of conduct and the disciplinary law of mediators, as well as issues concerning the mediators' training accreditation and the administration of the institution of mediation by the Central Mediation Committee of the Ministry of Justice. To a great extent, it repeats and enhances the pre-existing legal framework, but it also provides for the practical implementation of the mandatory initial mediation scheme, which now applies to a broader category of cases.[20] In particular:

[18] The mediator's fee was freely agreed by the parties by written agreement. If there was no written agreement Article 194 of the second Mediation Act set the mediator's minimum fee at EUR 170,00 for providing his services up to two hours whereas for service of more than two hours the minimum fee was set at EUR 100,00 per hour (no maximum was set); at the same time, even lower fees regarding maintenance disputes, small claims etc. were provided.

[19] Law 4640/2019. Mediation in civil and commercial matters—Further harmonization of the Greek legislation with the provisions of Directive Directive 2008/52/EC of the European Parliament and the Council of 21 May 2008 and other provisions, Government Gazette A 190.

[20] For an overview in the English language see Koumpli (2021b).

The Central Mediation Committee of the Ministry of Justice

The administration of the institution of mediation is entrusted to the Central Mediation Committee of the Ministry of Justice, a body firstly introduced by virtue of the second Mediation Act. The Central Mediation Committee consists of thirteen members, appointed by the Minister of Justice: (a) two judges or prosecutors of civil and criminal justice; (b) two university professors experienced in mediation, coming from more than one educational institution, but at least one from a law school; (c) two representatives of the plenary of the Bar Associations of the country; (d) two representatives of the Ministry of Justice; (e) two mediators representing professional agencies; and (f) three mediators following a call for interest. For each full member of the Central Mediation Committee a substitute shall be appointed under the same procedure. The most senior of the judiciary serves as chairman of the Central Mediation Committee. The term of office of the chairman and the members of the Committee shall be three years and may be renewed once. The members of the committee shall be prohibited from maintaining any cooperation with the mediators training bodies. The importance that the legislator gives to the Central Mediation Committee is depicted in the fact that it is composed of persons of recognized standing equipped with guarantees of independence in the performance of their duties.

The Mandatory Initial Mediation Session

In principle, civil and commercial law disputes can be voluntarily submitted to mediation as long as the parties have the authority to dispose of the subject matter of the dispute, namely, where the law does not require a court judgment for its resolution.[21] At the same time, a mandatory initial mediation session requirement is provided for the following categories of disputes: (a) family disputes (concerning lawsuits filed as of 15 January 2020), including cross-border family property disputes; (b) disputes under the standard civil procedure falling within the jurisdiction of the Single-Member Court of First Instance—when the value of the subject-matter of the dispute exceeds the amount of EUR 30.000,00—and the Multi-Member Court of First Instance (concerning lawsuits filed as of 1st July 2020); (c) disputes arising from contracts which contain a valid mediation clause (concerning lawsuits filed as of 30 November 2019).[22] Disputes where the State or public entities are parties are excluded from the mandatory initial mediation session requirement.[23] Also, under this regime mediation is primarily used as a tool to reduce court workload; it appears, however, that it further takes account of the

[21] Article 3(1) of the third Mediation Act.

[22] Articles 6(1) and 44 of the third Mediation Act, as amended.

[23] Article 6(2) of the third Mediation Act.

value of the subject matter of the dispute, so that small claims are not excessively burdened with procedural requirements eventually prohibiting access to justice.

In the above enumerated disputes, the mediator shall be appointed by mutual consent of the parties or the claimant shall submit a request for recourse to mediation to an accredited mediator included in the register of the Ministry of Justice. If the respondent does not agree on the person of the mediator, the latter is appointed by the Central Mediation Committee of the Ministry of Justice. The mediator shall notify the other party (or parties) of the request and arrange the date and place of the mandatory initial mediation session. This session takes place no later than twenty days from the day following the claimant's request to the mediator, extended up to thirty days when any of the parties resides abroad. The requirement of the mandatory initial mediation session is fulfilled if the parties and their lawyers appear before the mediator, even if they agree not to proceed to mediation. In such case, the record of the session is drawn by the mediator and shall be filed with the submissions of the parties before the court, constituting a condition for the admissibility of the hearing of the case. If the parties eventually agree to proceed to mediation, they draw the agreement to mediate and shall complete the mediation within forty days, unless they agree on a later date.[24]

The summons to the mandatory initial mediation session and the agreement to mediate in case of voluntary mediation suspend the statute of limitations, all deadlines regarding the exercise of the claims and rights in question as well as procedural deadlines during the mediation process. All deadlines continue counting again after the drafting of the record proving the failure of the mediation or the withdrawal statement from the mediation proceedings by any of the parties to the other party and the mediator or from the completion or annulment in any way of the mediation process.[25]

If a party who has been invited fails to attend the mandatory initial mediation session, the mediator will draft the relevant record and the other party shall submit it to the court. The court may then, in addition to its ruling on the merits, impose fines to litigants who were summoned in a mediation process but opted not to attend (ranging from EUR 100,00 to EUR 500,00), taking into account the overall behaviour of the party and the reasons for their non-attendance at the mediation session.[26]

CJEU preliminary reference rulings in the *Alassini*[27] and *Menini*[28] cases served as the basis for providing compatibility of the mandatory initial mediation session provisions with the protection of the fundamental right of the parties to have

[24] Article 7 of the third Mediation Act.

[25] Article 9 of the third Mediation Act.

[26] Article 7(6) of the third Mediation Act.

[27] CJEU, *Rosalba Alassini v Telecom Italia SpA*, C-317/08, *Filomena Califano v Wind SpA*, C-318/08, *Lucia Anna Giorgia Iacono v Telecom Italia SpA*, C-319/08, and *Multiservice Srl v Telecom Italia SpA*, C-320/08, judgment of 18 March 2010, ECLI:EU:C:2010:146.

[28] CJEU, *Livio Menini and Maria Antonia Rampanelli v Banco Popolare – Società Cooperativa*, judgment of 14 June 2017, C-75/016, ECLI:EU:C:2017:457.

effective recourse to justice. The ability of the parties to leave the mediation process at any time and to seek judicial recourse, the limited costs related to the mandatory initial mediation session,[29] the provision of a short period within which mediation shall be concluded as well as the suspension of prescription periods of all rights pending the mediation process confirm such compatibility. The right of recourse to justice might be affected by the introduction of mandatory mediation; the restriction in question, however, was considered by the Greek legislator as permitted, since the aim sought by the relevant provisions, namely the speedier and less expensive settlement of disputes and the lightening of the burden of the judicial system, to the benefit of the general interest, was considered proportionate to the restriction imposed on fundamental rights. Arguably, a particular feature of the mandatory mediation regime in Greece providing that the parties are required to attend the mediation process with their respective lawyers gives rise to costs together with the additional mediator's fees and may constitute a barrier to the access to justice. The exclusion of small claims from the scope of the requirement of a mandatory initial mediation session as well as the exclusion of both consumer disputes and small claims from the scope of the requirement to attend with a lawyer appear to speak for the compatibility of the Greek mediation regime with the case law of the CJEU.[30]

Following the current international trends, mediation is thereon transformed from an inherently voluntary and informal process to a pure regulatory tool aiming at saving resources in the administration of justice. The middle way introduced by the third Mediation Act scheme bridges the gap between mandatory and voluntary mediation in an attempt not to excessively obstruct the parties' right to access to justice. And, indeed, even if one accepts that mandatory elements in mediation may erode aspects of voluntariness and autonomy, there is no doubt that such elements can be a useful tool to encourage mediation on a wider scale. In this respect, the Greek quasi-compulsory scheme could be considered as a temporary expedient to encourage wider use of mediation in general so that it eventually becomes a "complementary" dispute resolution means. Since the application of the new regime, it appears that parties and lawyers are gradually gaining awareness about the advantages of mediation as an innovative tailor-made process that allows the parties to discover the core of their conflict and reach solutions that satisfy their interests, but could not be obtained in a courtroom. With regard to family and family property disputes, it seems that a certain progress has been made and numerous cases are being brought to mediation on a voluntary basis, irrespectively of the mandatory initial mediation session requirement.

---

[29]The mediator's fee in mandatory initial mediation session is in principle freely agreed by the parties by written agreement. If there is no written agreement, Article 18 of the third Mediation Act set the mediator's minimum fee for conducting the mandatory initial mediation session at EUR 5000.

[30]Koumpli (2021a).

The Regulation of the Mediation Process

According to the EU Mediation Directive and the Greek Mediation Acts consecutively implementing it, a 'cross-border dispute' shall be one in which at least one of the parties is domiciled or habitually resident in a EU Member State other than that of any other party on the date on which: (a) the parties agree to use mediation after the dispute has arisen; (b) mediation is ordered by a court of a EU Member State; (c) an obligation to use mediation arises under national or foreign law; or (d) an invitation is made to the parties by the court before which an action is already brought. It is further stated that a cross-border dispute shall also be one in which judicial proceedings or arbitration following mediation between the parties are initiated in a Member State other than that in which the parties were domiciled or habitually resident on the date on which the circumstances mentioned above under (a)-(c) occurred.[31] Remarkably, the criterion of the cross-border nature of a certain dispute according to the above is subjective, i.e., it is related to the person of the parties. Furthermore, it focuses exclusively on the permanent residence or habitual residence of the parties, without taking into account the place of mediation or other elements of foreignness, such as e.g., the nationality of the parties, the place of injury or the place of execution of the mediation agreement in relation to the place of its formation. Even though the provided definition is limited to 'EU cross-border disputes', this does not mean that a mediation process cannot take place in Greece when one or all the parties are, for instance, domiciled outside the EU. Such process may of course be defined as 'cross-border mediation' in the broad sense; yet, it may remain essentially unregulated by the Greek Mediation Act and, depending on the particular agreement of the parties, it may constitute either an institutional mediation or simply a 'wild mediation'. It should be highlighted that in the latter case no formal requirements concerning the qualities and the duties of the mediator are applicable. However, the parties may opt to subject the mediation to the Greek Mediation Act in the event that they intent to obtain an enforceable title in order to enforce the mediated agreement in Greece in case of violation of its terms.

According to the provisions of the Mediation Act,[32] the parties may in principle agree to have recourse to mediation before or after the dispute has arisen (mediation *ex voluntatis*). They may also be invited by a national court or, exclusively in child custody and parental care disputes,[33] be ordered by a national court to do so during

---

[31] Article 2 of Directive 2008/52/EC; Article 2(6) of the third Mediation Act. Broader definitions of the term are included in the UNCITRAL Model Law on International Commercial Mediation and International Settlement Agreements Resulting from Mediation, 2018 (amending the UNCITRAL Model Law on International Commercial Conciliation, 2002), https://uncitral.un.org/en/texts/mediation/modellaw/commercial_conciliation and the United Nations Convention on International Settlement Agreements Resulting from Mediation, 2018 (the "Singapore Convention on Mediation"), https://uncitral.un.org/en/texts/mediation/conventions/international_settlement_agreements.

[32] See Article 4 of the third Mediation Act.

[33] This way of mandatory recourse to mediation was introduced by Article 8 of Law 4800/2021. Reforms regarding parent-child relationships, other family law matters and further urgent

the pendency of a suit (mediation *ex juditio*). Mediation may further be ordered by another EU court as well as be imposed by another provision of law (mediation *ex lege*). Yet, it is not specified what 'recourse to mediation' means and, subsequently, when the mediation process begins. In an attempt to deal with this question, legal doctrine suggests that "what is critical is the time when the mediation procedure actually begins, i.e., the time when the parties appoint a mediator in order to start the mediation procedure to solve their dispute".[34]

In order to protect and ensure the validity of the parties' claims, the compatibility with rules regarding limitation and prescription periods as well as procedural deadlines is required, so that the parties will not be discouraged from referring to mediation due to the risk of extinction of their claims. In this respect, it is provided that the recourse to mediation or to mandatory initial mediation session suspends the statute of limitations and the prescription period as well as procedural deadlines for as long as the mediation procedure lasts. Limitation and prescription period as well as procedural deadlines that have been suspended, continue once the report of failure is drafted or a party serves the statement abandoning the mediation to the other party and the mediator or the procedure is in any other way terminated.[35]

The commencement of the mediation process presupposes the existence of an agreement to mediate. Such agreement is evidenced by virtue of a written document or the court records and is governed by the provisions of substantive contract law. The agreement to mediate can be concluded either separately or jointly, in the same document with the main contract as mediation clause. Even in the latter case, it constitutes an autonomous agreement, distinguished from the main contract. This means that the judge or the arbitrator deciding on a case where a mediation clause applies only has to verify the validity of such clause and not the validity of the entire contract. Even though the Mediation Act does not specify the content of the agreement to mediate, there is no doubt that a clear commitment to mediation constitutes the minimum requirement for the validity of such agreement.

The Mediation Act defines the mediator as "a third person in relation to the parties, who is asked to conduct mediation in an effective, competent and impartial way, assisting them to find a mutually acceptable solution to their dispute", providing also that he shall be accredited by the Ministry of Justice.[36] The appointment of the mediator may be based on a contract between him and the parties (governed by the law applicable under Rome I Regulation), on a public law instrument (judgment) or even de facto, without any existing relationship with the parties.[37] Before

provisions, Government Gazette A 81 (in force since 16 September 2021). In this case, the mediation shall be conducted by a mediator trained in family mediation and registered in a special registry of family mediators kept by the Central Mediation Committee of the Ministry of Justice, according to Ministerial Decision No. 41917οικ./26.08.2021, Government Gazette B 4017, as amended by Ministerial Decision No. 46181οικ./03.09.2021 Government Gazette B 4145.

[34] Klamaris and Chronopoulou (2013), p. 593.

[35] Article 9 of the third Mediation Act.

[36] Articles 2 and 12 of the third Mediation Act.

[37] Diamantopoulos and Koumpli (2014), p. 377; Diamantopoulos and Koumpli (2015), p. 324.

accepting his appointment, the mediator must verify that he has the appropriate expertise and premises to conduct the mediation and, upon request, he must disclose information concerning his expertise and experience to the parties. The mediator is also obliged to ensure that prior to the beginning of the mediation the parties have understood and expressly agreed on the terms and conditions of the agreement to mediate, including any provisions relating to obligations of confidentiality of the mediator and the parties.[38] He conducts the mediation according to the ethical provisions of the Mediation Act and the European Code of Conduct for Mediators,[39] being only liable for fraud in case of breach of his duties[40] (by contrast with arbitrators, who are also liable for gross negligence[41]).

The mediation process is regulated in a spirit of flexibility, given that the relative details are to a large extent determined by the mediator after consultation with the parties: the parties are free to agree with the mediator on the manner in which the mediation is to be conducted either by reference to a set of rules or otherwise. The lack of formality should not, however, be considered as introducing an out-of-law process. In an attempt to ensure the fairness of the process, there are framework provisions and basic principles governing its conduct. In particular:

The principle of confidentiality constitutes a fundamental element of the mediation process. Mediation shall be conducted in such a way as to respect confidentiality, unless the parties agree otherwise. The parties may bind themselves in writing to maintain confidentiality as to the contents of any agreement reached between them, unless the disclosure of its content is necessary for the enforcement of such agreement. None of the persons involved in the mediation procedure (e.g., mediators, parties, their attorneys etc.) shall be heard as witness in the future. Nor shall they be compelled to disclose information concerning the mediation process in subsequent court or arbitration proceedings, unless it is imposed by public policy rules and in particular when it is required in order to ensure the protection of children or to prevent harm to the physical or psychological integrity of a person.[42] The mediator, in particular, shall keep confidential all information arising out of or in connection with the mediation (including the fact that the mediation is to take place or has taken place), unless compelled by law or grounds of public policy to disclose it. Moreover, any information disclosed in confidence to mediators by one of the parties must not be disclosed to the other parties without permission, unless compelled by law.[43]

The existing legal framework, furthermore, introduces the principle of independence and impartiality of the mediator.[44] If there are any circumstances that may, or

[38] Article 15 of the third Mediation Act.

[39] Article 12(3) of the third Mediation Act.

[40] Article 5(7) of the third Mediation Act.

[41] Article 881 of the Code of Civil Procedure.

[42] Article 16 of the third Mediation Act.

[43] Article 5(4) and (5) of the third Mediation Act.

[44] Article 13 of the third Mediation Act.

may be seen to, affect a mediator's independence or give rise to a conflict of interests, the mediator must disclose those circumstances to the parties before acting or continuing to act—this duty being a continuing obligation throughout the process of mediation. Such circumstances include any personal or business relationship with one or more of the parties, any financial or other interest, direct or indirect, in the outcome of the mediation, as well as the mediator or a member of his firm having acted in any capacity other than mediator for one or more of the parties. In such cases the mediator may only agree to act or continue to act if he is certain of being able to carry out the mediation in full independence in order to ensure complete impartiality and the parties explicitly consent. Mediators are also obliged at all times to act—and endeavour to be seen to act—with impartiality towards the parties and be committed to serve all parties equally with respect to the process of mediation.

The parties can finish the mediation process at any time they wish, meaning that they can declare their will not to reach an agreement; the mediator, thus, shall proceed immediately to the termination of the procedure, drawing up and signing the relevant minutes together with the parties and their attorneys or alone. From a procedural point of view, following an unsuccessful mediation, the prescription period and procedural deadlines that were suspended shall continue. When the mediation was ordered by the court, the latter continues the proceedings after summons by any of the interested parties. When the parties referred to mediation before the commencement of the court proceedings, they can file a lawsuit concerning their claim. Of course, no judicial review procedures are provided in case of failure; at the same time, no second attempt to mediate is prohibited. Admittedly, even in case of failure, the parties will have obtained the benefit of at least discussing their dispute and trying to understand each other's positions. After the successful conclusion of the mediation process, the mediator, the parties and their attorneys sign the relevant minutes incorporating the mediation agreement. Each party[45] can submit the original document of the minutes to the competent court. Since their filing to the clerk of the court, the minutes recording a mediation agreement concerning a claim subject to enforcement constitute an enforceable title.[46] The law governing the mediation agreement is in principle determined by Rome I Regulation. As to agreements that may escape its ambit, the old provision of Article 25 of the Greek Civil Code on the law governing contractual obligations is still applicable.

[45] However, Article 6(1) of Directive 2008/52/EC requires both parties' consent even in this case. Therefore, the national provision is contrary to EU law as far as EU cross-border disputes are concerned. With regard to domestic disputes, the Greek legislator is free to regulate the matter, and hence there is no issue of incompatibility.

[46] Article 8 of the third Mediation Act.

3 Legal Issues of Mediation in Cross-Border Family Property Disputes

In principle, all civil-law aspects of property regimes of spouses and partners—such as the daily management of the property or the liquidation regime in cases of separation or death etc.—can be submitted to mediation, regardless of the nature and the location of the assets. Such disputes may also be associated with other issues dealing with the classification of property of either or both spouses/partners into different categories during and after marriage/partnership, the transfer of property from one category to the other one, the responsibility of one spouse/partner for liabilities and debts of the other spouse/partner, the powers, rights and obligations of either or both spouses/ partners with regard to property, the dissolution of the family property regime and the partition, distribution or liquidation of the property, the effects of the family property regime on a legal relationship between a spouse/ partner and third parties as well as the material validity of a matrimonial property agreement.

Moreover, such disputes can be submitted to mediation jointly with other disputes concerning, for example, maintenance or parental care, which may arise from divorce or the dissolution of the registered partnership. However, before opting for mediation, a suitability assessment is necessary in any case. And this assessment should take into account, for instance, the willingness of the parties to mediate, whether the views of one or both of them are too polarised for mediation, whether there are indications of domestic violence, whether there is incapacity resulting from alcohol or drug abuse as well as other indications of a severe imbalance in bargaining powers.

Given that in cross-border family cases more than one legal system is involved, it is important to take the laws of all legal systems concerned into consideration, as well as regional or international law applicable in a particular case. Mediators have a responsibility to draw the parties' attention to the importance of obtaining the relevant legal information and specialist legal advice, given that mediators, even those having the relevant specialist legal training, are not in a position to provide legal advice to the parties. Mediation in international family disputes needs to take into consideration the interrelation between the matters dealt with in mediation and issues of applicable law and jurisdiction. Legal information becomes particularly relevant with respect to two aspects: first, the content of the mediated agreement, which needs to be compatible with legal requirements and, second, the question of how to give legal effect to the mediated agreement in the legal systems concerned.

3.1 Issues of Applicable Law

In the context of cross-border family mediation, it must be investigated which law will govern (a) the agreement to submit the dispute to mediation, (b) the contract between the mediator and the parties, (c) the mediation process and the exercise of the duties of the mediator and the legal representatives of the parties (law of mediation or *lex mediationis*), (d) the subject of the mediation (law in mediation), as well as (e) the agreement resulting from the mediation. In this respect:

First, due to their contractual nature, the law applicable to the above issues is in principle defined by the provisions of Rome I Regulation[47] on the law applicable to contractual obligations.

Second, it has also been supported that in particular the obligations arising from the pre-contractual duty of the mediator to disclose any cases of conflict of interest, cases that may affect his independence, neutrality and impartiality, etc. are governed by the law defined by the provisions of Rome II Regulation[48] on the law applicable to non-contractual obligations.[49]

Third, mediation, being a substantive law—and not a procedural law—institution, is governed by the substantive provisions of the law that regulates the main relationship of the parties from which the dispute arose (*lex causae*).[50] These are the substantive provisions of the applicable law which govern the mediation process and the negotiations for the drawing up of the contracts. Consequently, from the point of view of Greek law, the parties are free to exclude the application of the substantive law provisions of the Greek Mediation Act[51] and to agree on the application of foreign substantive mediation law provisions. On the contrary, the parties cannot exclude the application of the procedural provisions of the Greek Mediation Act,[52] since procedural issues are regulated by the *lex fori*, in accordance with the principle *lex fori processum regit*.[53]

Fourth, in case of mediation in cross-border family property disputes the subject of the mediation (law in mediation) and the mediation agreement are governed by the law defined in Articles 20–35 of the twin Regulations.

It should also be noted that a situation may arise where among the different matters dealt within the mediated agreement some are at the free disposal of the parties—such as family property matters—and some are not (e.g., in some countries,

[47] Regulation (EC) No 593/2008 of the European Parliament and of the Council of 17 June 2008 on the law applicable to contractual obligations, OJ L 177, 4.7.2008, pp. 6–16.

[48] Regulation (EC) No 864/2007 of the European Parliament and of the Council of 11 July 2007 on the law applicable to non-contractual obligations, OJ L 199, 31.7.2007, pp. 40–49.

[49] Michailidou (2019), p. 423.

[50] Tsikrikas (2014), p. 291.

[51] Such as, for example, Article 3(1) regarding the mediatable disputes, Article 5 on the mediation process, Article 9 specifically regarding the suspension of the statute of limitations, or Articles 12–16 on the obligations of the mediator.

[52] Such as, for example, Article 3(2) on the obligation of the lawyer to inform his client about the mediability of his dispute before filing a lawsuit before Greek courts, on penalty of inadmissibility of the hearing, Articles 6 and 7 on the mandatory initial mediation session in case of the particular before the Greek courts, Article 8 on the enforceability of the mediation agreement or Article 9 specifically on the suspension of procedural deadlines.

[53] See instead of others Kerameus (1997), p. 378.

matters concerning custody, child support etc.). In this case, and according to the applicable law, the agreement becomes immediately binding on the parties in relation to the former matters, while the latter part of the agreement may depend on court approval. In Greek law, after the enactment of Law 4800/2021 introducing compulsory recourse to mediation by court order in case of disputes concerning child custody and parental care, the 'mediability' of the latter is undisputable.

Giving legal effect to a mediation agreement will often require the involvement of a court, be it for registration purposes or for turning the agreement into a court order. Hence, considering which court(s) may have jurisdiction on the issues that are to be included in the mediation agreement is important, as is the question of applicable law. It may also be that the involvement of more than one judicial or administrative authority in the process of giving legal effect to the content of that agreement becomes necessary.

3.2 *Issues of Recognition and Enforcement of the Mediation Agreement*

It should be emphasised that not every agreement which is legally binding on the parties in one legal system is also automatically enforceable in that legal system. The enforcement of foreign mediation agreements in a certain state is governed by the law of that state, i.e., by the *lex fori*, according to the aforementioned principle *lex fori processum regit*. As concerns rendering an agreement which has become enforceable (by embodiment in a court order or otherwise) in one legal system legally binding and enforceable in the relevant other legal system there are generally two pathways which can be considered:

First, the pathway of recognition and enforcement in the second State, either because an international, regional or bi-lateral instrument provides for the recognition or because a foreign court order can otherwise be recognised in that legal system in accordance with the law of the second State. Second, the pathway of taking the agreement itself to the second State and making the necessary arrangements to render the agreement binding and enforceable in this State.

The European Mediation Directive does not contain provisions on the enforcement in a Member State of mediation agreements that have been made enforceable in another Member State. Foreign mediation agreements on family property disputes that have been made enforceable in a Member State could only be recognised and declared enforceable in Greece—and vice versa—by virtue of Articles 58–60 of the twin Regulations[54] on the recognition and enforcement of authentic instruments and

[54]Given that Regulation (EC) No 805/2004 of the European Parliament and of the Council of 21 April 2004 creating a European Enforcement Order for uncontested claims, OJ L 143, 30.4.2004, pp. 15–39, does not apply to family property disputes. Similarly, family disputes are also excluded from the scope of the United Nations Convention on International Settlement Agreements Resulting

court settlements.[55] In this case, it must be examined whether the mediation agreement in question constitutes 'authentic instrument' or 'court settlement' in the meaning of the Regulations. 'Authentic instrument' means a document in a matter of the matrimonial property regime/property consequences of a registered partnership which has been formally drawn up or registered as an authentic instrument in a Member State and the authenticity of which relates to the signature and the content of the authentic instrument, and has been established by a public authority or other authority empowered for that purpose by the Member State of origin. 'Court settlement' means a settlement in a matter of the matrimonial property regime/ property consequences of a registered partnership which has been approved by a court, or concluded before a court in the course of proceedings. If the mediation agreement does not constitute 'authentic instrument' or 'court settlement'—which is the case of the mediation agreements issued in accordance with the Greek Mediation Act—it cannot be made enforceable through the simplified procedure of the twin Regulations, but it can be made enforceable by virtue of the provisions of the national law, such as Article 905 of the Greek Code of Civil Procedure on the declaration of enforceability of foreign enforceable titles, or of a relevant international treaty signed between the two Member States.

Foreign mediation agreements reached outside the European Union, which are registered as an authentic instrument and are enforceable according to the law of the country of origin, shall become enforceable in Greece in accordance with the provisions of Article 57 of the Lugano Convention of 2007[56] (with regard to Norway, Switzerland and Iceland) or any existing bilateral treaties, otherwise in accordance with Article 905 of the Greek Code of Civil Procedure on the declaration of enforceability of foreign enforceable titles.

If a foreign agreement—reached either within or outside the European Union—has not been recorded in an authentic instrument, it can be made enforceable according to Article 904 of the Greek Code of Civil Procedure, i.e., (a) by being incorporated in a notarial act; (b) after the issuance of an order of payment when the agreement concerns the recognition of a money claim; (c) when they are incorporated in the minutes recording court proceedings embodying the settlement of the parties under Article 293(1) of the Greek Code of Civil Procedure.

Based on the above considerations, the ideal situation would be that the twin Regulations provide for simplified recognition and enforcement of mediated

from Mediation, 2018 (the "Singapore Convention on Mediation"), https://uncitral.un.org/en/texts/mediation/conventions/international_settlement_agreements.

[55] Excluding the provisions on the recognition and enforcement of decisions, given that mediation agreements, even when incorporated in court decisions or judicially validated, cannot fall within the scope of the term 'decision'. According to the EU approach, a 'decision' must emanate from a judicial body deciding on its own authority on the issues between the parties. Cf. CJEU, C-414/92, *Solo Kleinmotoren*, 02.06.1994, ECLI: ECLI:EU:C:1994:221, para. 17· CJEU, C-39/02, *Maersk Olie & Gas A/S*, 14.10.2004, ECLI: ECLI:EU:C:2004:615, para. 45.

[56] Convention on jurisdiction and the recognition and enforcement of judgments in civil and commercial matters of 30.10.2007, OJ L 339, 21.12.2007, 1.

agreements from one Member State to the other. Co-operation between the administrative/judicial authorities of the different Member States concerned may be necessary when it comes to ensuring the enforceability of the agreement in the different jurisdictions. In any case, states should also facilitate simple procedures through which mediation agreements can, on the request of the parties, be approved and rendered enforceable by a competent authority.

It is moreover to be highlighted that in the event that the mediation agreement deals with real property, it is also necessary to be embodied in a notarial act and to be registered at the Land Registry.[57] Where a mediation agreement covers a wide range of subjects, the terms of the agreement should include that its entry into force will be conditional upon the completion of the registration at the Land Registry. In such cases, it may be advisable to refer to the outcome of mediation as a 'provisional agreement' and to reflect this in the title and wording of the document recording the agreed solution.

4 Processual Dimension of Mediation in Cross-Border Family Property Disputes of Spouses and Partners

Some of the most significant aspects relating to the procedural dimension and the best practices of mediation in cross-border family property disputes can be summarized as follows[58]:

4.1 Safeguards of Quality

To guarantee the quality of mediation, it is indispensable that those conducting mediation have undergone appropriate training. To safeguard the quality of international family mediation, mediation services should be monitored and evaluated, ideally by a neutral body. The Greek Mediation Act currently in force contains detailed provisions on the qualifications of the mediators and their mandatory basic and advanced training, the qualifications of training providers and the curriculum of the basic and advanced training as well as the accreditation of mediators by the Ministry of Justice.[59]

---

[57] Article 8(4) of the third Mediation Act.

[58] In this respect, see among others Moore (2014); Paul and Kiesewetter (2014); Carter and Watts (2016); Lack and Goh (2019).

[59] Articles 12 and 22–28 of the third Mediation Act.

4.2 *Direct or Indirect Mediation*

'Direct mediation' can be defined as the mediation in which both parties directly and simultaneously participate in the mediation sessions with the mediator, either in a face-to-face meeting with the mediator or in a long-distance meeting through teleconferencing facilities or communication over the Internet. Conversely, the term 'indirect mediation' refers to mediation in which the parties do not directly meet one another during the mediation but each meet with the mediator separately. The separate meetings with the mediator can be held across two separate states or in the same state with mediation taking place at different times ('shuttle mediation') or at the same time but in different rooms ('caucus mediation'). It is, of course, also possible for a mediation process to include both indirect and direct mediation. For example, a direct mediation can be accompanied or preceded by caucus meetings, where the mediator meets with each party separately. Whether direct or indirect mediation is most appropriate in the individual case will depend on the circumstances of the case (e.g., the costs related to geographical location, possible allegations of domestic violence etc.). The decision is also closely linked to that of determining the place of mediation, once a face-to-face meeting has been identified as the way forward. The third Greek Mediation Act explicitly provides for the direct and/or indirect conduct of both the mandatory initial mediation session and the mediation process, based on the assessment of the mediator.[60]

4.3 *Single or Co-Mediation*

Particularly in highly conflictual cross-border family cases, the use of co-mediation should be encouraged where feasible. Co-mediation is beneficial in providing the experience, knowledge and methodology of two mediators, which increases the likelihood of arriving at an agreed outcome. However, there may be cases where co-mediation is not feasible. Co-mediation is likely to be more expensive than single mediation. Furthermore, if the two mediators have not co-mediated before, there may be a risk that they will need time to adapt to the different dynamics of co-mediation. This points to the advantages of single mediation by a mediator with experience in mediating disputes in cross-border family cases, which is likely to be less costly, may be easier to schedule and does not involve the risk that the methodologies of two mediators who have not co-mediated before will conflict. The third Greek Mediation Act explicitly provides that the mediator shall be one, unless the parties agree in writing that there shall be more mediators.[61]

[60] Articles 5(4) and 7(3) of the third Mediation Act.

[61] Article 5(2) of the third Mediation Act.

4.4 Methods of Mediation: Bi-Cultural, Bi-Lingual, Bi-Gender and Bi-Professional Schemes

A special form of co-mediation is bi-cultural, bilingual mediation. This addresses the specific needs for intercultural competence as well as language skills when mediating between parties from different States of origin with different mother tongues. According to this model, mediation is to be conducted by two experienced family mediators: one from each party's State of origin and cultural background. Where different languages are spoken in the States of origin, the mediators will bring with them the necessary language skills, although it has to be highlighted that at least one of them needs to have a good understanding of the other language involved.

There are two further issues that some of the mediation schemes setup for international family disputes using bi-national mediation try to balance, i.e., the gender and professional expertise of the mediators. Co-mediation in these schemes is conducted by one female and one male mediator, one with a legal background and one with a socio-psychological background. This allows for the combining of professional expertise and cultural competence in handling different mediation issues. The big advantage of 'bi-cultural', 'bi-lingual' co-mediation is that it may provide a confidence building framework for the parties, creating an atmosphere where the parties feel understood and assisted in their communication by someone from their own linguistic and cultural background. In view however of the possible danger of a party identifying him- or herself with one of the mediators and considering this person as a representative in the mediation, the mediators need always to highlight their role as neutral and impartial third parties.[62]

Communication in the preferred language might also be facilitated through the use of interpretation. Where interpretation is considered an option, the interpreter has to be chosen diligently and needs to be well prepared and aware of the highly sensitive nature of the conversation, and of the emotional atmosphere of the mediation, so as not to add a further risk of misunderstanding and jeopardise an amicable resolution. Furthermore, safeguards concerning confidentiality of mediation communications must be extended to include the interpreter(s).

It should be noted that the successful implementation of the above models necessarily depends on the availability of financial resources and appropriate, skilled mediators.

5 Concluding Remarks

The foregoing analysis demonstrates the broadness and complexity of the mediation regulatory and processual framework in case of cross-border family disputes, and in particular disputes concerning family property issues. Although the need to delimit

[62] Cf. HCCH (2012), Guide to Good Practice Child Abduction Convention: Part V – Mediation, https://www.hcch.net/en/publications-and-studies/details4/?pid=6561.

cross-border mediation by legal rules and to include it in the legal order is not disputed, and the Greek legal framework provides detail regulation, it should not be overlooked that the multitude and fragmented nature of legal regulations at international and EU level can, on the one hand, limit the flexibility of the procedure, and, on the other hand, contribute to the recourse to the judicial process for the resolution of disputes that will arise during the application of these provisions. The paradoxical phenomenon of litigation in relation to mediation, i.e., in relation to a process designed to avoid litigation ('disputing irony'), has already been observed in the USA.[63]

For the time being, there is a relative reluctance to establish an autonomous—international or EU—regulatory framework for cross-border mediation across the spectrum of private disputes, which will include family law disputes. However, it must be pointed out that if a single international or EU regulation seems difficult because of the high degree of consensus required, this obviously cannot be the case for national regulation. Indeed, the establishment of an effective mechanism for the cross-border enforcement of mediation agreements is expected to contribute to the strengthening of trust and the development and establishment of mediation in the resolution of cross-border family disputes.

The previous analysis also highlighted the peculiarities of the cross-border family mediation process, which require specific qualifications and skills of the mediator, beyond those necessary for common mediation.

Given that the field of cross-border family mediation is under constant development and formation, the continuation of the scientific as well as jurisprudential debate around its regulatory and processual dimension is expected with particular interest.

References

Carter A, Watts S (2016) The role of language interpretation in providing a quality mediation process. Contemp Asia Arbitr J 9(2):301–316

Coben J, Thompson P (2006) Disputing irony: a systematic look at litigation about mediation. Harv Neg Law Rev 11:43–146

Diamantopoulos G, Koumpli V (2014) On mediation law in Greece. Revue hellénique de droit international:361–394

Diamantopoulos G, Koumpli V (2015) Mediation: the Greek ADR journey through time. In: Esplugues C, Marquis L (eds) New developments in civil and commercial mediation. Springer International Publishing, Switzerland, pp 313–343

Esplugues C (2014) Civil and commercial mediation in the EU after the transposition of Directive 2008/52/EC. In: Esplugues C (ed) Civil and commercial mediation in Europe: cross-border mediation – vol II. Intersentia, Cambridge, pp 485–771

European Parliament – Directorate General for Internal Policies (2014) 'Rebooting' the Mediation Directive: Assessing the Limited Impact of its Implementation and Proposing Measures to

[63] Coben and Thompson (2006).

Increase the Number of Mediations in the EU, http://www.europarl.europa.eu/RegData/etudes/etudes/join/2014/493042/IPOL-JURI_ET(2014)493042_EN.pdf
HCCH (2012) Guide to Good Practice Child Abduction Convention: Part V – Mediation, https://www.hcch.net/en/publications-and-studies/details4/?pid=6561
Kerameus K (1997) Enforcement in the international context. RCADI 264
Klamaris N, Chronopoulou C (2013) Mediation in Greece: a contemporary procedural approach to resolving disputes. In: Hopt K, Steffek F (eds) Mediation. Principles and regulation in comparative perspective. Oxford, Oxford University Press, pp 585–604
Koumpli V (2017) The regulation of mediation in cross-border disputes: the model of Greece. In: Roth M, Geistlinger M (eds) Yearbook of international arbitration and ADR – vol V. Dike/NWV, Zurich/Vienna, pp 269–284
Koumpli V (2019) A further step towards institutionalization of mediation in Greece: recent developments after Law 4512/2018. In: Roth M, Geistlinger M (eds) Yearbook of International Arbitration and ADR – vol VI. Dike/NWV, Zurich/Vienna, pp 267–276
Koumpli V (2021a) Greece: Institutionalizing Mediation Through Mandatory Initial Mediation Session (Law 4640/2019). Kluwer Mediation Blog, http://mediationblog.kluwerarbitration.com/2020/01/20/greece-institutionalizing-mediation-through-mandatory-initial-mediation-session-law-4640-2019/
Koumpli V (2021b) A further step towards institutionalization of mediation in Greece: recent developments after Law 4640/2019. In: Roth M, Geistlinger M (eds) Yearbook of International Arbitration and ADR – vol VII. Dike/NWV, Zurich/Vienna, pp 223–232
Lack J, Goh A (2019) The importance of process-design when selecting a mediator for cross-border disputes. WhosWhoLegal http://lawtech.ch/wp-content/uploads/2016/03/WWL-Mediation-2019-Article-Lawtech-Final-version.pdf
Michailidou Ch (2019) Procedural and substantive issues of mandatory mediation and its limits in cross-border cases – the example of the Greek legislation. In: Cadiet L, Hess B, Requejo Isidro M (eds) Privatizing dispute resolution. Trends and limits, studies of the Max Planck Institute for International, European and Regulatory Procedural Law – vol 18. Nomos Verlagsgesellschaft Baden-Baden, pp 393–432
Moore C (2014) The mediation process. Practical strategies for resolving conflicts, 3rd edn. Jossey Bass, San Francisco
Paul C, Kiesewetter S (eds) (2014) Cross-border family mediation. International parental child abduction, custody and access cases, 2nd edn. Wolfgang Metzner Verlag, Frankfurt
Tsikrikas D (2014) Verfahrensrechtliche und kollisionsrechtliche Fragen der Mediation. ZZPInt 19: 281–297

Part II
European Law Section

EU Trade Mark and Brexit

Iza Razija Mešević

1 Introduction

Six years ago, on 23 June 2016, the citizens of the United Kingdom of Great Britain and Northern Ireland (UK) made a historical decision by voting in a referendum to leave the European Union (EU) by 52% to 48% in favour of this step.[1] Although for many of us the UK exit (Brexit) seemed a highly unlikely scenario, we were proven wrong on the morning of 24 June and faced a completely new reality.[2] However, the vote itself proved to be only the tip of the iceberg, since Brexit opened up, not only for the EU, but also for the UK administration, a Pandora's box full of questions and issues never posed before. Although legal uncertainty burdened nearly every step in the process of the UK's withdrawal from the EU,[3] this article is devoted to a very specific one: namely, the legal and practical concerns that Brexit raised with regard to EU-wide Intellectual Property Rights (IPR), more specifically the EU trade mark

[1] BBC (2016).

[2] Bazerkoska (2016), p. 54.

[3] Markakis (2017), p. 23.

I. R. Mešević (✉)
University of Sarajevo, Sarajevo, Bosnia and Herzegovina
e-mail: ir.mesevic@pfsa.unsa.ba

I. Kunda et al. (eds.), *Balkan Yearbook of European and International Law 2022*, Balkan Yearbook of European and International Law 2022,
https://doi.org/10.1007/978-3-031-29432-7_7

(EUTM),[4] as well as the current solutions to them offered by the Withdrawal Agreement.[5]

2 Brexit

Prior to 2009 and the entry into force of the Treaty of Lisbon,[6] there was no procedure under the EU Treaties for the voluntary withdrawal of a Member State from the EU.[7] Today, this option is embedded in Article 50 of the Treaty on European Union (TEU).[8] The withdrawing Members State is required to notify the European Council of its intention, after which the EU and that state will negotiate and conclude an agreement setting out the arrangements for its withdrawal (Article 50(2)). The EU Treaties cease to apply to that state from the date of the entry into force of the withdrawal agreement or, failing that, two years after the deposit of the notification of intention to withdraw, provided there is no extension of this period (Article 50(3)). The UK government gave the above-mentioned notice to the European Council in March 2017[9] and the Withdrawal Agreement between the remaining Member States of the EU (EU27) was agreed on 19 October 2019, signed on 24 January 2020 and entered into force on 1 February 2020.[10]

The objective of this Agreement (Article 1) was to set out arrangements for the withdrawal of the UK from the EU and the European Atomic Energy Community (Euratom). According to its Preamble, the law of the EU and of Euratom in its entirety ceased to apply to the UK from the date of the entry into force of the Agreement. However, the latter included various separation provisions aimed to prevent disruption and to provide legal certainty to citizens and economic operators. The Preamble also underlined that there is a need to take all necessary steps to begin as soon as possible from the date of the entry into force of the Agreement, the formal negotiations of one or several agreements governing the future relationship between the EU27 and the UK.

[4]Other IPRs with a unitary effect were affected by Brexit as well, in particular the Community Design and the Community Plant Variety. However, the impact of this new development will also have consequences on the Unitary Patent System, Protected Designations of Origin and Protected Geographical Indications, supplementary protection certificates for medicinal products and plant protection products, as well as further developments in the field of copyright law.

[5]Agreement on the withdrawal of the United Kingdom of Great Britain and Northern Ireland from the European Union and the European Atomic Energy Community (2019/C 384 I/01).

[6]Treaty of Lisbon amending the Treaty on European Union and the Treaty establishing the European Community, signed at Lisbon, 13 December 2007, Art. 49a.

[7]Jones (2018), p. 7ff.

[8]The Treaty on European Union (consolidated version), 2012.

[9]United Kingdom notification under Article 50 TEU, 29 March 2017.

[10]European Commission, The EU-UK Withdrawal Agreement. Timeline of “Article 50” negotiations on the Withdrawal Agreement.

According to Article 126 of the Agreement, there is also a transition or implementation period, which started on the date of the entry into force of this Agreement and ended on 31 December 2020. This period gave both sides some "breathing space" and time to discuss the mentioned future relationship between the UK and the EU on all matters, including the protection of IPRs. As a result, the EU-UK Trade and Cooperation Agreement[11] was concluded on 30 December 2020, setting out preferential arrangements, among others, also in area of IPRs. The latter agreement was applied provisionally as of 1 January 2021 and entered into force on 1 May 2021.

3 Brexit and IPRs

Brexit introduced a challenging and intense time for all sectors and industries, as well as for areas of law. However, the impact of this historical step was very specific with regard to IPRs, in particular those with unitary effect.

The era of global trade and the knowledge economy requires worldwide, or at least broad regional, protection of IPRs. We must also not overlook that law-making in this field is in general under the influence of international aspects and trade,[12] so harmonised legislation and the simplification of procedures for obtaining transnational protection play a significant role.[13] Consequently, the policies and plans for international IP protection of globally operating companies in general follow their business policies and strategies.[14] The EU made a crucial contribution in this process by harmonising aspects of IPRs in the Member States, which were of significance for the proper functioning of the single market, and even more so by establishing supranational IPRs such as the EUTM[15] or the Community design. These strategic reforms provided for legal certainty for European and overseas businesses with regard to protection of their IPRs, but also reduced the costs of registration and simplified and centralised administrative procedures for obtaining rights.

However, Brexit disrupted this trend of legal certainty, and its goal now, to a certain extent, was different from one of harmonisation and internationalisation. Its objective was to reclaim national autonomy regarding the replacement, or revision,

[11] Trade and Cooperation Agreement between the European Union and the European Atomic Energy Community, of the one part, and the United Kingdom of Great Britain and Northern Ireland, of the other part (2021/L 149/10).

[12] George (2017), p. 141.

[13] Pegram (2019), p. 15.

[14] Ibid, p. 14.

[15] The EUTM was first established in 1993 as a Community trade mark (CTM) with Council Regulation (EC) No 40/94 of 20 December 1993 on the Community trade mark (CTM Regulation).

of EU legislation with national laws and policies, and of the jurisprudence of the Court of Justice of the EU (CJEU) with the jurisprudence of national courts.[16]

Notwithstanding the above, the consequences of Brexit are different with regard to particular IPRs (copyright, patents, trade marks, designs. . .), since they have been "Europeanised at different speeds"[17] and by means of different instruments (directives and/or regulations). Therefore, the scope and content of the protection of IPRs (e.g. copyright) which were predominantly subject to the EU harmonisation process (directives) were presumed to remain the same at least for a certain period. Subsequently, the potential work of revising and unravelling UK laws to remove the elements of the underlying EU legislation is likely to take many years.[18] Hence, it is inevitable that the latter will continue to be relevant in the UK with regard to these IPRs.[19] On the other hand, the EU regulations which introduced supranational IPRs, such as the EUTM, or the Community design, have ceased to have effect in the UK immediately, without the UK Parliament or Government having to do anything,[20] simultaneously imposing burdening uncertainty, especially for the right holders of those IPRs.

4 Brexit and the EU Trade Mark System

It must not be disregarded that the EU trade mark system is based on two pillars—the Trade Mark Directive[21] harmonising substantive trade mark law in the Member States, and the EUTM Regulation,[22] establishing an EUTM with unitary effect.

As stated above,[23] the effects of Brexit on the UK trade mark legislation are likely to take time. Nevertheless, although the trade mark law in the UK is heavily influenced by EU harmonisation in this field,[24] as well as by the judicial interpretation of the CJEU and the fact that the EUTM also had an extended effect on this territory, the UK courts in the past continuously showed their mistrust of certain concepts introduced by the EU legislator. Among other things, these were the broad definition of a subject matter that could be protected as a trade mark, the scope of

[16] Dinwoodie and Dreyfuss (2018), p. 967 *et seq.*; George (2017), p. 150.

[17] Arnold et al. (2017), p. 1.

[18] Dinwoodie and Dreyfuss (2018), p. 983; Arnold et al. (2017), p. 2.

[19] Forrester (2018), p. 45.

[20] Arnold et al. (2017), p. 2.

[21] Directive (EU) 2015/2436 of the European Parliament and of the Council of 16 December 2015 to approximate the laws of the Member States relating to trade marks.

[22] Regulation (EU) 2017/1001 of the European Parliament and of the Council of 14 June 2017 on the European Union Trade Mark.

[23] See *supra*: 3. Brexit and IPRs.

[24] Dinwoodie and Dreyfuss (2018), p. 972.

protection of a trade mark, but also even the EU-wide exhaustion of rights.[25] Hence, an element of uncertainty with regard to future legislative developments in the UK will remain for current or future right holders of a national UK trade mark. Moreover, apart from the fact that the UK gained legislative autonomy concerning trade mark legislation, it is also no longer subject to the jurisdiction of the CJEU. Consequently, even without substantive legislative changes in this area, interpretations by the UK courts of national trade mark law influenced by the Trade Mark Directive might in the future be different from those offered by the CJEU. Yet, it can be hoped that the future case law of the CJEU will still have some persuasive value.[26]

As for the EUTM, which is governed by the EUTM Regulation, it was immediately clear that Brexit's effect would be far more immediate and drastic, since the latter would automatically cease to have effect on the UK, and the geographical coverage, and thus the scope of protection of the EUTM, would also be reduced. Hence, for the right holders of existing EUTMs, as well as for EUTM applicants, UK representatives before the EU Intellectual Property Office (EUIPO), the EUIPO itself, licensors and licensees of EUTMs, but also other interested parties, Brexit meant for a while a true "leap in the dark".[27] Speculation, fears and worries were addressed and potential scenarios were constructed on how to safeguard existing rights and positions with minimum costs and administrative burdens on one hand, and maximum commercial certainty and stability on the other. Although it was on one hand clear that the political decision on these issues would take a while and that individual initiative would be required to cushion some of the immediate consequences, it was obvious on the other that the impact would be softer if the post-Brexit relationship between the UK and EU stayed close.[28]

However, before we further elaborate the particular issues that were detected with regard to EUTMs and Brexit, it seems relevant to point out that Brexit was not actually the first challenge that the EUTM System faced involving a change in the geographical scope of this supranational right. The first challenge was the enlargement of the EU.

5 Enlargement

It is undeniable that Brexit posed an unprecedented situation for the EUTM system. Until then, the challenge that this unitary right had been facing was the opposite—the accession of new states to the EU and not the exit of current ones. Perhaps the former test was even more demanding, but is was taken under foreseeable and

[25] Ibid, p 972 *et seq.* and Fn. 29.

[26] Loney et al. (2017), p. 33.

[27] Bazerkoska (2016), p. 55.

[28] Traub et al. (2016), p. 12.

controlled circumstances, since the accession process for new Member States takes years and is predominantly managed and channelled by the EU-side at the negotiating table. With Brexit, the situation was rather different. However, both situations deal with the issue of the territorial scope of EUTMs—the enlargement with its expansion, and Brexit with its reduction.

As for the enlargements, it was important to create a balance between the interests of right holders of CTMs and those of prior national trade marks in new Member States, and to ensure legal certainty in general.[29] Then, for the first time in 2004, the fifth (biggest) enlargement of the EU with 10 new Member States (Cyprus, Estonia, Hungary, Latvia, Lithuania, Malta, Poland, Czech Republic, Slovakia and Slovenia) also meant a geographical expansion of a unitary trade mark right (CTM) to new territories. This development meant not only that the laws of the new Member States had to be aligned with the *acquis communautaire* in this field, but also the CTM system, the Office for Harmonisation in the Internal Market (OHIM, now EUIPO), and the accompanying EU legislation needed to be adjusted to new circumstances.[30] Originally, the CTM Regulation had no provisions covering the question of enlargement and the extension of registered CTMs and CTM applications to new, associated countries, as well as concerning a solution to the issue of conflicting marks from new Member States.[31] Hence, in Annex II of the Accession Treaty,[32] the CTM Regulation was amended with a new Article 142a, governing, in short, the automatic extension of the registered CTMs and CTM applications filed before the date of accession to the territory of new Member States (Article 142a(1)). The goal was to preserve the unitary character of the CTM without any additional financial, or administrative burden for the existing CTM right holders and CTM applicants.[33] Apart from these main principles, Article 142a also regulated the fact that such CTM applications could not be refused due to the absolute grounds for refusal that emerged with the accession of the new Member States, the conditions to oppose such applications, due to earlier rights from the new Member States, the question of the declaration of invalidity of CTMs registered prior to the accession, and the possibility of prohibition of use of CTMs in the new Member States (Article 142a (2)-(5)).[34] Although the provided solutions were beneficial for the CTM right holders, regarding the no-cost and no-burden extension of their rights to new territories,[35] it was inevitable that this new situation posed a budgetary challenge

[29] Folliard-Monguiral and Rogers (2004), p. 48.

[30] Ibid.

[31] Pretnar (1997), p. 186 *et seq.*

[32] Part 4 (C)(I) of the 2003 Act of Accession, p. 342.

[33] Folliard-Monguiral and Rogers (2004), p. 49; Kresbach and Grögerova (2007), p. 153; Boesch (2005), p. 100.

[34] For more details, see Folliard-Monguiral and Rogers (2004), p. 49 *et seq.*

[35] Kresbach and Grögerova (2007), p. 156.

for OHIM, among other things, due to the translation costs related to the new Member States' languages.[36]

The next, sixth and seventh, enlargements that took place in 2007 (Bulgaria and Romania)[37] and in 2013 (Croatia)[38] were easier to handle since the OHIM and the CTM system were prepared for this challenge.[39]

There were most certainly a number of questions raised during the enlargement which had their relative equivalent in the Brexit process, such as the potential extension of registered EUTMs and pending EUTM applications to the UK as national trade marks and trade mark applications. Other questions, such as the status of EUTM representatives from the UK, enforcement, genuine use, etc., were different. In any case, the emphasis put on legal certainty and balance of interests in the enlargement process was the same as for the unravelling Brexit procedure, both for the EU27 and the UK side.

6 Anticipated Issues

Between the referendum and the Withdrawal Agreement, there were a number of issues raised and scenarios drafted by the legal practitioners and scholars in the field of trade mark law concerning how Brexit would affect the EUTM system. The level of uncertainty, as well as the stakes, were very high at that time, while the EUTM representatives, EUTM right holders and applicants, as well as other interested parties, were awaiting political intervention.

The most common, general question raised was whether the outcome of this process would be a so-called "hard/clean" or a "soft" Brexit and, if the latter, what solutions[40] would be offered. Although these two terms or scenarios were interpreted differently, especially with regard to the context in which they were used, they can in general be simplified and reduced to the level and scope of change in the pre-Brexit arrangements between the EU and the UK that would occur after the final departure.[41] Depending on this outcome, the level of adjustment that the holders of EUTM rights would have had to face given the new circumstances would

---

[36]Folliard-Monguiral and Rogers (2004), p. 57 *et seq.*

[37]Annex III, Point 1.I of the 2005 Act of Accession, p. 231.

[38]Annex III, point 2(I) of the 2012 Act of Accession, p. 41.

[39]Kresbach and Grögerova (2007), p. 153.

[40]One offered solution was the so-called "Swiss option", meaning the UK not being a part of the EEA, but rejoining EFTA and negotiating agreements with the EU with regard to harmonisation with the EU IPR laws, but retaining sovereignty to deviate from it (George (2017), p. 170 *et seq.*). Also, the prospect of a "softer" Brexit with regard to the EUTM system would have meant a change in EU legislation that would allow the UK to remain within the EUIPO, in which case EUTMs and decisions of the Boards of Appeal could remain applicable also after Brexit (Ibid, p. 152).

[41]George (2017), p. 138 *et seq.*

be different.[42] However, even in the case of a "soft" Brexit, it was inevitable for them to be prepared for the new conditions. In the following sections, we elaborate only some of the main new issues and challenges that were identified along the way.

6.1 Existing EUTMs

The first and obvious concern raised in this context was the urgency for the existing (registered) EUTMs to be protected in the UK after Brexit as national trade marks with as few formalities and costs as possible. The effect of Brexit on the EUTM Regulation was clear[43] and since the EUTM is a unitary right (Article 1(2) of the EUTM Regulation), post-Brexit, all existing EUTMs would cease to have effect in the UK. However, considering the disastrous commercial effects that such an abrupt limitation of territorial scope of protection would have on the right holders of those EUTMs and the UK economy, a number of "transitional packages" following that breaking point were offered. The anticipated solutions that resonated most are probably those drafted by the Chartered Institute of Trade Mark Attorneys (CITMA) and all of which were based on already seen historical scenarios.[44] The CITMA offered seven potential options, some of which could have been implemented unilaterally by the UK and others, which required bilateral arrangements with the EU, thereby clearly preferring those minimising the costs and resource burden to businesses, while maximising legal certainty.

The possible scenarios, in short, were:

UK Plus
The EUTM system is extended to cover all EU Member states plus the UK. As a consequence, all existing EUTMs would cover both the UK and EU.

The Jersey Model
The UK unilaterally deems EUTM registrations to have effect in the UK, without the need for formal entry in the UK Intellectual Property Office (UKIPO), or any other action. This scenario is comparable to the enforcement of EUTMs in Jersey, which is not a part of the EU, as well as some British colonies, which protect on their territory designs registered in the UK.[45]

The Montenegro Model
All existing EUTM registrations would be automatically entered in the UKIPO as UK trade mark registrations with the same scope of protection, registration date and, where applicable, priority and seniority. This model was inspired by the solution

[42] Ibid, p. 140.

[43] See *supra*: Sect. 3. Brexit and IPRs.

[44] Arnold et al. (2017), p. 2.

[45] Ibid, p. 3.

adopted when the Montenegrin trade mark system separated from the Serbian system.[46]

The Tuvalu Model
Similar to the Montenegro model. However, the existing EUTM registrations would be entered in the UKIPO only if the right owner so requires. Again, comparable with the Montenegro model, this system was influenced by the solution used when the Tuvalu's trade mark system separated from the UK system.[47]

Veto
This scenario is based on the Tuvalu model. However, the UKIPO would retain the right to veto to refuse registration.

The Republic of Ireland Model
The EUTM right holders would be able to enforce their rights until the renewal of the EUTM in the EU and the UK. They would also have an "opt-in" possibility, in the sense that they could create a corresponding UK trade mark registration when renewing the EUTM registration, or up to a cut-off period, after which it would no longer be possible. This system is similar to the one used when the Irish and UK trade mark systems were separated.[48]

Conversion
This system resembles the existing mechanism for the conversion of EUTMs into national trade marks, with the exception that the EUTM registration would continue to exist. The new UK applications would retain the application date of the EUTM registration and would be fully examined by the UKIPO.

However, very soon after CITMA published this list of potential scenarios, it was clear that the most pragmatic choice would be the so-called "Montenegro-plus model", meaning that all existing EUTMs would be entered in the UKIPO on Brexit day, while retaining their registration, priority and seniority dates.[49] In any case, it was clear that very soon the UKIPO would face a tremendous increase in workload.[50]

While waiting to see which, if any, of these options would be transformed into an actual political decision, many EUTM right holders opted for topping up their trade mark portfolios regarding their most important EUTMs with additional UK national trade marks to provide for some certainty. However, the downside to this strategy was the inability to use the priority date of an already existing EUTM and, of course, the additional costs and administrative procedures. Although this double preventative filing was in particular non-lucrative for larger trade mark portfolios, the number

[46] Ibid.

[47] Ibid.

[48] Ibid.

[49] Loney et al. (2017), p. 33.

[50] Traub et al. (2016), p. 13.

of UK trade mark applications, predominantly from the US and China, increased after Brexit by 33% in August 2016.[51]

Nevertheless, after the initial period of unpredictability, the UK government repeatedly confirmed that it would grant new, equivalent UK rights (so-called "UK-child rights")[52] to all right holders (with an "opt-out" possibility) of registered EUTMs and that this "cloning process" would be performed free of charge and with a minimum administrative burden.[53] In other words, no EUTMs would be lost, regardless of a deal or no-deal Brexit.[54]

6.2 *Use It or Lose It*

The concept of the genuine use of an EUTM is embedded in Article 18 of the EUTM Regulation which stipulates that, if the right holder has not put his EUTM in use in the EU in connection with the goods or services in respect of which it is registered within five years following registration, or if such use has been suspended during an uninterrupted period of five years, such an EUTM is subject to revocation. Hence, there was a concern that EUTM holders (predominately those based in the UK), who solely used their EUTMs on the territory of UK, would potentially be under the risk of revocation[55] if the pre-Brexit use of an EUTM was not taken into consideration.[56]

Contrary to the question of the position of the existing EUTMs in the UK territory post departure, which was mostly reliant on a certain political intervention, the risk of revocation was something that the right holders potentially had the chance of preventing. They could do this, for example, by beginning to use their EUTMs also on a trans-border basis (in other EU Member States) after the notification on the intention to withdraw was made by the UK in accordance with Article 50 TEU, which, however, involved additional costs for them and perhaps was not even in accordance with their business strategy.[57] Having said that, many right holders were reassured when the UK government confirmed that also the EUTMs (potentially converted to national UK trade marks) used in the remaining 27 EU countries within five years before exit day would not be vulnerable to revocation due to non-use.[58]

---

[51] Nurton (2016), p. 1.

[52] Potts et al. (2019), p. 27.

[53] Clark (2019), p. 24; Potts et al. (2019), p. 27.

[54] Potts et al. (2019), p. 27.

[55] Dinwoodie and Dreyfuss (2018), p. 984; Traub et al. (2016), p. 13; Advocates for International Development, Kirkland & Ellis International LLP (2017), p. 5.

[56] Arnold et al. (2017), p. 3.

[57] Ibid, p 4; Dinwoodie and Dreyfuss (2018), p. 984; Traub et al. (2016), p. 14.

[58] Clark (2019), p. 25 *et seq.*

6.3 Pending EUTM Applications and Other Procedures

Since "soft" Brexit very soon appeared to be only wishful thinking, it was evident that an EUTM application filed after the transition period (31 December 2020) would only cover the territory of the EU27. As a consequence, in future, applicants who aim to obtain trade mark protection in the EU, as well as in the UK, would have to make two separate applications—one to the EUIPO and the other to the UKIPO—which would result in an increase of costs regarding the protection and maintenance of rights.[59]

However, there was still the question of which scenario was likely to happen with regard to the pending EUTM applications filed before the end of the transition period. As in the case of existing EUTMs,[60] the precautionary measure was to re-file in the UKIPO in order to obtain a UK trade mark, although with the same disadvantages (costs and priority). Here also, after a period of uncertainty, a transition period of nine months from the exit was announced when the UKIPO would recognise all filing dates and claims to earlier priority and UK seniority related to the corresponding EUTM application.[61]

Another question raised and closely related to the matter of pending applications was one concerning the pending opposition, invalidity and appeal proceedings at the time of Brexit.[62] Regarding this issue, the EUIPO indicated in 2019[63] that before withdrawal day, opposition and EUTM invalidity proceedings, based solely on UK rights, would be treated as usual. However, as from withdrawal day, any opposition or invalidity request based solely on a UK right would be dismissed.

6.4 Representatives

In accordance with Article 120(1)(a) of the EUTM Regulation, there are three requirements for professional representatives before the EUIPO: that they are nationals of a member state of the European Economic Area (EEA); that they have a place of business or employment in an EEA member state; and that they are entitled to act before a national office (or the Benelux office) in an EEA member state. Since the EEA comprises EU Member States and three EEA EFTA states (Iceland, Liechtenstein and Norway), the question was what the position of UK representatives would be after the actual UK departure from the EU, which does not follow the so-called "Norway Option" (leaving the EU, not the EEA by re-joining EFTA[64]).

---

[59] Traub et al. (2016), p. 13.

[60] See *supra*: Sect. 6.1. Existing EUTMS.

[61] Clark (2019), p. 26; Potts et al. (2019), p. 27.

[62] Loney et al. (2017), p. 33.

[63] EUIPO (2019), Brexit - Update, 8 May 2019.

[64] George (2017), p. 168.

Consequently, the UK would become a third country in terms of the EEA Agreement, and the UK IPR professionals would no longer fulfil the requirements of Article 120 of the EUTM Regulation. So, their goal was to retain their status at least for an interim period in order to develop and implement new business strategies, or to give right holders/clients the opportunity to find new representatives.[65]

As Nurton[66] rather charmingly stated: "Panic is not a quality you normally associate with patent and trademark attorneys…". However, the UK decision to leave the EU almost resulted in such a reaction, since EUIPO-related work represents a substantial part of their income.[67] CITMA conducted research in 2017 and established that UK trademark attorneys are involved in nearly one quarter (23.7%) of all EUTMs.[68]

In comparison to EUTM right holders or applicants, some of whom became proactive and others decided to "sit it out" and wait for political decision-makers to rule, the majority of IPR firms from the UK chose the former approach. They started implementing "survival strategies", for example by establishing offices in EU Member States, or expanding existing ones, as well as looking for options for merger, or preparing to qualify in other EU jurisdictions.[69] Developing a network of offices in a number of Member States was also an option.[70] Another "fear" of trade mark attorneys was that even if they managed to adapt to the new circumstances, Brexit would still have an effect on their business, because it would create the impression with clients that they could no longer provide legal counsel as effectively as attorneys from the EU Member States.[71] In particular, from the perspective of overseas companies, this development could mean that they would potentially choose non-UK firms as professional representatives in EUIPO and for IP/trademark litigation, since the UK would no longer be used as an EU base.[72]

6.5 Enforcement

The EUTM Regulation (Article 123) introduced EUTM Courts in the Member States, which can also issue pan-European injunctions (Article 131(2)). However, after the departure of the UK, the consequences in this regard are twofold. On one hand, the UK court system no longer has EUTM courts, and the power of injunctions

[65] Nurton (2017), p. 24.
[66] Ibid, p. 23.
[67] Ibid.
[68] Clark (2019), p. 26.
[69] Nurton (2017), p. 23.
[70] Ibid, p. 26.
[71] Ibid, p. 24.
[72] Pegram (2019), p. 16.

issued by UK courts no longer extends to the EU27 Member States.[73] On the other hand, it was an open question, if the pan-European injunctions issued by the EUTM Courts in the EU27 Member States could under certain conditions still be effective in the UK. The repercussion of this development is, that trade mark infringements would have to be separately litigated in the UK and the EU.[74] Bringing two sets of proceedings in the case of a trade mark violation to the EU (EUTM Court) and to the UK (a national court) leads to an increase in litigation costs for the right holders.[75] One of the proposals made in this context was to use the period of possibility of EU-wide enforcement (injunctions) and to tackle all the current cases of infringement.[76] Apart from the issue of injunctions, another concern was identified, namely one regarding the status of pending EUTM litigation after the actual departure of the UK, since, at that point, as mentioned above, the UK courts would cease to be EUTM Courts and would stop having jurisdiction over EUTMs.[77]

6.6 *EUTM Licences*

Another matter raised was the impact of Brexit on EUTM licences, in particular in cases where the licensed territory is, or includes, the UK and where no existing UK national trade marks were currently included in the licence.[78] The latter was an even greater concern, since the provisions on EUTM licences embedded in the EUTM Regulation (Articles 25 and 26) and those applying to UK national trade marks differ to a certain extent.[79] Included here, for example, are provisions with regard to the scope of rights of a non-exclusive licensee to enforce the national UK trade mark against third parties in its own name, or the right of the licensee to obtain compensation for damages suffered due to infringement.[80] Another dilemma addressed in this regard was whether, even in the case of a transposition of EUTMs into the UKIPO register after the actual Brexit, the new UK trade marks deriving from the EUTMs would automatically be included in the existing licence without a need to amend them.[81]

Consequently, even before the final word of the Withdrawal Agreement, there was an urge to review and amend existing licensing agreements,[82] or to use the

---

[73] Khwaja et al. (2017), p. 47.
[74] Traub et al. (2016), p. 12.
[75] Ibid, p. 13.
[76] Ibid, p. 15.
[77] Aries (2016), p. 10.
[78] Ibid.
[79] Ibid.
[80] Ibid, p. 11 *et seq.*
[81] Ibid, p. 13.
[82] Traub et al. (2016), p. 14.

opportunity, if those agreements were currently being (re-)negotiated, to clarify their geographical scope (the EU and/or the UK), or contract out certain provisions.[83] Considering, at that time, the potential conversion of EUTMs into UK national trade marks, it seemed advisable to amend the agreements with regard to the list of rights in order for them to cover both if that should apply.[84] Further, the question of choice of governing law and the choice of jurisdiction was also taken into account, in particular in cases where the law governing the contractual side of the licence was different from the law governing the validity, infringement or enforcement of trade marks.[85] The latter was of importance due to the fact that, as stated above,[86] UK courts would not be able to issue pan-European injunctions for EUTMs.

7 Developments Before the Withdrawal Agreement

In September 2017, the European Commission published a Position Paper on IPRs (Position Paper)[87] regarding the main principles of the EU's standpoint in this regard, to be presented to the UK in the context of negotiations under Article 50 TEU. This document to an extent ended the period of complete uncertainty and gave the interested parties, foremost EUTM right holders and applicants, some reassurance on what the negotiating position of the EU is in respect of a few of the above-elaborated pending issues and concerns.

In the Position Paper, the Commission clearly identified three key issues that would appear due to the UK exit with regard to IPRs, namely the scope of protection of certain IPRs in the UK, the treatment of applications for those rights and the question of exhaustion of rights. It also underlined that this uncertainty would affect the conditions under which goods that are placed on the market in the EU before the withdrawal date could continue to circulate between the EU27 and the UK.

In relation to unitary IPRs and with the EUTMs in particular, the Commission stressed that the future Withdrawal Agreement should ensure certain principles. Firstly, that the protection enjoyed in the UK on the basis of EU law of IPRs having a unitary character within the EU before the withdrawal date is not undermined by the withdrawal. The latter in the sense that there should be an automatic recognition of such an IPR in the UK on the basis of the existing unitary IPR. There should also be no financial costs for the right holders, and the administrative burden should be kept to a minimum. Basically, the proposed solution follows the so-called

[83] Aries (2016), p. 10.

[84] Potts et al. (2019), p. 28.

[85] Ibid, p. 29.

[86] See *supra*: Sect. 6.5. Enforcement.

[87] European Commission, Position paper transmitted to EU27 on Intellectual Property Rights (including geographical indications), 6 September 2017.

"Montenegro solution" suggested by CITMA,[88] as elaborated above.[89] Moreover, the implementation of this principle should include the determination of the renewal dates, the respect of priority and seniority principles and the adaptation of "genuine use" requirements (in the case of no genuine use in the UK prior to the withdrawal) and "reputation" rules (regarding trade marks having reputation in the EU) to the specific situation under consideration. Resistance to this solution from the UK side was expected. The latter mainly because of the costs of transfer that would fall on them, the cluttering of the UKIPO with EU IPRs, the right holders of which might not even need or want to have UK-specific protection, and the lack of a *bona fide* declaration of "intent to use" the trade mark in this solution, which is usually a requirement for UK trade mark registration.[90]

With regard to the pending applications for unitary IPRs submitted before the withdrawal date (and also the EUTM), the Position Paper included the solution that the applicants should be entitled to priority dates in respect of such applications when applying (after the withdrawal date) for an equivalent IPR in the UK

Furthermore, a position was taken in this document also considering the exhaustion of rights. The latter in the sense that IPRs exhausted in the EU prior to withdrawal should remain exhausted in both the EU27 territory and in the UK territory and that the conditions for exhaustion concerning each IPR should be those defined by EU law.

It was clear that the EU had not taken a position on all the dilemmas that were pressing for the EUTM community. Furthermore, the Position Paper only represented the standpoint of one side in the negotiating process. For example, apart from the issue of enforcement of EUTMs, one of the main questions that was omitted was the one on representation before the EUIPO.[91] In addition, the relevance of the proposed solution regarding the exhaustion of rights was "tarnished" by the open question about the scope (national or international) of exhaustion of rights that the UK would adopt after actual withdrawal.[92]

8 Withdrawal Agreement

The importance of IPRs for both the EU and the UK is mirrored in the fact that there is a whole section (Title IV, Articles 54–61) of the Withdrawal Agreement dedicated especially to the new regime for these rights.[93] The latter was to be expected considering the economic relevance of IPRs in the EU and UK. Besides, the

[88] Loney (2018), p. 1.

[89] See *supra*: Sect. 6.1. Existing EUTMS.

[90] Loney (2018), p. 1.

[91] Ibid.

[92] Loney et al. (2017), p. 33; Traub et al. (2016), p. 14.

[93] Clark (2019), p. 26.

legislative effort that was put in by the EU to establish standards for their protection clearly showed that there is mutual interest in establishing an arrangement of withdrawal to ensure stability in this field following Brexit.[94] A very important contribution to this stability is also given by the circumstance that throughout the transition period EU law remained applicable to and in the UK, which included the EUTM Regulation. Nevertheless, we must stress that some of the EUTM-relevant provisions of the Withdrawal Agreement regulate few of the burning issues discussed in this paper *pro futuro*, whilst others only for the transition period[95] that ended on 31 December 2020. Furthermore, particular dilemmas have only even been indirectly the subject of its regulation.

However, as the Preamble of the Withdrawal Agreement announced, several other agreements governing the future relationship between the EU27 and UK were also be negotiated after its entry in force. Consequently, the abovementioned EU-UK Trade and Cooperation Agreement was concluded, that we will briefly refer to later in this paper.[96]

8.1 Representation

Article 97 of the Withdrawal Agreement is not situated in Title IV dedicated to IPRs. However, it raises the question of representation in ongoing proceedings before the EUIPO, which was one of the main concerns for the EUTM representatives from the UK.[97]

Applied to this category, the Agreement regulates that a person who is authorised to represent a party before the EUIPO in accordance with EU law (Article 120 of the EUTM Regulation (Professional representatives)) and who was representing that party in a procedure brought before the EUTM before the end of the transition period may continue to represent that party in that procedure and will in every respect be treated as a professional representative authorised to represent. The latter applies to all stages of the procedure before that Office.

The effect of this provision of the Withdrawal Agreement is, in some cases, obviously extended beyond the transition period, depending on the type of the ongoing procedure (application, opposition, appeal, etc.) and the date when the pending procedure was commenced (e.g., before or immediately after the entry into force of the Withdrawal Agreement, or at the end of the transition period). What this meant for the (former) EUTM representatives from the UK is that, if they did not adjust their business activities in some of the above- elaborated manners[98]

[94] George (2017), p. 135.

[95] See *supra:* Sect. 2. Brexit.

[96] See *infra*: Sect. 9. Future relations.

[97] See *supra*: Sect. 6.4. Representatives.

[98] Ibid.

and thus do not fulfil the three cumulative conditions of Article 120 of the EUTM Regulation, they are not authorised to represent parties in proceedings before the EUIPO initiated after the transition period.[99]

8.2 *Title IV of the Withdrawal Agreement*

As mentioned above, this title of the Agreement is devoted solely to IPRs (Articles 54–61). However, since these provisions refer to a variety of rights (e.g. Community plant variety, Community design), in the following section, we will refer only to the provisions relevant to EUTMs.

8.2.1 Continued Protection of Registered EUTMs in the UK

The provision of Article 54 of the Withdrawal Agreement ensures legal certainty and relief for the right holders of the existing EUTMs in the sense that the geographical scope of their rights will not be reduced on the departure of the UK. However, we can no longer speak of a unitary effect of those rights with regard to the territory of the UK, but of a "coupling of rights" or a "family of rights" composed of an EUTM and a corresponding, new, national UK trade mark. This solution also releases EUTM right holders of the financial burden of preventative double filing in the UK and the negative effect of loss of priority.[100]

The "heart" of Article 54 is the implementation of the "Montenegro Model"[101] in the sense that the EUTMs which were registered before the end of the transition period are, without any re-examination, converted into registered and enforceable national UK trade marks under UK law, consisting of the same sign, for the same goods or services. Furthermore, the UK "child trade marks" enjoy the date of filing or the date of priority of the corresponding EUTM and, if applicable, the seniority of a (prior) UK trade mark (Article 54(5)). UK trade marks arising from the corresponding EUTMs have as their first renewal date the renewal date of the EUTMs in question (Article 54(4)). What is also very important to EUTM right holders and resembles the solution applied to the extension of EUTMs during EU enlargements[102] is that the registration of corresponding UK Trade marks is conducted free of charge by the UKIPO, using the data available in the registry of the EUIPO (Article 55), which this institution provides. However, this solution is

[99] See also EUIPO, Notice to Stakeholders, 20 June 2020 and EUIPO, Impact of the UK's withdrawal from the EU – EUTMs and RCDs, 21 January 2021.

[100] See *supra*: Sect. 6.1. Existing EUTMs.

[101] Ibid.

[102] See *supra*: Sect. 5. Enlargement.

without prejudice to renewal fees that may apply at the time of renewal of the EUTM (Article 55(4)).

The cloning of the existing approximately 1.4 million EUTMs into the UKIPO register represents an obvious administrative burden for this institution. The registration procedure does not require a separate application or any particular administrative procedure (Article 55). The right holders of EUTMs are not required to have a correspondence address in the UK in the three years following the end of the transition period. The UKIPO announced at that point that it will not create corresponding UK trade mark rights on 31 January 2020, but at the end of the transition period.[103] In order to prevent the cluttering of the register, an "opt-out request" (after January 2021) has been introduced for EUTM right holders, if they are not interested in a corresponding UK trade mark. However, this possibility is excluded if the comparable UK right has been used in the UK, the right was assigned or licensed or there is an agreement in relation to it, or litigation has been initiated based on that comparable UK right.[104]

Moreover, Article 54(3) stipulates that if an EUTM original right is declared invalid or revoked in the EU as a result of an administrative or judicial procedure, which was ongoing on the last day of the transition period (until 31 December 2020), the corresponding right in the UK will also be declared invalid or revoked (Article 54(3)). The date of effect of the declaration or revocation in the UK is same as in the EU. Nevertheless, the UK is not obliged to declare invalid or to revoke the corresponding right in the UK where the grounds for the invalidity or revocation of the EUTM do not apply in the UK.

In addition, the Withdrawal Agreement also gave an answer to the above-elaborated dilemma of genuine use.[105] It stipulates that the new UK trade mark will not be liable to revocation on the ground that the corresponding EUTM was not put into genuine use in the territory of the UK before the end of the transition period (Article 54(5)). The same applies vice versa with regard to the genuine use of an EUTM. Its use in the UK until the end of the transition period will be taken into account, which means in practice that an EUTM which has only been used in the UK cannot be revoked for non-use in the EU until 31 December 2025.[106]

Finally, the new, national UK trade marks arising from EUTMs which have acquired reputation in the EU in accordance with EU law benefited from that reputation until the end of the transition period. However, after 31 December 2020, the reputation of the corresponding UK trade mark is based on its use in the UK (Article 54(5).

---

[103] UKIPO, Intellectual property and the transition period, 31 January 2020.

[104] UKIPO, Guidance: EU trade mark protection and comparable UK trade marks from 1 January 2021. Opting out of the comparable UK Trade Mark, 30 January 2020.

[105] See *supra*: Sect. 6.2. Use It or Lose It.

[106] Valuiskich (2020).

8.2.2 Pending EUTM Applications and Other Procedures

According to Article 59(1) of the Withdrawal Agreement, a right of priority was established in favour of an EUTM application filed before the end of the transition period.[107] If such an application was accorded a date of filing, the applicant has, for the same trade mark in respect of goods or services, which are identical with or contained within those for which the application has been filed in the EU, the right to file an application in the UK within nine months from the end of the transition period. The latter window was closed on 30 September 2021. Such an application was deemed to have the same filing date and date of priority as the corresponding application filed in the EU and, where appropriate, the seniority of a(n) (earlier) trade mark of the UK. In other words, EUTM applications were not automatically extended to the UK, as existing EUTMs.[108]

However, pending applications are in general subject to opposition and it could have been the situation that the latter was based solely on an older UK trade mark. In such a case, the contested EUTM was registered in the EU. However, if the applicant decided to use the benefit of the provision of Article 59(1) and re-file in the UK, the new application was open for opposition based on any prior UK marks, and the opposition procedure was conducted at the UKIPO.[109] With regard to pending cancellation proceedings, the outcome was similar to that concerning opposition. Having said that, if he cancellation of a registered and cloned EUTM was based solely on UK prior rights, EU proceedings was concluded, and the EUTM remained registered in the EU. However, a new and separate cancellation procedure could have been initiated in the UK in respect of a corresponding UK trade mark.[110]

8.2.3 Exhaustion of Rights

Finally, the question of exhaustion of rights was regulated by the Withdrawal Agreement. However, legal certainty was secured only for the transition period (Article 61). Accordingly, IPRs which were exhausted both in the Union and in the United Kingdom before the end of that period under the conditions provided for by EU law also remained exhausted both in the EU and in the UK. However, at that point the question remained, what would happen after 1 January 2020 (the end of the transition period). Then, goods placed on the UK market by, or with the consent of, the right holder after that date might have, depending on the scope of exhaustion introduced in the UK, no longer be considered exhausted in the EEA, which in particular meant that persons exporting goods incorporating trade marks from the

[107] UKIPO, Intellectual property and the transition period, 31 January 2020.

[108] Valuiskich (2020).

[109] Ibid.

[110] Ibid.

UK to the EEA might need the right holder's consent.[111] In order to resolve this issue, a consultation process has been launched in June 2021 with the aim to determine, what would be the most appropriate regime for the exhaustion of IP rights and how to implement it.[112] The proposed regimes included the "do nothing" approach (UK +), the national regime, the international regime and a mixed system.[113] After the consultation was closed, it was concluded that "...there is not enough data available to understand the economic impact of any of the alternatives to the current UK+ regime. As a result, it has not been possible to make a decision based on the criteria originally intended."[114] Accordingly, the current exhaustion regime will remain in force until further decision.

8.2.4 Enforcement

Article 67(1) of the Withdrawal Agreement shed some light on the jurisdiction issues regarding legal proceedings initiated before the end of the transition period. Specifically, after the end of that period, the provisions regarding jurisdiction of the EUTM Regulation apply in the United Kingdom, as well as in the EU Member States in situations involving the UK in respect of legal proceedings instituted before the end of the transition period, and proceedings or actions that are related to such legal proceedings pursuant to Articles 29, 30 and 31 of Regulation (EU) No 1215/2012.[115,116] Nevertheless, it must be underlined that any remedies issued by the UK courts will only apply to the comparable UK mark.

[111] UKIPO, Guidance: Exhaustion of IP rights and parallel trade from 1 January 2021, 30 January 2020.

[112] UKIPO, Closed consultation. Consultation document on the UK's future regime for exhaustion of IP rights, 18 January 2022.

[113] Walters (2021), p. 1 and UKIPO, Closed consultation. Consultation document on the UK's future regime for exhaustion of IP rights, 18 January 2022.

[114] UKIPO, UK's future exhaustion of intellectual property rights regime, 18 January 2022.

[115] Regulation (EU) No 1215/2012 of the European Parliament and of the Council of 12 December 2012 on jurisdiction and the recognition and enforcement of judgments in civil and commercial matters.

[116] EUIPO, Notice to Stakeholders, 20 June 2020; European Commission, Questions and Answers on the United Kingdom's withdrawal from the European Union on 31 January 2020, 24 January 2020.

9 Future Relations

In February 2020, after the terms of the withdrawal were clear, the UK Government published a document outlining its approach to negotiations with regard to establishing a future relationship with the EU.[117] Considering IPRs, it was stated, that the future agreement should include an IPR chapter that secures mutual assurances to provide high standards of protection for IP rights, including registered IPRs, meaning also trade marks.[118]

Furthermore, some substantive changes to UK trade mark legislation were announced by UKIPO, which, among other things, would also regulate the question of EUTMs which are the subject of licences.[119] These will continue to have effect in the UK and will be treated as if they applied to cloned UK trade marks. However, the registration of these licences will not be conducted automatically into the UKIPO register. Hence, it is important for the interested parties to become proactive. Then, the UKIPO extended the period within which such licences, already registered at the EUIPO before 1 January 2021, must be recorded for a corresponding UK trade mark to 12 months from 1 January 2021.

Finally, the EU-UK Trade and Cooperation Agreement was concluded and entered into force and its Title V is devoted to IPRs. With regard to trade marks (Section 2, Arts. 236-244), questions such as classification, signs which may constitute a trade mark, rights conferred by a trade mark, the registration procedure, well-known trade marks, exceptions to rights, grounds for revocation, the right to prohibit preparatory acts in relation to the use of packaging or other means and bad-faith applications were tackled. Apart from the latter, the Agreement, among others also addresses the issues of the enforcement of IPRs (Arts. 256 *et seq.*).

10 Conclusion

Having in mind the unpredictability that plagued the EUTM community in the first post-Brexit years, we can now with a satisfying level of certainty claim that the dust has settled on many of the posed dilemmas. The Withdrawal Agreement has established legal certainty primarily for EUTM right holders and applicants, whilst urging them yet again to stay alert and actively participate in the shaping of their future trade mark portfolio (the opt-out opportunity and re-filing of pending applications). As was clear in the early stages of preparation for the UK departure, the unitary effect of the EUTM could not be preserved, but the current solutions come very close to the next best thing. Many other questions concerning future relations

[117] HM Government (2020), p. 16.

[118] Chapter 23: Intellectual Property.

[119] UKIPO, Guidance: EU trade mark protection and comparable UK trade marks from 1 January 2021, 30 January 2020.

between EU and the UK regarding IPRs, were resolved in the EU-UK Trade and Cooperation Agreement. It will also be very interesting to observe whether or not the corresponding UK trade marks will develop an existence and destiny of their own, or if they will still be treated in their right owners' business strategies as part of the main EUTM. Finally, other developments that need to be closely watched are the extent to which the UK trade mark legislation will diverge in time from the principles arising from EU law and how will the exhaustion regime in the UK be regulated in the future.

Other Sources

Advocates for International Development, Kirkland & Ellis International LLP (2017) Brexit Briefing: Impact on Intellectual Property Rights. http://www.a4id.org/wp-content/uploads/2017/02/Brexit-Briefing-Impact-on-Intellectual-Property-Rights.pdf. Accessed 19 May 2022.

Agreement on the withdrawal of the United Kingdom of Great Britain and Northern Ireland from the European Union and the European Atomic Energy Community (2019/C 384 I/01). Official Journal of the European Union, C 384, 12 Nov 2019.

Agreement on the withdrawal of the United Kingdom of Great Britain and Northern Ireland from the European Union and the European Atomic Energy Community (2019/C 384 I/01). Official Journal of the European Union, L 149, 30 April 2021.

Annex III, point 2(I) of the 2012 Act of Accession, OJ L 112, 24 April 2012, p 41.

Annex II, Part 4 (C)(I) of the 2003 Act of Accession, OJ L 236, 23 September 2003, p. 342.

Annex III, Point 1.I of the 2005 Act of Accession, OJ L 157, 21 June 2005, p. 231.

Consolidated version of the Treaty on European Union, OJ C 326, 26 October 2012.

Council Regulation (EC) No 40/94 of 20 December 1993 on the Community trade mark. OJ L 11, 14 Jan 1994.

Directive (EU) 2015/2436 of the European Parliament and of the Council of 16 December 2015 to approximate the laws of the Member States relating to trade marks. OJ L 335, 23 December 2015.

EUIPO (2020) Brexit Information Hub, 18 June 2020. https://euipo.europa.eu/ohimportal/en/Brexit-q-and-a. Accessed 9 July 2020

EUIPO (2019) Brexit - Update, 8 May 2019. https://euipo.europa.eu/ohimportal/en. Accessed 2 July 2020

EUIPO (2020) Notice to stakeholders, 20 June 2020. https://euipo.europa.eu/tunnel-web/secure/webdav/guest/document_library/contentPdfs/Brexit/EC_EUIPO_Notice_trademarks_and_designs_18_June_2020_en.pdf. Accessed 21 May 2022

EUIPO (2021) Impact of the UK's withdrawal from the EU – EUTMs and RCDs, 21 January 2021. https://euipo.europa.eu/ohimportal/en/law/brexit-q-and-a/representatives. Accessed 21 May 2022

European Commission (2020) Draft text of the Agreement on the New Partnership with the United Kingdom, 18 March 2020. https://ec.europa.eu/info/sites/info/files/200318-draft-agreement-gen.pdf. Accessed 8 July 2020

European Commission (n. d.) The EU-UK Withdrawal Agreement. Timeline of 'Article 50' negotiations on the Withdrawal Agreement. https://ec.europa.eu/info/european-union-and-united-kingdom-forging-new-partnership/eu-uk-withdrawal-agreement_en. Accessed 23 June 2020

European Commission (2017) Position paper transmitted to EU27 on intellectual property rights (including geographical indications) TF50 (2017) 11 – Commission to EU 27, 6 September 2017. https://ec.europa.eu/commission/sites/beta-political/files/position-paper-intellectual-property-rights_en.pdf. Accessed 5 July 2020

European Commission (2020) Questions and answers on the United Kingdom's withdrawal from the European Union on 31 January 2020, 24 January 2020. https://ec.europa.eu/commission/presscorner/detail/en/qanda_20_104. Accessed 8 July 2020

HM Government (2020) The future relationship with the EU. The UK's approach to negotiations. https://assets.publishing.service.gov.uk/government/uploads/system/uploads/attachment_data/file/868874/The_Future_Relationship_with_the_EU.pdf. Accessed 7 July 2020

Regulation (EU) 2017/1001 of the European Parliament and of the Council of 14 June 2017 on the European Union trade mark, OJ L 154, 16 June 2017.

Regulation (EU) No 1215/2012 of the European Parliament and of the Council of 12 December 2012 on jurisdiction and the recognition and enforcement of judgments in civil and commercial matters, OJ L 351, 20 Dec 2012.

Treaty of Lisbon amending the Treaty on European Union and the Treaty establishing the European Community, signed at Lisbon, 13 December 2007, OJ C 306, 17 December 2007.

UKIPO (2020) Guidance: Exhaustion of IP rights and parallel trade from 1 January 2021, 30 January 2020. https://www.gov.uk/guidance/exhaustion-of-ip-rights-and-parallel-trade-after-the-transition-period. Accessed 19 May 2022

UKIPO (2020) Guidance: EU trade mark protection and comparable UK trade marks from 1 January 2021, 30 January 2020. https://www.gov.uk/guidance/eu-trademark-protection-and-comparable-uk-trademarks#opting-out-of-the-comparable-uk-trade-mark. Accessed 19 May 2022

UKIPO (2020) Intellectual property and the transition period, 31 January 2020. https://www.gov.uk/government/news/intellectual-property-and-the-transition-period. Accessed 6 July 2020

UKIPO (2022) Closed consultation. Consultation document on the UK's future regime for exhaustion of IP rights, 18 January 2022. https://www.gov.uk/government/consultations/uks-future-exhaustion-of-intellectual-property-rights-regime/the-uks-future-regime-for-the-exhaustion-of-ip-rights. Accessed 19 May 2022.

UKIPO (2022) UKIPO, UK's future exhaustion of intellectual property rights regime, 18 January 2022. https://www.gov.uk/government/consultations/uks-future-exhaustion-of-intellectual-property-rights-regime. Accessed 21 May 2022.
United Kingdom notification under Article 50 TEU (2017), 29 March 2017 http://data.consilium.europa.eu/doc/document/XT-20001-2017-INIT/en/pdf. Accessed 20 May 2022

References

Bibliography

Aries N (2016) Brexit implications for trade marks. Int J Franch Law 14(6):9–13
Arnold R, Bently L, Derclaye E, Dinwoodie G (2017) The legal consequences of Brexit through the lens of IP law. https://doi.org/10.2139/ssrn.2917219. Accessed 27 June 2020
Bazerkoska J (2016) View from the Balkans: Brexit and the possible implications on the candidate countries for EU membership. Iustinianus Primus Law Rev 7(2):52–58
BBC (2016) EU referendum results. https://www.bbc.com/news/politics/eu_referendum/results. Accessed 27 June 2020
Boesch E (2005) Die Auswirkungen der Erweiterung der EU auf die Gemeinschaftsmarke, Vorteile und Schwierigkeiten in Zusammenhang mit der Erstreckung der Gemeinschaftsmarke. ÖBI 3: 100
Clark T (2019) The future for EU IP in the UK. Manag Intellect Prop 281:23–26
Dinwoodie GB, Dreyfuss RC (2018) Brexit and IP: the great unrevealing? Cardozo Law Rev 39(3): 967–995
Folliard-Monguiral A, Rogers D (2004) The Community trade mark and designs system and the enlargement of the European Union. Eur Intellect Prop Rev 26(2):48–58
Forrester I (2018) European Union law in the UK after Brexit. Judicial Rev 23(1):45–64
George A (2017) Restructuring intellectual property jurisdiction post-Brexit: strategic considerations for the European Union and Britain. Brooklyn J Int Law 43(1):131–189
Jones DL (2018) Brexit and the future of English law. Vic Univ Wellington Law Rev 49(1):1–22
Khwaja S, Shaw A, von Gerlach L, Kacperek E, de Dampierre M, Valot A (2017) Guide to trade mark forum shopping in Europe. Manag Intellect Prop 269:44–47
Kresbach G, Grögerova V (2007) Die Gemeinschaftsmarke nach dem Beitritt von Bulgarien und Rumänien zur Europäischen Union. ÖBl 4:153–156
Loney M (2018) Analysing the European Commission's Brexit position for IP. Manag Intellect Prop:1–1
Loney M, Nurton J, Rahhal N, Tan S (2017) The 10 trade mark topics to watch. Manag Intellect Prop 267:31–38
Markakis M (2017) Legal issues arising from the Brexit referendum: UK and EU constitutional analysis. Int J Legal Inform 45(1):14–23
Nurton J (2016) Revealed: filing trends at the UK IPO post-Brexit. Manag Intellect Prop:1–1
Nurton J (2017) How UK IP firms hope to survive Brexit. Manag Intellect Prop 269:23–26
Pegram J (2019) What Brexit means for non-EU IP owners. Manag Intellect Prop 280:13–16
Potts B, Stone D, Feldges J, Livneh K, Shen D (2019) Practical preparations for Brexit: a global perspective. Manag Intellect Prop 281:27–30

Pretnar B (1997) Is the future enlargement of the European Union an immediate issue for the Community trade mark system? Eur Intellect Prop Rev 19(4):185–187
Traub F, Haleen I, Clay A (2016) Brexit – what next for intellectual property rights? IP Litigator 22(4):11–15
Valuiskich E (2020) Trade marks in post-Brexit world. https://www.finnegan.com/en/insights/blogs/european-ip-blog/trade-marks-in-post-brexit-world.html. Accessed 20 May 2022
Walters M (2021) Opinion: tired of Brexit? The exhaustion is still to come! Managing Intellectual Property: N. PAG

Part III
International Law Section

From Rule by Law to the Rule of Law: Main Obstacles to Establishing the Rule of Law in Bosnia and Herzegovina

Benjamin Nurkić

1 Introduction

The establishment of a state based on the rule of law (hereinafter: RoL) and democratic institutions has been and remains the main goal of the international community when it comes to the states of the former Socialist Federal Republic of Yugoslavia (hereinafter: the former Yugoslavia) and this objective has been achieved in some states like the Republic of Slovenia and Republic of Croatia, which was confirmed with their accession to the European Union, whereas Bosnia and Herzegovina (hereinafter: B&H) failed in achieve a sufficient degree of the RoL to gain entry into the European Union.[1] This paper discusses the transition from the rule-by-law system to the system formally based on the RoL principle. The process of institutional development on principles of the RoL has been analyzed and researched to a much lesser extent than the democratization process.[2]

Rule by law[3] is a term coined to describe 'the RoL' in states with authoritarian regimes. In such governmental systems the principles of constitutionality and legality are formally followed however, these laws do not serve to protect the citizens but to strengthen and further legitimize the government. Rule by law can also represent a synonym for 'thin' or formal definition of the RoL.[4] According to Moustafa and Ginsburg, such systems have developed an institutional system that has, to some

[1] On the role of the international community in the establishing the rule of law in B&H see: Hogić (2020); Coman (2017).

[2] See: Campbell (1998), pp. 165–245; Kirbis and Flere (2017), p. 125.

[3] Sajó (1995), pp. 97–104.

[4] On rule by law also see: Dyzenhaus (2021).

B. Nurkić (✉)
University of Tuzla, Faculty of Law, Tuzla, Bosnia and Herzegovina
e-mail: bnurkic@bih.net.ba

I. Kunda et al. (eds.), *Balkan Yearbook of European and International Law 2022*,
Balkan Yearbook of European and International Law 2022,
https://doi.org/10.1007/978-3-031-29432-7_8

degree, judicial autonomy whose primary function is to: establish social control and sideline political opponents, legitimize and legalize regime's actions, control the work of administrative officers and maintain cohesion among ruling elites, meet economic obligations, i.e. present state safe for foreign investments.[5] Or, as Dyzenhaus observes, rule by law argues that there is no more to law than what the holder of supreme legislative power chooses to enact, regardless of what the content is.[6] Rule by law 'is associated with a certain form of authoritarianism, whereby a strong man uses law as a means of subordinating citizens but refuses to acknowledge any legal constraints on his own actions. This is a fake rule of law, critics say, because it is not motivated by any real love of legality.'[7]

On the other hand, the RoL represents a principle that is often associated with constitutionalism and constitutional state, which is a narrow view of the RoL compared to what it really means in contemporary context. We shall use the definition given by Hisahi Owada, a judge at the International Court of Justice, who listed the following key components of the RoL: the supremacy of the law; equality before the law; separation of powers; the independence of the judiciary; the international RoL in relation to the individual.[8] In this regard, the transition from the rule-by-law system to the system based on the RoL implies the change in understanding of the whole concept of the RoL—transition from understanding the law as a government's tool to it being an instrument for the restriction of authorities.[9]

2 Socio-Economic Specificities of the Former Yugoslavia

In terms of system rigidity and the centralization of economic activities, the former Yugoslavia was different compared to other communist countries. 'Decentralized totalitarianism' and 'soft totalitarianism' are terms used to describe the former Yugoslav political system.[10] Therefore, Edvard Kardelj, the principal ideologist in former Yugoslavia, wrote that the Soviet Union formed an independent executive apparatus that created independent bureaucratic caste with specific social interests. Unlike the Soviet Union, the former Yugoslavia formally advocated for direct democracy embodied in works councils.[11] The Soviet model was also criticized because of the establishment of typical dictatorship instead of the proletariat

[5] Moustafa and Ginsburg (2008), pp. 1–13.

[6] Dyzenhaus (2021), p. 261.

[7] Waldron (2021), p. 96.

[8] Bingham (2010), pp. 172–173.

[9] For further information on the difference between the rule-by-law principle and the rule of law refer to: Tushnet (2014), pp. 79–92.

[10] Andjelić (2003), pp. 26, 35.

[11] Bensosn (2001), pp. 96–97.

dictatorship.[12] The 1963 Constitution formally confirms the will for democratization and establishment of constitutional state.[13] Thus, the former Yugoslavia, along Poland, became the only communist state to introduce constitutional control before the fall of the Berlin Wall.[14] In this context the three distinct phenomena typical for the former Yugoslav state are: increased political activity through institutions and not the party, decentralized economy, and innovation of ruling communist regime.[15] Direct democracy, workers' self-management and constitutional state became main characteristics that formally differentiated the former Yugoslavia from other communist states. Although the separation from the Communist Bloc and turning towards democratization and constitutional state marked the political progress of the former Yugoslavia.

However, the former Yugoslavia, as other communist states, also faced the issue of institutionalizing political power, which was a historical problem for all states with the socialist model of government.[16] Interest rate policy, which was in existence until 1982, confirms that the former Yugoslavia had typical socialist economy although workers' self-management differentiated it from other socialist states.[17] Workers' self-management never had the opportunity to reach its full potential due to the unwillingness of political authority in Yugoslavia to hand the power to the workers, therefore the workers' self-management really never existed since the politics ruled all economic processes.[18] Market socialism never existed in practice, since there was no distribution of power between the Party and enterprises which were supposed to conduct business based on the principles of market economy, that is the existence or non-existence of profit determined the survival of the enterprise.[19] Such a principle never really existed since the future of the enterprise was determined by the government and not the market. Additionally, there were limitations to the organization of private companies in terms of the number of employees such company could hire, which was not in accordance with market principles.[20]

Representatives in self-management bodies were not in contact with the voters, while local government did not have the actual power. In place of democratization there was bureaucratization and technocratization of the state and economic power.[21] Direct democracy was implemented only formally since the whole election process

[12] Lapenna (1972), p. 214.
[13] Maksimović (1965), pp. 164–167.
[14] Sadurski (2014), p. 6.
[15] Fisk (1971), pp. 279–280.
[16] Ibid, p. 278.
[17] Uvalić (1992), pp. 105–106.
[18] Ibid, p. 214.
[19] Bensosn (2001), p. 132.
[20] Lapenna (1972), p. 216.
[21] Leonardson and Mirčev (1979), p. 193.

was controlled by the Party.[22] Citizens' participation in political processes was really low mostly due to doubt that political processes could be influenced. Furthermore, lack of knowledge on the importance of participation and political processes as well as non-awareness of political culture resulted in abstinence of citizens' participation in political processes.[23] So direct democracy was just an empty slogan which existed only on paper. Absence of democratic frameworks and economic non-functionality were some of the reasons for the fall of the former Yugoslavia.[24]

3 The Former Yugoslav Legal System: Rule by Law or RoL?

Constitutions of the socialist countries were just a cover for the political reality, and they reflected the Party's objectives in places where there were no true Party restrictions and guarantees for citizens' freedoms.[25] The Party of Yugoslavia considered constitutionalism to be extremely important for political stability and economic dynamics.[26] The Yugoslav Constitution of 1974 formally guaranteed the principle of constitutionality, legality and the protection of individuals' rights,[27] but this is not enough in order to claim that Yugoslav legal system was based on the RoL and for that purpose we will analyze the relations between judiciary and the Party, the protection of human rights in the former Yugoslavia and the efficacy of institutional work control in state institutions.

3.1 Judiciary and the Party Relations

The Yugoslav Constitutional Court (YCC) was established in 1963 following the adoption of a new constitution, aiming to solve interinstitutional conflicts and to protect the Constitution and legislations from bureaucratic power abuse.[28] Yugoslavia had a structured state form based on the RoL with judicial, executive, and legislative branches and the Constitution, which clearly guaranteed individual rights and the protection of constitutionality and legality. In essence, all major decisions were made by the Party while the less important decisions were made by the state

---

[22] Bensosn (2001), p. 98.

[23] Leonardson and Mirčev (1979), pp. 193–194.

[24] Bensosn (2001), p. 132.

[25] Baričević (2007), p. 206.

[26] Fisk (1971), p. 282.

[27] The 1974 Yugoslav Constitution in Title III governed the rights and the duties of the citizen, while Title IV governed the principles of constitutionality and legality.

[28] Fisk (1971), p. 293.

institutions.[29] Judiciary was a tool in hands of the Party and did not set any limitations to the actions of the Party. Unlike other rigid communist regimes, the ruling regime in Yugoslavia limited influence of judiciary institutions in a more subtle way. Primarily it was done by limiting tenures and appointments of judges.

The duration of judicial tenure for the YCC judges and ordinary court judges was 8 years, but the YCC judges were not eligible for re-election after the completion of the term.[30] In such legal circumstances judges could not be independent so in practice they behaved in accordance with the interests of authorities in order to keep their bench, and because it was especially difficult for the former judges to find employment if they were not re-elected. Certainly, such problem did not exist for the YCC judges since there was no possibility for re-election, therefore the judiciary independence was the weakest at its lowest levels.[31] Issuing limitations on the duration of judicial tenure made the formal regulation of judiciary independence to be pointless. Another problem was the election process, i.e. the criteria used for the appointment of judges. Article 230 of the Yugoslav Constitution provided criteria for persons having judicial authority:

> Judges of ordinary courts shall be elected and relieved of office in a way, under conditions and by a procedure which shall ensure professional expertise and moral-political capabilities for the exercise of judicial functions and assure judicial independence in the administration of justice.[32]

Moral-political suitability was another name for obedience to the ruling regime. Moreover, a moral-political suitability was in conflict with international commitments that the former Yugoslavia undertook in relation to the prohibition of discrimination based on the political views of individuals. In essence, a moral-political suitability actually meant obligatory membership in the Party. This is supported by the fact that 87.2% of judges were members of the Party in 1979, which means that judges were just servants of the communist regime and not a tool for prevention of arbitrariness on the part of authorities. No attempts were made to hide the political interference of the Party with the judicial proceedings.[33] Judiciary was just an instrument in the hands of regime with a task to legitimize and legalize procedures of the authority.

[29] Ibid, p. 293.

[30] Article 381 of the 1974 Yugoslav Constitution provides the duration of judicial tenure for the YCC, whereas the election of ordinary court judges was regulated in Article 230 of the Constitution which states that judges are elected for a cpecific time period and can be re-elected.

[31] See: Macfarlane (1990), pp. 129–130.

[32] Article 230 of the 1974 Yugoslav Constitution.

[33] Macfarlane (1990), p. 130.

3.2 *Protection of Human Rights in the Former Yugoslavia*

The constitutions of the Eastern Bloc states had special sections on the rights of individuals but usually with special clauses such as 'unless otherwise foreseen by law' or 'unless otherwise restricted by law'.[34] The similar thing could also be seen in the former Yugoslavia, where the Yugoslav Constitution guaranteed the rights of individuals, but were limited by the Criminal Code, especially the freedom of speech.[35]

Limiting the freedom of speech led, not only to the protection of ruling authority, but it also led to abuse of power by state officials.[36] By limiting the freedom of speech the former Yugoslavia, as other communist states, tried to save ruling regime from criticism, under the pretext of socialist self-governing democratic order. Also, there was an attempt to portray the former Yugoslavia to international community as a more progressive state in comparison to other communist states in terms of the protection of human rights.

In the former Yugoslavia, individuals' rights were restricted by the Criminal Code. Thus, the Yugoslav Criminal Code (The Criminal Code) in Article XV sanctioned offences against self-governing socialist system and safety of Yugoslavia. According to the Article 114 of the Criminal Code the penalty minimum of one year was sanctioning the following offences: acting against authority of the working class and working people, acting against socio-economic system or self-governing system, unconstitutional actions for the purpose of overthrowing the government, attack on economic system, and attack on brotherhood and unity and equality of peoples.[37] The Criminal Code limited in great detail and extent any form of criticism of the Yugoslav legal order and ruling regime.

YCC declined in 1988 to review the constitutionality of this Article. With these regulations the former Yugoslavia was in breach of international commitments regarding the Universal Declaration of Human Rights (Universal Declaration). In late 1990s, the Amnesty International published a book on the former Yugoslav political prisoners who were incarcerated against the Universal Declaration. The Criminal Code provisions on protection of Yugoslav legal order were mostly used against political opponents, and one of the major issues was that there was no differentiation between violent and non-violent acts, meaning, propaganda and violent acts were classified in the same way.[38] This was the evidence of classic non-democratic treatment of citizens, and state had to show it was acting in such manner as a prevention measure against the enemies of the system.

Application of the Criminal Code became problematic in front of the United Nations Commission on Human Rights. Yugoslav representative determined that in

[34] Elster (1991), p. 265.

[35] Macfarlane (1990), p. 138.

[36] Ibid, p. 138.

[37] Ibid, pp. 122–123.

[38] Ibid, pp. 123–125.

a multi-national state it is difficult to distinguish between propaganda and violent acts, but on that occasion, he tried to persuade the attendees that the then Yugoslavia sanctioned only people who wanted to endanger public order and safety. German expert Tomuschat on that occasion expressed his concern that the Criminal Code Articles in question were used to prevent free discission about the then Yugoslav legal system. A proof that the German expert's concern was justified is the Committee of the Assembly for Jurisprudence statistics from 1984 which analyzed the work of republican prosecution offices and prosecution offices in provinces, where it was said 763 criminal proceedings were carried out for political offences and 501 (65%) for speech crimes. Of course, not everyone supported the mentioned norms, therefore, at the legal experts' meeting on criminal law in Ljubljana in 1985. Marjanović, a legal expert from Macedonia, argued against such norms that limited the freedom of speech: 'Socialism, he declared, cannot be defended with closed lips and bowed head.'[39] Another problem with human rights protection in the former Yugoslavia were judges who accepted positivism's understanding of law. The then Yugoslav legal system was strictly formalized, and in such legal culture, judges were instruments for mechanical application of legal text in judicial decision-making. Legal syllogism was the main method of decision-making process, where deciding cases on formal ground was more important rather than merits. The then Yugoslav legal system was developed on Marxist ideology and on Hans Kelsen's theory,[40] who strongly opposed the application of general principles such as human rights in judicial decision-making.[41] According to Degan, it is unknown whether any court in former Yugoslavia in its decision referred to any international convention or international customs related to human rights, although former Yugoslavia was a member state of most international treaties on human rights in force at that time.[42] Civil law system in force in the former Yugoslavia was not selected only because the former Yugoslavia followed the traditions of the European Continental legal systems, but rather due to the fact that states with authoritarian government, according to Moustafa and Ginsburg, often tend to organize their legal order based on civil law system because it has better mechanisms to ensure limitation of judicial power by legislators.[43] Ethnic nationalism was the third problem in the protection of human rights in Yugoslavia. Although Marxist state ideology was against nationalistic divisions, Yugoslavia did not strictly follow such ideology. Such practice was not only present in Yugoslavia, because Marxism was not always in conflict with nationalism, therefore, Soviet communism was a continuation of Russian expansionism. As well, the then Yugoslav communists did not get the support of the people through ideology but because of the way in which national issues were solved. In that way the then Yugoslav communism can be characterized as national

---

[39] Ibid, pp. 126–127.

[40] Karčić (2020).

[41] Stone Sweet (2003), pp. 2767–2768.

[42] Degan (2011), pp. 25.

[43] Moustafa and Ginsburg (2008), pp. 18–19.

communism.[44] Baričević states that in 1948–1974 period, the Yugoslav constitutional system was dominated by class principle as opposed to national identity, while in 1974–1991 period national identity gains the same level of importance as a class principle.[45] Nationalism showed its destructive nature against the RoL just before the dissolution of the former Yugoslavia, during and after armed conflict on the territory of the former Yugoslavia,[46] so the question of ethnic nationalism and the RoL will be discussed in the part of the paper on the development of the RoL in B&H. Right before the dissolution of the former Yugoslavia there was a wide ethnicization of judicial power which in itself could have indicated what consequences nationalism would leave on all Yugoslav citizens causing armed conflicts across the former Yugoslavia but also problems in the development of the RoL in post-Yugoslavian states.[47]

3.3 Efficiency of Institutional Control Over the Work of State Institutions

Problematic relations between the judiciary and the Party and the protection of human rights in the former Yugoslavia all together had enormous impact on the efficacy of institutional work control in state institutions. As many other countries, The former Yugoslavia faced the issue of civil servants' work control. The problem of control was reflected in the fact that the Yugoslav authorities did not have reliable information on the quality of civil servants' work because there was no real freedom of speech and thus public criticism of the government, therefore, the only source of information for the then Yugoslav authorities were civil servants who conveyed a distorted image the civil service work quality, and public did not give real criticism because of restrictions on freedom of speech.

This endangered the government's goal to create an effective and law-abiding system of government. As opposed to that, civil servants who behaved arbitrarily were not sanctioned for such behavior because criticism was not allowed.[48] It definitely influenced the economic activity in the state so the total external debt of Yugoslavia in 1980s was 2 billion dollars.[49] Yugoslavia was not effective in the institutional governance, although, unlike in other communist states it developed principles for the protection of constitutionality and legality. It was only an illusion of institutional functioning which at lower level behaved arbitrarily while the higher-level institutions, aside the Party which was the main policy maker, did not have any

[44] Sekulić (1992), pp. 116–121.

[45] Baričević (2007), p. 207.

[46] See: Rusinow (1991).

[47] Cohen (1992), p. 313.

[48] Macfarlane (1990), p. 138.

[49] Andjelić (2003), p. 49.

significant role in the creation of political processes. In that context, there was quasi-constitutionalism in the former Yugoslavia based on the rule-by-law system.[50]

4 The Dissolution of the Former Yugoslavia and the Transition from the Rule-By-Law System to a System Based on the RoL in B&H

The General Framework Agreement for Peace in B&H (the Dayton Agreement) ended the armed conflict in B&H in 1995, but signing the agreement not only ended the armed conflict, but also established a completely different legal order, from the one that had previously existed when B&H was a part of the former Yugoslavia. After the declaration of independence, B&H maintained a similar constitution it had as the former Yugoslav republic.[51] The new Constitution entered into force upon signing of the Dayton Agreement, which is part of Annex IV of the Dayton Agreement and which confirms the continuity of B&H, but also brings innovations that were not applied in the legal tradition of Yugoslavia and B&H.[52] The most important change in the legal life of B&H was an explicit turn to the RoL.

4.1 The Constitution of B&H and the RoL

Unlike the Constitution of Yugoslavia, the constitution adopted with the signing of the Dayton Agreement, brought about an explicit turn towards the RoL. Article I (2) of the Constitution of B&H (hereinafter: CB&H) states: 'Bosnia and Herzegovina shall be a democratic state, which shall operate under the rule of law and with free and democratic elections.'[53] In addition to the declarative turn towards the RoL, the CB&H creates preconditions for the implementation of the RoL, in a way that guarantees the legal supremacy and the protection of internationally recognized human rights. The legal supremacy is evident in the role of the Constitutional Court of B&H (hereinafter: CCB&H), which guarantees compliance with, not only constitution and acts, but also the European Convention for the Protection of Human Rights and Fundamental Freedoms (ECHR) and other rules of international law. Therefore, the CCB&H has three jurisdictions. The first is to resolve any

[50] Baričević (2007), p. 208.

[51] Constitution of the Republic of B&H, the country's official name from 1992 to 1995, was very similar to the constitution the repulic had as a part of Yugoslavia, with a lot of articles and very detailed regulation.

[52] The new Constitution is thus an example of an Anglo-American legal tradition with a small number of members and very general regulations.

[53] Article I(2) of the CB&H.

dispute that arises between the Entities or between B&H and an Entity or Entities, or between institutions of B&H. The jurisdiction of the CCB&H but not limited to, is to examine whether an Entity's decision to establish a special parallel relationship with a neighboring state is consistent with the CB&H, and jurisdiction over issues whether any provision of an Entity's constitution or a law of an Entity is compatible with the CB&H. The second is the appellate jurisdiction over issues arising for a review of a final judgement. The third jurisdiction relates to concrete constitutional review, where each court in B&H is allowed to initiate a request for the review of law constitutionality concerning whether a law, on whose validity its decision depends, is compatible with the CB&H. In that case the CB&H determines not only whether the law is constitutional, but also its compliance with the ECHR, other laws in B&H and general rules of international law.[54] Therefore, the CB&H has supremacy over all laws and other legal provisions.[55] The second characteristic of the CB&H is the guarantee of human rights. The CB&H prescribes the protection of human rights like no other constitution in the world.[56] No other constitution, like the CB&H guarantees the implementation of international human rights treaties.[57] Nevertheless, the ECHR has a central role in the CB&H. Thus, Article II(2) states that the human rights and freedoms set forth in the ECHR will apply directly in B&H and will have legal supremacy.[58] Paragraph 6 of the same article states that all institutions in B&H, including all courts, agencies, governmental organs, and instrumentalities operated by or within the Entities are obliged to apply the rights listed in the ECHR.[59] As well, Article III/3(b) of the CB&H states that general principles of international law shall be an integral part of the law of B&H and the Entities.[60] As we have already stated, in the event that any of the courts refers any law for the review of its constitutionality, the CCB&H does not assess whether a specific law is only in accordance with the CB&H and the laws of B&H, but also with the ECHR and general rules of international law that can be applied in that particular case.

The CB&H implements a monist system, since it supports the interference from the international law on the internal B&H system for the protection of human rights without the approval of the legislative power.[61] Unlike the Yugoslav Constitution which prescribed that constitutional rights can be limited by law, the CB&H limits the legislator from introducing new norms which could limit the rights guaranteed by

[54] The position and competencies of the CCB&H are regulated by Article VI of the CB&H. Provisions on the jurisdiction of the CCB&H are regulated by Article VI (3).

[55] Išerić (2019), p. 6.

[56] Chandler (2000), p. 92.

[57] Annex I of the CB&H lists the international agreements that will be applied in B&H, regardless of whether B&H has ratified them or not.

[58] Direct application guarantees the application of the provisions of the ECHR without the need to ratify the ECHR.

[59] Article II(6) of the CB&H.

[60] Article III/3 (b) of the CB&H.

[61] Vehabović (2006), pp. 54–60.

the CB&H. Namely, Article X of the Constitution states no amendment may eliminate or diminish any of the rights and freedoms referred to in Article II of the Constitution.[62] In this respect, the CB&H, unlike the Constitution of Yugoslavia, created a better legal framework for the implementation of the RoL, because it enabled the international protection of human beings, without the active role of the legislature in the ratification of international treaties. Formally, the Constitution of Yugoslavia guaranteed the supremacy of law through the protection of constitutionality and legality, but in practice, the Party had supremacy. The CB&H also guarantees the protection of constitutionality and legality, with one important distinction, a monistic approach that enables the protection of human rights through the application of international instruments.

4.2 The CB&H and Ethnic Exclusivism

The CB&H created the preconditions for the development of the RoL. But in addition to being an instrument for the development of a democratic society, the CB&H was also an instrument in achieving a long-awaited peace so it contains certain provisions that guarantee exclusive rights only to members of certain ethnic groups, which some see as contrary to the RoL and human rights. The creation of exclusive rights for certain ethnic groups is already implied at in the Preamble of the CB&H, which reads: 'Bosniacs, Croats, and Serbs, as constituent peoples (along with Others), and citizens of B&H hereby determine that the CB&H is as follows.'[63] Basis of the constitutional legitimacy in B&H is significantly different from other democratic countries. Democratic countries have the generally accepted principle of people's sovereignty. The decision-making process in these institutions is based on this principle. This is not opposed to the increasingly common collective protection of the respective national, linguistic, religious, and other collectivities. The starting point of the CB&H which enables ethnic exclusivism is in the aforementioned Preamble of the CB&H and in this way, at least two particularities of the constitutional order of B&H are set.[64] The constituent peoples[65] have gained the importance of a constitutional category. In the Preamble of the CB&H, the constituent peoples are placed in the first place, which leads to the conclusion that the CB&H gives priority to the ethnicity over the position of citizen. The model of the constituency of

[62] Article X of the CB&H.

[63] Preamble of the CB&H.

[64] Trnka (2009), pp. 4–5.

[65] Trnka himself pointed out: 'In syntagm 'constitutent peoples', the word *peoples* denotes ethnonational identity, that is a special national identity and not the people (populus) as a collective of individuals, memebers of one state. The term 'constituent' etymologically means basic, integral, elemental, important, that determines. The word derives from latin word 'constituo', which as verb means to appoint, regulate, set up, establish, form; and as a noun 'constitution' it means internal structure, order, organization, institution (political), constitutuion, law.' Trnka (2000), pp. 49–50.

the people as it exists in B&H is unique, but also discriminatory.[66] Discrimination is evident in the establishment of exclusive ethnic rights, which prevents citizens who are not members of the constituent peoples to exercise the same rights. Ethnic exclusivism at state level can be seen in the manner the members of the Presidency and delegates in the House of Peoples of the Parliamentary Assembly of B&H are elected. So Article IV(1) of the CB&H states: 'The House of Peoples shall comprise 15 Delegates, two-thirds from the Federation (including five Croats and five Bosniacs) and one-third from the Republika Srpska (five Serbs).',[67] whereas Article V of the CB&H states: 'The Presidency of B&H shall consist of three Members: one Bosniac and one Croat, each directly elected from the territory of the Federation, and one Serb directly elected from the territory of the Republika Srpska.'[68] We can see that seats for members of the Presidency and delegates in the House of Peoples of B&H are strictly reserved for the constituent peoples, which the European Court of Human Rights (ECtHR) determined to be in conflict with the ECHR.

The ECtHR judgments in cases *Sejdić and Finci v. B&H*[69] and *Zornić v. B&H*[70] best depict the inconsistency of the constituent people model with the provisions of the ECHR, but also with the RoL. The ECtHR in these judgements established that the CB&H contains discriminatory provisions against persons not belonging to one of the three constituent peoples with regard to active and passive suffrage. Specifically, the ECtHR has determined that persons who are not members of the constituent peoples cannot stand for the president elections and cannot be elected to the House of Peoples of B&H. In this regard, the ECtHR found a violation of Article 14[71] in conjunction with Article 3 of Protocol 1[72] to the European Convention and Article 1 of Protocol 12[73] to the European Convention. In the judgment in *Zornić v. B&H*, the ECtHR, referring to the previous judgment in *Sejdić and Finci*, found:

> In Sejdić and Finci the Court observed that when the impugned constitutional provisions were put in place a very fragile ceasefire was in effect on the ground and that the provisions were designed to end a brutal conflict marked by genocide and 'ethnic cleansing'. The nature of the conflict was such that the approval of the 'constituent peoples' was necessary to ensure peace. However, now, more than eighteen years after the end of the tragic conflict, there could no longer be any reason for the maintenance of the contested constitutional provisions. The Court expects that democratic arrangements will be made without further delay. In view of the need to ensure effective political democracy, the Court considers that the time has come for a political system which will provide every citizen of B&H with the right to stand for elections to the Presidency and the House of Peoples of B&H without discrimination

[66] See: Decision U-5/98 of the CCB&H which states that the principle of constituent peoples is determined as 'overarching' principle of the CB&H with which the Entities must fully comply.

[67] Article IV of the CB&H.

[68] Article V of the CB&H.

[69] Case of Sejdić and Finci v. B&H (Applications nos. 27996/06 and 34836/06).

[70] Case of Zornić v. B&H (Application no. 3681/06).

[71] Article 14 of ECHR.

[72] Article 3 of Protocol No. 1 ECHR.

[73] Article 1 of Protocol No. 12 ECHR.

> based on ethnic affiliation and without granting special rights for constituent people to the exclusion of minorities or citizens of B&H.[74]

The implications of the ECHR judgment, which have not yet been enforced, have a dual effect on B&H, that is, B&H has an international obligation as a state that has ratified the ECHR to enforce the ECtHR judgments, but B&H also has an internal obligation to enforce those judgments because the monistic nature of the constitutional provisions translates international obligations into domestic legal obligations.[75] In this sense, the CB&H is between the RoL and ethnic democracy and faces the problem of contradictions between the predominance of ethnic groups and civil equality.[76] The CB&H has the characteristics of constitutional nationalism, as Hayden defines it as a constitutional structure that privileges the members of ethnic nation over other residents in a particular state.[77]

5 Building the RoL in B&H: A New Constitution, the Same Obstacles

The CB&H provides a better legal framework for the development of the RoL from the one that existed in Yugoslavia. Although the adoption of the CB&H has created a better legal framework for the implementation of the RoL, B&H has been facing inherited obstacles to the implementation of the RoL. So, the problems that existed in the former Yugoslavia continue to exist in B&H.

5.1 Relations Between the CCB&H (the Judiciary) and Political Parties in B&H

What preceded the dissolution of the former Yugoslavia was the introduction of a multi-party system in 1990, when the Party lost its primacy in political processes. After the end of the armed conflict in B&H, the same political parties that were the key players during the war continue to rule in peace.[78] The nationalist rhetoric, which was the cause of the war, continued after the war, putting the interests of ethnic groups before the interests of the state and the RoL. The multi-party system initiated the process of democratization in B&H, but it also contributed to the growth of ethnic nationalism. Parties founded before the armed conflict in B&H were

[74] Case of Zornić v. B&H (Application no. 3681/06).

[75] See: Begić (2016).

[76] Perry (2005), pp. 215–216. Also see: Bassuener (2017).

[77] Rangelov (2014), pp. 23–24.

[78] Party of Democratic Action (SDA), Croation Democratic Union (HDZ), Serb Democratic Party (SDS).

founded in order to protect the interests of their respective ethnic group and even though in their programs they formally advocated for the protection of democratic values and the RoL, in practice this was not the case. Consequently, after the war the entire legal order was ethnicized, even more than what the CB&H allows and the interests of political parties also prevail over the institutions of B&H.

After signing the peace agreement and once the nationalists formed the government it became impossible to establish the RoL, because belonging to a particular ethnic group was more important than any law.[79] The spread of nationalist politics became legitimate during the war and turning one group against the other which weakened the legal order and created a certain amount of uncertainty. Although the CB&H bases its legitimacy to some extent on the protection of collective ethnic rights, it is not the only basis for the legitimacy of the CB&H, but with nationalists coming to power, ethnicity became the only source of legitimacy. In fact, even though the CB&H guarantees privileged rights to certain ethnic groups, it is not only committed to the protection of certain collectives, but the CB&H has a basis of legitimacy in the protection of human rights, the RoL and democratic values. However, when nationalists gained power, the strength of law and state institutions diminished in the process of ensuring the legitimacy of legal order based on the RoL.[80]

The election of judges of the CCB&H is regulated by Article VI of the CB&H, which stipulates that four judges are elected from the territory of the Federation of B&H (FB&H), and two judges are elected from the Republic of Srpska (RS), while the ECtHR president elects three judges after consulting the President of the state. Apart from that, it is stated that judges who are elected must be prominent lawyers of high moral standing.[81] The CB&H does not prescribe any other condition for the election of judges of the CCB&H, not even the ethnicity of the individual who is elected, which is logical from the aspect of the RoL, since judges should protect the principles of the constitutional state and the principles of the RoL, and not the interests of ethnic groups. But the actions of B&H institutions, especially the House of Representatives of the FB&H and the National Assembly of the RS, led to the custom of electing judges for the CCB&H consisting of two Bosniak judges and two Croat judges from the FB&H and two Serb judges from the RS.[82]

The established constitutional custom is not in line with the RoL and human rights guaranteed by the CB&H. Therefore, as Išerić states, the mentioned constitutional custom is *contra constitutionem* and is not in accordance with the CB&H.[83] Thus, the institution in charge of protecting the RoL and human rights falls under the influence of nationalist policies and its integrity is damaged by the fact that the method of election itself is not in line with the RoL and human rights. That same

[79] Andjelić (2003), p. 196.

[80] Perry (2005), pp. 7–10.

[81] Article VI of the Constitution B&H.

[82] See: Išerić (2017).

[83] Ibid.

institution should protect those values, which sometimes seems absurd when the very manner in which the CCB&H judges are elected is not in accordance with those values.[84] According to Joseph Marko, a former judge of the CCB&H, some of the CCB&H judges act as protectors of the constituent peoples, not the CB&H.[85] This proves that nationalist rule and the RoL cannot coexist, as nationalists base their power on ethnic representation, while the RoL requires that all citizens be treated equally, regardless of their ethnicity, so ethnic policies create norms that privilege members of certain ethnic groups where such norms should not exist. In addition, the said constitutional custom was created in order to control the institution with the supreme authority in the protection of the RoL, much like the Party controlled the judiciary in the former Yugoslavia by appointing mostly judges who were members of the Party. The ethno-nationalist parties, with the stated custom, decided to bring the CCB&H under control by ethnic criteria.

Re-building the impaired and distressed judiciary sector is the main condition for the establishing the rule of law.[86] Unfortunately, B&H is an example that the introduction of multi-party elections without the establishment of institutions that will guarantee the RoL, especially in a country with strong ethno-nationalism, will not lead to democratization, but to ethnicization and strengthening of political parties instead of state institutions.[87] As Paddy Ashdown points out: 'This, above all, was the mistake we made in B&H (...) It is much more important to establish the rule of law quickly than to establish democracy quickly. Because without the former, the latter is soon undermined. In B&H, we got these priorities the wrong way round.'[88]

In the case of Krstan Simović, a former judge of the CCB&H, who was removed from office for jeopardizing the independence of the CCB&H, after the discovery of a letter sent to Milorad Dodik, the president of the Alliance of Independent Social Democrats (SNSD) in which Simović stated that he is available should the president need help with the staff selection and any other professional assistance, adding that they need to achieve a higher degree of cooperation.[89] This is a positive example of the functioning of the RoL in B&H, but it does not deny the fact that the judges of the CCB&H, as we have already stated, have acted as protectors of the constituent peoples instead of being protectors of the CB&H. The second example is the case of the president of High Judicial and Prosecutorial Council of B&H (the Council) Milan Tegeltija, who as the president of the institution in charge of ensuring the independence of the judiciary in B&H, stated for Radio Free Europe:

> I did say that according to the Law on the High Judicial and Prosecutorial Council, I am a RS representative. We have obligations towards RS because of the Law on the High Judicial and

[84] See: Sahadžić (2013).

[85] Išerić (2017), p. 23.

[86] Hrle (2016), p. 61. Also, on the building the rule of law in post-conflict societies see: Stromseth (2021).

[87] Blagovčanin (2020), pp. 20–25.

[88] See: Chandler (2004), p. 313.

[89] Ademović et al. (2012), p. 171.

> Prosecutorial Council that was created by the Agreement on the transfer of certain competencies.[90]

The statement was made during an extra-institutional gathering organized by Milorad Dodik after the CCB&H's judgement, which declared Article 53 of the Law on Agricultural Land of the RS unconstitutional.[91] Gathering was organized so that all Serbs working in the institutions of B&H would make an agreement on future activities in the institutions of B&H and possible blockades. This shows that individuals who were supposed to guarantee the independence of the judiciary are essentially working in the interest of ethno-national policies. This is a negative example because Milan Tegeltija was never sanctioned for his statement and actions. The third example is case of Haris Zahiragić, a young SDA activist who made guest appearance on the national television FACE TV to talk about ventilators scandal that happened at the beginning of the COVID-19 pandemic,[92] and who admitted that if he learned details about the participants in the scandal, he would not share his findings with prosecutors office but he would inform his party.[93] In that context, the one-party system that existed in Yugoslavia was replaced by the multi-party system, which did not bring democratization, but partitocracy and ethnicization of the political and legal system of B&H.

5.2 *Efficiency of Human Rights Protection in B&H*

The protection of human rights in B&H faces two problems, one is the European model of constitutional review and the positivist concept of law by the judiciary. Although the CB&H is written in the Anglo-American style, the CB&H prescribes a European model the protection of constitutionality, which means that only the CCB&H can review the constitutionality of statutes. Thus, Article VI of the CB&H prescribes two types of review, abstract review of constitutionality and concrete review of constitutionality. According to the CB&H, abstract constitutional review applies to:

> Disputes may be referred only by a member of the Presidency, by the Chair of the Council of Ministers, by the Chair or a Deputy Chair of either chamber of the Parliamentary Assembly, by one-fourth of the members of either chamber of the Parliamentary Assembly, or by one-fourth of either chamber of a legislature of an Entity.[94]

---

[90] Statement by Milan Tegeltija given for Radio Free Europe, available at: https://www.slobodnaevropa.org/a/vsts-tegeltija-ustavni-sud-bih/30434809.html. Accessed 3 March 2021.

[91] The Decision of the CCB&H: U-8/19.

[92] See: Nurkić and Jahić (2020).

[93] Haris Zahiragić guest appearance in the FACE TV program, available at: https://www.fokus.ba/vijesti/bih/zahiragic-kad-sam-se-uclanio-u-sda-bilo-je-puno-nepostenih-sad-ih-pola-ih-nema/1758488/. Accessed 3 March 2021.

[94] Article VI(3) of the CB&H.

On the other hand, the concrete review of constitutionality applies on issues referred by any court in B&H concerning whether a law, on whose validity its decision depends, is constitutional. The paper does not analyze the appellate jurisdiction of the CCB&H, which is most common and covers only individual legal acts, so in that sense it does not refer to the protection of constitutionality, that is, putting unconstitutional laws out of force. Using law to violate human rights is a characteristic of the rule-by-law system, and therefore constant constitutional review of laws, in terms of the protection of constitutionality and human rights, increases the degree of RoL and reduces the degree of rule by law. Ordinary courts have also the obligation to protect the RoL or as Begić points out, the obligation of ordinary courts in B&H is to ensure properly guaranteed rights and freedoms unless citizens initiate individual proceedings before them.'[95]

As Trnka refers, the issue with the abstract review of constitutionality in B&H is that the CB&H set active proponents for review of constitutionality very closely, and thus immobilized the activities of the CCB&H, in terms of putting unconstitutional legal regulations out of force.[96] Due to the monopoly position of the CCB&H in terms of protection of constitutionality, the protection of human rights is largely limited due to the narrow circle of proponents for the protection of constitutionality. An alternative offered for the protection of constitutionality, and thus the protection of human rights, is a concrete constitutional review that allows any court to request the evaluation law's constitutionality that is to be applied in a particular case.

Concrete constitutional review in the European model of constitutional review remains the only way for the active participation of ordinary courts in the review of constitutionality.[97] The problem with concrete constitutional review is that ordinary courts, both in B&H[98] and in Eastern European countries, have the lowest rate of requests for concrete constitutional review. This issue is characteristic for states that are in the process of transition from an authoritarian government to democratic.[99] In this regard B&H has the issue with legal positivism, which also existed in the former Yugoslavia. Ordinary court judges apply the law mechanically, without broader law application, and therefore there is no concrete control of constitutionality, more precisely, judges do not view themselves as the third pillar of power, but a mechanism for enforcing laws passed by the legislature.

In this sense, the judiciary in B&H, similar to other post-socialist countries, fears to become a true judicial power.[100] This leads to application of unconstitutional legal regulations by judges, which makes it impossible to establish the RoL. When the

---

[95] Begić (2017), p. 83.

[96] Trnka (2006), pp. 367–368.

[97] Sadurski (2014), pp. 36–37.

[98] Since the entry into force of the CB&H until the moment of writing of this paper, concrete review of constitutionality has been initiated 52 times. Data is avaliable at: http://www.ccbh.ba/odluke/. Accessed 5 April 2022.

[99] Sadurski (2014), p. 35.

[100] Ibid, p. 68.

CCB&H is immobilized due to a narrow circle of proponents and where judges lack courage and use legal positivism, regardless how broadly the CB&H protects human rights, if it is not used in practice, the RoL remains just a letter on paper.

In essence, the concrete review of constitutionality is applied only when ordinary courts suspect the unconstitutionality of the law, and in cases where courts are convinced that the law is unconstitutional, they should apply the provisions of the constitution directly.[101] Unfortunately, the concrete review of constitutionality has not been developed in B&H, nor the direct application of constitutional provisions by ordinary courts, although the CB&H itself stipulates that all institutions, including courts, are obliged to apply the ECHR. More frequent constitutional review would greatly help alleviate the positivist understanding and application of law by ordinary courts, also because the CCB&H has practiced the application of the ECHR in its judgments.[102] The problem of legal positivism was also identified in the Expert's Report on Rule of Law issues in B&H (Report), known as Priebe Report, states that in many areas, legislation in B&H is in line with European and other international standards, but there is a considerable gap between legislation and practice, and the positivist and formalistic behavior of many office holders often appears as a real obstacle to proper implementation of such standards.[103] Also, this problem can be explained by the fact that B&H throughout history has been developing 'subservient legal culture'[104] where the interest of the state is more important than the human rights of citizens.

For the protection of constitutionality, as well as human rights, concrete review of constitutionality is much more important than abstract review, because in that way the legal system reacts faster in eliminating unconstitutional regulations. On this issue Ackerman points:

> if a court must wait for a specific complaint by an ordinary individual, it may take a while before a bitterly politicized dispute makes its way into the judges' chambers"; and this pause, and the resultant "cooling down" of the political passions, "provides the court with a valuable political resource to sustain itself as part of the new constitutional order.[105]

This is particularly evident in B&H. Application of certain laws in B&H has had a great legal impact and evaluating these laws as unconstitutional has no merit due to their effect, so the legal system in B&H has developed a sort of practice to apply unconstitutional legislation.

The first unconstitutional law that had negative consequences and still can be seen, especially when it comes to the privatization process, was the Law on Ownership Transformation passed in 1994 by the FB&H, during the armed conflict, which prescribed the transformation of publicly owned property into state property. Such an important law and adopted during the war is certainly unconstitutional, but it

[101] Ibid, p. 37.

[102] See: Ademović et al. (2012).

[103] Expert Report on Rule of Law issues in B&H, para 20.

[104] On 'subservient legal culture' see: Hasanbegović (2021).

[105] Sadurski (2014), p. 94.

also implied what would follow, and that was plunder of public property, with devastating effects on B&H's economy.[106] Such law has never been declared unconstitutional, although the very manner in which it was enacted, that is, the circumstances in which it was enacted, imply its unconstitutionality.

Another law that brought adverse legal consequences is the Law on Bankruptcy Proceedings of Federation B&H. The law was passed in 2006 and put the workers of economic entities who filed for bankruptcy in unfavorable position by limiting employees' pay claims to only last eight months regardless of the number of unpaid wages. Such legislation is contrary to the human rights guaranteed by the ECHR, but also other international treaties,[107] which was confirmed by the Constitutional Court of the FB&H in 2016, declaring the said law unconstitutional.[108] However, the said law had legal consequences and restricted the rights of workers for ten years, and courts applied it regularly, without requesting a review of the constitutionality of the said law. Such a practice has harmed thousands of workers, and the very verdict of the Constitutional Court of the FB&H loses its significance when the law had such adverse consequences that it is impossible to annul. In the above example, we can see legal system of B&H suffered consequences because of inaction and fear in ordinary courts, when it was necessary to protect the RoL and human rights. Although the CB&H created a solid legal framework for the protection of the RoL, the inaction of ordinary courts and the positivist approach to law and its application, human rights are not protected to the extent prescribed by the CB&H. Immobility of the CCB&H, which developed a high-level practice of the protection of human rights, prevents efficient and effective protection of human rights and the RoL.

5.3 *Efficiency of State Institutions in B&H*

The two main characteristics of institutions in B&H are inertia and corruption. B&H like all other postcommunist societies is simply obsessed with corruption.[109] Additionally, B&H was ruled by the Ottoman Empire, therefore B&H is simultaneously a post-communist and post-ottoman state. That fact has double negative influences on fighting against corruption.[110] Similar to the situation in the former Yugoslavia, corruption is a consequence of the balance of power between political parties, the judiciary, and the possibility of protecting human rights. Of course another reason is the armed conflict which consequently created new political elite to replace the

[106] Begić (2014), pp. 35–36.

[107] Begić and Razić (2015), pp. 56–66.

[108] Decision of the Constitutional Court of the Federation of B&H, U-27/15.

[109] Krastev (2005), p. 323.

[110] See Uberti (2018), p. 35. Uberti proved that '(...) the countries that experienced socialist or Ottoman rule for a longer period of time tend to have more corruption today.'

communists, and was based on the control of previous regime's state resources and the incorporation of the old nomenclature into the new system, which led to economic and social inequality.[111] Moreover, the achievements of pluralism and economic liberalism have been nullified by corruption, and the very source of corruption lies in the fact that ethnically defined political parties control the administrative, judicial and other state authorities.[112] Also, it is essential to notice that 'administrative corruption is simply an unavoidable consequence of Bosnia's ongoing transition from a managed to a market economy.'[113] As shown in Corruption Perceptions Index released by Transparency International, B&H ranks among the worst in Europe.[114] Also, according to the International Crisis Group, much of the corruption is caused by '(...) the existence of unreasonable and irrational tax codes and business regulations that force much economic activity underground.'[115] Of course, one of the reasons why B&H has a problem with widespread corruption is the transition from managed economy to a market economy. Another problem is the culture in B&H because 'Where roles and relationships prevail over rules and regulations, it is essential to change the culture.'[116] Therefore, one of the key factors for fighting against corruption in B&H is establishing the rule of law culture, where rules and procedures will be more important than roles and relationships. In that sense, B&H is a good example of 'partial reform syndrome' in the fight against the corruption,[117] because B&H still did not face the causes of the corruption.

The inertia of the legal system in B&H, which is evident from the numerous CCB&H decisions on the violation of right to trial in reasonable time,[118] is in fact an indicator that legal system in B&H does not function in the interest of citizens. Courts are slow in executive and labor disputes, but are very efficient in defamation trials of journalists where accusations are mostly made by politicians.[119] This shows that judges are instruments of authorities, which also confirms the Alan Uzelac's statement that the instrumentalist concept of law that judges apply is one of the relics of the past system that still exists in the states formed after the dissolution of the former Yugoslavia.[120]

---

[111] Bieber (2006), p. 34.

[112] Friedman (2004), p. 85.

[113] Donais (2013), p. 202.

[114] Corruption Perceptions Index, available at: https://www.transparency.org/en/cpi/2020/index/nzl. Accessed 5 March 2021.

[115] Friedman (2004), p. 104.

[116] Pajić (2002), p. 126.

[117] Donais (2013), p. 203.

[118] Expert Report on Rule of Law issues in B&H, para 34.

[119] Koga štiti bh pravosuđe: Pravna država najefikasnija u procesuiranju novinara za „klevetu", available at: https://inforadar.ba/koga-stiti-bh-pravosude-pravna-drzava-najefikasnija-u-procesuiranju-novinara-za-klevetu/. Accessed 5 March 2021.

[120] Uzelac (2010), pp. 379–388.

Of course, all of these obstacles, in establishing the rule of law, are intertwined. Corruption is caused by non-adequately protection of human rights, i.e., inertia of the legal system because people are looking for other means how to satisfy their rights. Also, partitocracy causes distrust in state institutions, so B&H citizens use connections in parties to satisfy their rights. In that sense, corruption is the consequence of all of these problems, lack of adequate protection of human rights, relations between parties and the judiciary, and inertia of the legal system.

6 Conclusion

'The rule of law, a functioning prerequisite for (...) liberal democracy, is absent'[121] in B&H. The current legal system of B&H was created in specific circumstances, primarily with the task of stopping the armed conflict, and that aim is fulfilled.[122] But in addition to stopping the conflict, the new constitutional order aimed to create a system based on the RoL and the protection of human rights. Based on the presented facts, we conclude that the CB&H has not fulfilled its function in ensuring the RoL and that all those obstacles for the implementation of the RoL that existed in Yugoslavia are inherited in the legal system of B&H. The causes of these problems are inherited from the former Yugoslavia, but also from the Ottoman Empire, and these causes are authoritarian political culture and 'subservient legal culture'. In this context, Edin Sarčević seems correct to state that B&H is currently between a 'constitutional and authoritarian state' due to the provisions of the CB&H, which favor certain ethnic groups and at the same time postulates the principle of the RoL.[123] Thus, B&H is currently between an authoritarian rule-by-law system and the RoL. But this is not only, as Edin Sarčević points out, due to the CB&H determined by ethnicity, but also, as explained in the paper, due to keeping the relics of the past system in the newly created system in B&H. Changing the CB&H according to the ECtHR judgments related to the abolition of privileges granted to the constituent peoples is one of the preconditions for the implementation of the RoL in full capacity, but it will not be sufficient for the full implementation of the RoL. The CB&H had a good starting position for building the RoL,[124] but the judicial proceedings in practice and relations between political parties and the judiciary, the inefficiency in human rights protection and ultimately the inefficiency of state institutions at all levels are not the result of ethnic privileges in the CB&H, but inherited problems from the former Yugoslavia. The CB&H provides a better legal framework for the protection of the RoL than the former Yugoslav legal system, but the potential of the CB&H has not been used, because the direct application of the

[121] Kmezić (2020), p. 195.

[122] See: Chandler (2006).

[123] Šarčević (2009), pp. 68–75.

[124] Chandler (2000), p. 92.

ECHR by the CCB&H and ordinary courts and the review of the constitutionality that would put an end to the rule of unconstitutional legal regulations, are possibilities provided by the CB&H, but currently not used. Therefore, B&H is the state of 'unfounded normative optimism', as Hasanbegović calls the states where formal protection of human rights is not founded in the culture of that state.[125] In this regard, the basis of B&H's legal order certainly is not the RoL, but the 'rule of unconstitutional regulations' and the 'rule of ethnically defined interests'. If it wishes to achieve the rule of law, B&H, primarily has to face the causes of the existing obstacles. Without that, B&H will not be able to make true progress in establishing the RoL.

Case-Law

ECtHR, Case of Sejdić and Finci v. B&H (Applications nos. 27996/06 and 34836/06).
ECtHR, Case of Zornić v. Bosnia and Herzegovina (Application no. 3681/06).
Constitutional Court of the Federation of BiH, Decision, U-27/15.

References

Ademović N, Joseph M, Marković G (2012) Ustavno pravno Bosne i Hercegovine. Fondacija Konrad Adenauer, Sarajevo
Andjelić N (2003) Bosnia-Herzegovina: the end of a legacy. Frank Cass, London
Baričević V (2007) The constitutions of socialist Yugoslavia and successor countries: continuities or discontinuities in the understanding of constitutional identity. Anali hrvatskog politološkog društva 4:203–225
Bassuener K (2017) A durable oligarchy: Bosnia and Herzegovina's false post-war democratic transition. In: Ramet SP, Hassenstab CM, Listhaug O (eds) Building democracy in the Yugoslav successor states: accomplishments, setbacks, and challenges since 1990. Cambridge University Press, Cambridge, pp 216–255. https://doi.org/10.1017/9781316848289.010
Begić Z (2014) War, peace and the protests. In: Arsenijević D (ed) Unbribable Bosnia and gensburg Herzegovina. Nomos, Baden Baden, pp 35–44
Begić Z (2016) Legal capacities of the Dayton constitution in the process of accession of Bosnia and Herzegovina to European Union. J Polit Law 9:11–20. https://doi.org/10.5539/jpl.v9n1p11
Begić Z (2017) Position of ordinary courts in direct implementation of constitutional norms: new perspective in the case of legislative silence in Bosnia and Herzegovina. In: Rainer A, Roth H (eds) Constitutional courts and ordinary courts: cooperation or conflict? Universitätsverlag Regensburg, Regensburg, pp 59–77
Begić Z, Razić S (2015) Constitutionality of the Bankruptcy proceedings in the federation of Bosnia and Herzegovina: how did we kill working class. Društveni ogledi – Časopis za pravnu teoriju i praksu 2:49–69
Bensosn L (2001) Yugoslavia: a concise history. Palgrave Macmillan, New York

[125] Hasanbegović (2021), pp. 123–139.

Bieber F (2006) Post-War Bosnia ethnicity, inequality and public sector governance. Palgrave Macmillan, New York.

Bingham T (2010) The rule of law. Penguin Books, London

Blagovčanin S (2020) The rule of the Cartel. Transparency international Bosna i Hercegovina, Banja Luka.

Campbell D (1998) National destruction: violence, identity, and justice in Bosnia. University Press of Minnesota, Minnesota

Chandler D (2000) Bosnia: faking democracy after Dayton. Pluto Press, London

Chandler D (2004) Imposing the 'rule of law': the lessons of bih for peacebuildingin iraq. Int Peacekeep 11(2):312–333. https://doi.org/10.1080/1353331042000237292

Chandler D (2006) State-building in Bosnia: the limits of informal 'trusteeship'. Int J Peace Stud:17–38

Cohen LJ (1992) Post-federalism and judicial change in Yugoslavia: the rise of ethno-political justice. Int Polit Sci Rev 13:301–319

Coman R (2017) Rule of law promotion: US and EU experiences in Bosnia and Herzegovina, and Ukraine. In: Hadjiisky M, Pal LA, Walker C (eds) Public policy transfer: micro-dynamics and macro-effects New Horizons in Public Policy series. Edward Elgar Publishing Limited, Cheltenham, pp 151–173. https://doi.org/10.4337/9781785368042.00015

Degan ĐV (2011) Međunarodno pravo. Školska knjiga, Zagreb

Donais T (2013) Power politics and the rule of law in post-Dayton Bosnia. Stud Soc Just 7(2): 189–210. https://doi.org/10.26522/ssj.v7i2.1043

Dyzenhaus D (2021) Thomas Hobbes and the rule by law tradition. In: Meierhenrich J, Loughlin M (eds) The Cambridge companion to the rule of law. Cambridge University Press, Cambridge, pp 261–277. https://doi.org/10.1017/9781108600569.015

Elster J (1991) Constitutionalism in Eastern Europe: an introduction. Univ Chicago Law Rev 58: 447–482

Fisk WM (1971) The constitutionalism movement in Yugoslavia: a preliminary survey. Slavic Rev 30:277–297

Friedman F (2004) Bosnia and Herzegovina: a polity on the brink. Routledge, London

Haris Zahiragić guest appearance in the FACE TV program, Available at: https://www.fokus.ba/vijesti/bih/zahiragic-kad-sam-se-uclanio-u-sda-bilo-je-puno-nepostenih-sad-ih-pola-ih-nema/1758488/. Accessed 3 March 2021

Hasanbegović J (2021) Ka filozofiji prava kao filozofiji ljudskih prava. Dosije studio, Beograd

Hogić N (2020) The European Union's rule of law promotion in the Western Balkans: building a rule of law constituency. Croatian Yearb Eur Law Policy 1:197–223

Hrle MS (2016) Building the rule of law: judicial reform in Bosnia and Herzegovina. In: Keil S, Perry V (eds) State-building and democratization in Bosnia and Herzegovina. Routledge, Oxon, pp 61–82

Išerić H (2017) Izbor domaćih sudija Ustavnog suda Bosne i Hercegovine kao ustavni običaj contra constitutionem (Election of National Judges of the Constitutional Court of Bosnia and Herzegovina as a Contra Constitutionem Constitutional Practice). Pravna misao 11-12:17–47

Išerić H (2019) Uloga Ustavnog suda BiH u profiliranju federalnog uređenja BiH (The Role of the Constitutional Court in Profiling the Federal Structure of BiH). Sveske za javno pravo 38:44–69

Karčić F (2020) A study on legal formalism in the former Yugoslavia and its successor states. The Centre for Integrity in the Defence Sector

Kirbis A, Flere S (2017) Political culture in the Yugoslav successor states. In: Ramet SP, Hassenstab CM, Listhaug O (eds) Building democracy in the Yugoslav successor states: accomplishments, setbacks, and challenges since 1990. Cambridge University Press, Cambridge, pp 108–134. https://doi.org/10.1017/9781316848289.006

Kmezić M (2020) Rule of law and democracy in the Western Balkans: addressing the gap between policies and practice. Southeast Eur Black Sea Stud 20(1):183–198. https://doi.org/10.1080/14683857.2019.1706257

Koga štiti bh pravosuđe: Pravna država najefikasnija u procesuiranju novinara za "klevetu", Available at: https://inforadar.ba/koga-stiti-bh-pravosude-pravna-drzava-najefikasnija-u-procesuiranju-novinara-za-klevetu/
Krastev I (2005) Corruption, anti-corruption sentiments, and the rule of law. In: Czarnota A, Krygier M, Sadurski W (eds) Rethinking the rule of law after communism. Central European University Press, Budapest/New York, pp 323–341
Lapenna I (1972) Main features of the Yugoslav constitution 1946–1971. Int Comp Law Q 21:209–229
Leonardson GS, Mirčev D (1979) A structure for participatory democracy in the local community: the Yugoslav constitution of 1974. Comp Polit 11:189–203
Macfarlane LJ (1990) Human rights: realities and possibilities. Palgrave Macmillan
Maksimović I (1965) Constitutional socialism in Yugoslavia. ANNALS Am Acad Polit Soc Sci, 358: 159-169.
Moustafa T, Ginsburg T (2008) Introduction: the functions of courts in authoritarian politics. In: Ginsburg T, Moustafa T (eds) Rule by law: the politics of courts in authoritarian regimes. Cambridge University Press, New York, pp 1–13
Nurkić B, Jahić A (2020) The rule of law crisis and self-incurred immaturity. J Lib Int Aff 6:67–79. https://doi.org/10.47305/JLIA2060067n
Pajić Z (2002) Chapter 7 the role of institutions in peace building: (Rule of Law in Bosnia and Herzegovina). In: Butler F (ed) Human rights protection. Brill-Nijhoff, Leiden, pp 111–133. https://doi.org/10.1163/9789004480841_010
Perry V (2005) Ethnic democracy in Bosnia and Herzegovina: containing the spectre?. The Fate of Ethnic Democracy in Post Communist Europe, 209–239
Rangelov I (2014) Nationalism and the rule of law. Cambridge University Press, New York
Rusinow D (1991) Yugoslavia: Balkan breakup? Foreign Policy 83:143–159
Sadurski W (2014) Rights before courts: a study of constitutional courts in postcommunist states of Central and Eastern Europe. Springer, London
Sahadžić M (2013) Ustavni sud Bosnei Hercegovine: Mjesto na kojem se diskriminacija ukida ili mjesto na kojem diskriminacija doseže novu razinu? In: Banović D (ed) (Ne) budi ovca: O etničkoj diskriminaciji u BiH. Sarajevski otvoreni centar, Sarajevo, pp 30–31
Sajó A (1995) On old and new battles: obstacles to the rule of law in Eastern Europe. J Law Soc 22: 97–104
Šarčević E (2009) Dejtonski ustav: Karakteristike i karakteristični problemi. Konrad Adenauer Stiftung, Sarajevo
Sekulić D (1992) Nationalism versus democracy: legacies of Marxism. Int J Polit Cult Soc 6:113–132
Stone Sweet A (2003) Why Europe rejected American judicial review: and why it may not matter. Mich Law Rev 101:2744–2780
Stromseth JE (2021) Post-conflict rule of law. In: Meierhenrich J, Loughlin M (eds) The Cambridge companion to the rule of law. Cambridge University Press, Cambridge, pp 513–537. https://doi.org/10.1017/9781108600569.029
Tegeltija Milan's Statement Given to Radio Free Europe, Available at: https://www.slobodnaevropa.org/a/vsts-tegeltija-ustavni-sud-bih/30434809.html. Accessed 3 March 2021
Trnka K (2000) Konstitutivnost naroda. Vijeće Kongresa bošnjačkih intelektualaca, Sarajevo
Trnka K (2006) Ustavno pravo. Fakultet za javnu upravu, Sarajevo
Trnka K (2009) Specifičnosti ustavnog uređenja Bosne i Hercegovine. Nastanak–realizacija–perspektive. Revus 11:45–71
Tushnet M (2014) Rule by law or rule of law? Asia Pac Law Rev 22:79–92. https://doi.org/10.1080/10192557.2014.11745925
Uberti LJ (2018) Corruption in transition economies: socialist, Ottoman or structural? Econ Syst 42(4):533–555. https://doi.org/10.1016/j.ecosys.2018.05.001

Uvalić M (1992) Investment and property rights in Yugoslavia. Cambridge University Press, New York

Uzelac A (2010) Survival of the third legal tradition? Supreme Court Law Rev 49:379–388

Vehabović F (2006) Odnos Ustava Bosne i Hercegovine i Evropske konvencije za zaštitu ljudskih prava i osnovnih sloboda. Asocijacija Alumni Centra za interdisciplinarne postdiplomske studije, Sarajevo

Waldron J (2021) The rule of law and the role of courts. Glob Constit 10(1):91–105. https://doi.org/10.1017/S2045381720000283

Characterisation of Cryptoassets as a Separate Category of Digital Assets

Jura Golub

1 Introduction

The development of modern technology has posed new challenges to the legal order in terms of qualifying new types of subjects due to which legal entities enter into social relations, and from which legal relations are consequently derived. For a long time, the global community has focused on various types of digital assets such as cryptocurrencies, primarily for lucrative reasons, but also because of the unconventional way in which such assets are acquired and transferred in legal transactions. The aim of this paper is to define the concept of digital assets and, with special reference to cryptoassets, to consider the legal qualification of such assets. Given the fact that modern relationships involving cryptoassets are conducted over the Internet in digital form, questions of qualification of digital assets are becoming increasingly important.

Before delving deeper into what the concept of digital assets encompasses, it is worth recalling the basic conceptual definition of assets accepted by modern civil law doctrine in the continental European legal sphere. For better understanding, it is necessary to distinguish between assets and estate, as these terms are often mistakenly equated. Legal science defines assets in the legal sense as a set of subjective rights represented by a holder, and the objects to which these subjective rights refer can be quantified in monetary values.[1] On the other hand, an estate consists of goods

The work of doctoral student Jura Golub has been fully supported by the "Young researchers' career development project—training of doctoral students" of the Croatian Science Foundation.

[1] Klarić and Vedriš (2014), p. 97.

J. Golub (✉)
Josip Juraj Strossmayer University of Osijek, Faculty of Law, Osijek, Croatia
e-mail: jgolub@pravos.hr

I. Kunda et al. (eds.), *Balkan Yearbook of European and International Law 2022*, Balkan Yearbook of European and International Law 2022,
https://doi.org/10.1007/978-3-031-29432-7_9

treated as property of an individual who has certain subjective rights to these things. It is clear from the above that assets is a broader legal concept, which, in addition to the right to things, also includes those subjective rights whose objects are not exclusively things.[2] After the conceptual definition of assets in general, things become more interesting in the context of digital assets. Namely, the problematic question arises as to how cryptocurrencies and other types of cryptoassets should be qualified. Are they things, so that entities may acquire ownership rights and other rights *in rem* relating thereto? Or are they only certain rights in digital form with an exclusively obligatory character?

In order to answer the questions raised, the paper will analyze the private law regulation of cryptoassets *de lege lata* using a comparative method. The choice of legal order is conditioned by the existence of a certain regulation of cryptoassets from a private law aspect. Namely, many legal orders still do not explicitly regulate the private law aspect of cryptoassets. Also, the activity of certain foreign and international organizations in terms of proposing normative solutions related to the legal nature of cryptoassets will be reviewed.

2 Classification of Digital Assets

The concept of digital assets has been widely used for a long time, but there are difficulties in defining the content of digital assets. In reviewing the literature, one gets the impression that the definition of digital assets often omits certain types that can also be classified as digital assets. Progress in the definition of digital assets is primarily due to the standardisation of certain bodies. More recently, however, normative activity by certain national and supranational bodies has also contributed to the definition of certain types of digital assets.

The U.S. Uniform Law Commission (ULC) made a useful contribution to the definition of terms by adopting in 2015 the Revised Uniform Fiduciary Access to Digital Assets Act[3] (hereinafter:), which aims to allow a specific group of persons, such as executors or proxies, to access the testator's online user accounts.[4] Under , digital assets are defined as electronic records in which individuals have a right or interest. But they do not include the underlying asset or liability unless it is itself originally an electronic record. It is clear from the accompanying commentary that the definition of digital assets does not include underlying assets, such as funds in an online bank account. On the other hand, it does include all currently existing and

[2] Ibid., pp. 95–96.

[3] National Conference of Commissioners on Uniform State Laws (2015) Revised Uniform Fiduciary Access to Digital Assets Act. (hereinafter: RUFADAA) https://www.uniformlaws.org/viewdocument/final-act-with-comments-40?CommunityKey=f7237fc4-74c2-4728-81c6-b39a91ecdf22&tab=librarydocuments. Accessed 10 May 2022.

[4] Conway and Grattan (2017), p. 112.

future electronic records, i.e., information stored electronically on a user's computer and other digital devices, then content uploaded to websites, and digital ownership rights.[5] According to this definition, the term digital assets can include all electronically recorded information, regardless of where specific information is stored (Internet, computer, cell phone, etc.), which includes, for example, social networks, applications, and e-mail.[6] In addition, however, the interpretation of the concept of digital assets under should be broadened further. The reason for that is that underlying assets that were themselves originally recorded electronically, or assets that have an inherent electronic existence, are also considered digital assets. Specifically, cryptocurrencies, Internet domains, airline and hotel awards programmes are also considered digital assets as they all share the same characteristic—they exist solely in electronic form and cannot be represented in physical form.[7]

The European Law Institute (ELI) has given additional impetus to the definition of digital assets with its Principles on the Use of Digital Assets as Security (ELI Principles).[8] ELI, unlike the ULC, defines digital assets in more detail. According to ELI, a digital asset is any record or representation of value that is stored, displayed, and managed solely electronically through a virtual platform or database. It includes a record or representation of an asset that is tradable in the real world, regardless of whether the digital asset itself is held directly or through an account with an intermediary; it is subject to a right of control, enjoyment or use, regardless of whether those rights are legally characterised as proprietary, obligatory or of some other nature; and it can be transferred from one party to another, including by way of voluntary disposition.[9] Simply put, ELI adheres that digital assets have three basic characteristics. They are intangible assets expressed in electronic form; such assets confer certain rights on individuals, such as the right of access and enjoyment; and finally, an essential element of digital assets is their transferability. According to ELI, the broad concept of digital assets includes both cryptoassets and all non-cryptographically authenticated digital assets, as long as the digital assets have the characteristics mentioned above. For example, the types of digital assets include social media and other online accounts, cryptocurrencies, financial assets that exist only in electronic form, various types of tokens, etc.[10]

A somewhat simpler definition of digital assets has been provided by UNIDROIT. It states that digital assets are electronic records capable of being subject to control, where electronic records are information that cumulatively

[5]RUFADAA (2015).

[6]Walker (2017), pp. 53–54.

[7]Ibid., p. 54.

[8]European Law Institute (2022) ELI Principles on the Use of Digital Assets as Security. Report of the European Law Institute. https://www.europeanlawinstitute.eu/fileadmin/user_upload/p_eli/Publications/ELI_Principles_on_the_Use_of_Digital_Assets_as_Security.pdf. Accessed 10 May 2022.

[9]Ibid., p. 17.

[10]Ibid., pp. 18–19.

meets two criteria, i.e., that such information is stored in an electronic or other intangible medium and that it is capable of being retrieved.[11] This definition of digital assets under UNIDROIT will be very useful when considering the legal nature of cryptoassets.

Given the definitions presented above, the basic division of digital assets can be reduced to non-financial and financial digital assets, as well as cryptoassets as a separate category of digital assets.[12]

2.1 Financial and Non-Financial Digital Assets

The general division of assets into financial and non-financial assets is based on whether the holder of such an asset can assert a certain obligatory claim against other persons, i.e., whether the holder is entitled to a claim. If such an asset gives the holder the right to an obligatory claim against another person, it is a financial asset because its value is determined by the amount of the obligatory claim. Financial assets usually include equity interests (e.g. shares), liabilities (debt securities), derivatives, currencies, etc. The characteristic of these financial instruments as part of financial assets is that they are traded on the stock exchange or the OTC market.[13] On the other hand, non-financial assets are those assets whose value is derived from their use or from the ability of the asset to retain its value over time. Non-financial assets primarily include real estate with its capacity to store internal values, as well as various other types of assets. These assets include goods, services and intellectual property that are characterised by their usability or variability.[14]

It should be noted that the division of assets into financial and non-financial is not new, but in the context of digitalisation, especially tokenisation, it takes on a whole new meaning. Namely, all financial assets that have gone through the process of tokenisation are considered digital financial assets. Tokens represent existing financial assets and simplify the trading of financial instruments by trading tokens that represent, for example, a share or a bond. The main difference between digital financial assets and cryptoassets is that digital financial assets represented by a token are recorded in a common system of records and that these financial assets are subject to certain rights established by law.[15] The Virtual Financial Assets Act of the Republic of Malta, which defines virtual financial assets as any record on a digital medium used as a digital medium of exchange, a unit of account or a store of value, other than electronic money, a financial instrument, or a virtual token, supports the thesis that digital financial assets are a distinct type of asset different from traditional

[11] UNIDROIT (2022), p. 7.

[12] Allen et al. (2020), pp. 13–15.

[13] Lehmann (2017), p. 739.

[14] Allen et al. (2020), pp. 14–15.

[15] Allen et al. (2020), p. 15.

financial assets. However, the aforementioned Maltese act introduces a new type of digital asset or a DLT asset. This asset includes virtual tokens, virtual financial assets, electronic money, and financial instruments, if these assets use or depend on DLT technology, which is described below.[16]

In contrast to Malta, the German Banking Act (*Kreditwesengesetz*—KWG) classifies cryptoassets as financial instruments[17] along with other common financial instruments, such as shares, debt instruments, currencies, derivatives, etc.[18] French law, on the other hand, recognises tokens and virtual currencies as digital assets, but all those assets that resemble financial instruments are excluded from the definition of digital assets.[19] An interesting legal regulation comes from Liechtenstein, where the law (TVTG) does not explicitly define whether or not digital assets are also financial assets. However, under Liechtenstein law, tokens are defined as information (. . .) that may represent claims or membership rights against any person, rights *in rem* or other absolute or relative rights (. . .).[20] This definition of tokens includes various forms of financial and non-financial assets if they are tokenised. These forms include shares, debts, and virtual currencies, but also real estate.[21] Undoubtedly, all tokens to which Liechtenstein's law applies are considered assets.[22]

2.2 *Cryptoassets*

There are several variations in the literature related to the definition of cryptoassets. But the definition of cryptoassets mainly describes cryptoassets as a digital representation of value secured by cryptography and based on the use of Distributed Ledger Technology (DLT), i.e., supporting decentralised records of encrypted data.[23] A similar definition of cryptoassets was given by the European Commission in the Proposal for a Regulation of the European Parliament and of the Council on Markets in Crypto-assets and amending Directive (EU) 2019/1937 (hereinafter: MiCA), which defines a cryptoasset as a digital representation of value or rights

[16] § 2(2) Act No. XXX of 2018 – Virtual Financial Assets Act, 2018, Government Gazette of Malta No. 20,028 – 20.07.2018.

[17] Binder (2022), p. 7.

[18] § 1(11) of the German Banking Act (*Kreditwesengesetz*—KWG). https://www.gesetze-im-internet.de/kredwg/index.html. Accessed 20 May 2022.

[19] International Bar Associationa. A French point of view: from crypto assets to digital assets. https://www.ibanet.org/article/f59c675e-e95e-4c74-bdc3-ea5a42e8ef9c. Accessed 20 May 2022.

[20] Lehmann (2021), p. 155.

[21] Lehmann (2021), p. 155.

[22] Art. 4 of the Law of 3 October 2019 on Tokens and TT Service Providers (Token and TT Service Provider Act - TVTG) (Gesetz vom 3. Oktober 2019 über Token und VT-Dienstleister (Token- und VT-Dienstleister-Gesetz - TVTG)), Liechtensteinisches Landesgesetzblatt, 2019.301.

[23] Huang (2021), p. 98.

that can be transferred and stored electronically using DLT or similar technology.[24] However, it should be mentioned that there are legislations that do not explicitly include DLT technology in the definition of cryptoassets, but only require the existence of an electronic form. For example, the German KWG defines cryptoassets as digital representations of value that are not issued or guaranteed by any central bank or public body and do not have the legal status of currency or money. On the other hand, these assets are used by any person or entity by agreement or actual practice as a means of exchange or payment accepted or for investment purposes and can be transmitted, stored and traded electronically.[25] An example from French law indicates the desire for greater technological neutrality and does not explicitly mention DLT technology, but uses the term of shared electronic recording system, which shares certain features with DLT technology.[26] The situation is similar with Liechtenstein, where instead of DLT technology, the concept of "trustworthy technologies" (TT) has been introduced, which are defined as technologies that ensure the integrity of tokens, the clear assignment of tokens to TT identifiers and the disposal of tokens.[27] The commitment of the MiCA proposal should be supported not only towards DLT technology, but also towards "similar technologies", with regard to possible future technological development and easier harmonisation with national concepts.

To better understand the topic, it is necessary to contextualise DLT, which is often associated and sometimes even mistakenly equated with blockchain technology. Indeed, the purpose of DLT is to enable the exchange and update of information in a distributed and decentralised manner.[28] DLT should be understood as a special encrypted database that contains a kind of register in which the transactions of participants are recorded.[29] However, decentralisation and distribution are the characteristics of this database, which means that the system consists of interconnected computers that act as nodes and can be geographically located anywhere in the world.[30] One of the main characteristics of DLT is that there is no central authority, a kind of intermediary, that monitors or manages the system. But this function is performed by networked computers or nodes, which is a main characteristic of a decentralised database.[31] DLT technology defined in this way is followed by blockchain technology, which has gained greater notoriety thanks to Bitcoin cryptocurrency. Namely, since DLT technology is the basis of blockchain, the

[24] Art. 3(1)(2) of the Proposal for a Regulation of the European Parliament and of the Council on Markets in Crypto-assets, and amending Directive (EU) 2019/1937, COM/2020/593 final (hereinafter: MiCA).

[25] §1 (11) KWG.

[26] Lehmann (2021), p. 153.

[27] Lehmann (2021), p. 154.

[28] Huang (2021), p. 98.

[29] Garcimartin Alferez and Sanchez Fernandez (2020), p. 407.

[30] Low and Mik (2020), p. 137.

[31] Low and Mik (2020), p. 137.

blockchain protocol itself consists of networked computers (nodes). These computers cryptographically identify users and verify their mutual transactions before recording such a transaction in the system. Users identify themselves with cryptographic keys, both a public key, which acts as an address, and a private key, which is a password. Since there are computers or nodes in DLT technology, each of them maintains a complete copy of the verified transactions of the blockchain ledger, and data packets containing the recorded transaction data are called blocks. Each of these blocks is linked to the next block by a digital signature, creating a chain that allows a blockchain to act as a ledger that only authorised network members can access. Since all transactions are recorded in all nodes, transactions always leave an indelible mark and it is not possible to change the data, as is the case when the data is only held by a central authority.[32]

According to the current classification, there are four subtypes of cryptoassets: exchange tokens, utility tokens, security tokens and Stablecoins.[33]

Exchange tokens are used as a digital means of payment or exchange, such as Bitcoin, by far the best-known virtual cryptocurrency.[34] Although the use of the term cryptocurrency is widespread, there are certain characteristics of exchange tokens that indicate irregularities compared to traditional currencies. Namely, the characteristic of cryptocurrencies is that they have no long-term intrinsic value. This means that they are extremely volatile due to significant fluctuations in market value in a short period of time. In addition, a fee is charged when cryptocurrencies are used as a means of payment or exchange. This is not the case with payments made by using traditional currencies, and finally, for the reasons mentioned above, virtual currencies are not used as units of account, while traditional currencies continue to be used for this purpose.[35]

However, in some legal orders there is doubt whether cryptocurrencies are a means of payment or a means of exchange. Namely, it still follows that priority should be given to the qualification of cryptocurrencies as a means of payment, although not a legal means of payment.[36] For example, Croatian law defines a contract of exchange as a contract in which one contracting party undertakes to transfer ownership of a certain thing or transfer a certain right to the other contracting party.[37] However, since Croatian law does not qualify cryptocurrencies as things, nor does a specific right derive from cryptocurrencies, there are obvious legal difficulties in qualifying cryptocurrencies as an object of exchange.[38]

It should be noted that it is wrong to equate virtual currencies with electronic money, although virtual currencies are also in the form of electronic records. Indeed,

[32] HCCH (2022), pp. 3–4.

[33] Cooper (2021), p. 623.

[34] Allen et al. (2020), p. 10.

[35] Wu (2020), p. 3.

[36] Perkušić (2020), p. 279.

[37] Perkušić (2020), p. 279.

[38] Perkušić (2020), p. 279.

as far as the conceptual definition of virtual currencies is concerned, the provision of Article 2(d) of Directive 2019/713[39] according to which virtual currency is a digital representation of value that is not issued or guaranteed by a central bank or a public authority, is not necessarily linked to a legally established currency and does not have the legal status of currency or money. However, it is accepted by natural or legal persons as a medium of exchange, and can be transferred, stored and traded electronically. On the other hand, electronic money as a means of payment is an electronic store of monetary value used for making payment transactions, provided that the issuer has previously received funds in the form of payment accepted by persons other than the electronic money issuer and that electronic money is recognised and regulated by positive law.[40] It can be concluded that the main difference is that electronic money, as the name suggests, has the legal status of money and is indirectly guaranteed by a central bank. The reason for that is that electronic money is based on a monetary value previously deposited with the electronic money issuer.

Furthermore, with regard to virtual currencies, it is also necessary to point out that, in addition to cryptocurrencies, there are also platform-based digital currencies. The particular difference is that platform-based digital currencies are controlled by the platforms themselves These platforms set the business rules, and the purpose of platform-based digital currencies is not to compete with legal tender, but to improve the business performance of the companies that use them.[41] On the other hand, cryptocurrencies are the opposite of platform-based digital currencies because the purpose of cryptocurrencies is to compete with legal tender and their ultimate goal is to become a universal means of payment. Another important difference is that cryptocurrencies are based on decentralised systems and there is no centralised entity that manages and is responsible for transactions.[42]

Utility tokens give their holders access to specific digital goods or services provided by or located on a system based on DLT technology.[43] In this case, it is an advance payment for goods or services before you receive them, i.e., the token is worth as much as the service for which the token is purchased.[44] Within the meaning of the Malta Virtual Financial Assets Act, this type of token is considered a virtual token because it is a record on a digital medium. Its benefit, value or application is limited solely to the acquisition of goods or services on the DLT platform on which

[39] Directive (EU) 2019/713 of the European Parliament and of the Council of 17 April 2019 on combating fraud and counterfeiting of non-cash means of payment and replacing Council Framework Decision 2001/413/JHA PE/89/2018/REV/3, OJ L 123, 10.5.2019, pp. 18–29.

[40] Perkušić and Slakoper (2017), p. 70.

[41] Ibid., pp. 80–81.

[42] Ibid., pp. 82–83.

[43] Cooper (2021), p. 623.

[44] Wu (2020), p. 4.

or in relation to which virtual tokens were issued, or within a limited DLT platform network.[45]

Security tokens in business confer a specific right or interest to the holder.[46] In fact, it is a type of security like bonds or shares that allows the holder to demand payment from the debtor or, for example, the payment of dividends if they are profit shares.[47]

Finally, *Stablecoins* should be understood as cryptoassets pegged to another type of assets such as gold or even a legal national currency.[48] The purpose of pegging this type of cryptoassets to traditional forms of assets is to reduce the risk of volatility and it is predicted that Stablecoin could be converted to national legal currencies in centralised stock markets in the future. Nevertheless, the initiative is currently under consideration due to a high risk of money laundering and other types of fraud.[49]

Given the previous taxonomy of cryptoassets, it is possible to make a fundamental distinction according to what a crypto token represents. Namely, exchange tokens do not represent any specific right for the holder, while on the contrary, other types of tokens represent a specific right. It can be a right to a certain thing or an obligatory claim towards a certain person.[50] For that person, the token holder's claim represents a certain obligation. Accordingly, tokens as cryptoassets can be divided into exogenous and endogenous.[51] Endogenous tokens have no link to anything external to the crypto system, and such tokens, like cryptocurrencies, represent assets in themselves.[52] On the other hand, exogenous tokens have a link to something external to the crypto system. For example, exogenous tokens can be linked to securities, things, or rights of an obligatory character.[53]

However, the Law Commission (England and Wales) in its consultation paper "Digital assets" does not accept such a division in the context of the characterisation of cryptoassets. The Law Commission justifies this for two reasons. First, Law Commission considers the legal nature of tokens within the crypto system, independent of the connection to something external.[54] As another, even more important reason, the Law Commission argues that separate consideration of the legal nature of exogenous and endogenous tokens is unnecessary.[55] For the reason that even endogenous tokens can still have a link with something external, indicating as an

[45] § 2(2) Act No. XXX of 2018 – Virtual Financial Assets Act, 2018, Government Gazette of Malta No. 20,028 – 20.07.2018.

[46] Cooper (2021), p. 623.

[47] Wu (2020), p. 4.

[48] Ibid.

[49] Wu (2020), p. 3.

[50] Allen et al. (2022), p. 26.

[51] Law Commission (2022a), p. 282.

[52] Ibid.

[53] Ibid.

[54] Ibid., p. 283.

[55] Ibid.

example Colored Coins.[56] Namely, the Colored Coins protocol covers information about small amounts of Bitcoin as a cryptocurrency, and such metadata can be used, for example, to represent an external thing.[57]

2.3 *What Does MiCA Regulate?*

Considering the above definition of cryptoassets according to MiCA, it is opportune to outline the content of the MiCA proposal. In 2020, the European Commission, as an integral part of the Digital Financial Package, proposed MiCA for the purpose of setting the legal framework for the unregulated segment of cryptoassets.[58] This legal framework applies to all cryptoassets that are not regulated by other Union acts on financial services.[59] The goals of MICA are to strengthen legal certainty, support innovation, protect consumers and investors, and financial stability in terms of cryptoassets.[60] The scope of MiCA refers to persons who issue cryptoassets or provide services related to cryptoassets in the EU.[61] However, financial instruments, electronic money, deposits, structured deposits and securitization are excluded from the scope of application.[62] MiCA introduces a series of rules to ensure compliance and transparency in the work of issuers and service providers related to cryptoassets.[63] MiCA proposes rules related to capital requirements, custody of assets and the way to exercise the rights of investors against issuers of cryptoassets.[64] The rules apply to entities that apply for authorization to provide services on the single European market.[65] In this sense, every entity that submits a request for approval is obliged to have a registered office in a certain Member State. Approval issued by one Member State will be valid in all other Member States.[66] According to MiCA, three basic types of cryptoassets are distinguished: (1) asset-referenced tokens[67]; (2) electronic money tokens[68]; and (3) the remaining category of

[56] Ibid.

[57] Ibid.

[58] Ferreira et al. (2021), p. 13.

[59] Maia and Dos Santos (2022), p. 60.

[60] Ferreira et al. (2021), p. 13.

[61] MiCA, art 2(1).

[62] MiCA, art 2(2).

[63] Ferreira et al. (2021), p. 13.

[64] Ibid.

[65] Ibid.

[66] Maia and Dos Santos (2022), p. 63.

[67] According to article 3(1)(3) of MiCA, asset-referenced token is a type of cryptoasset that purports to maintain a stable value by referring to the value of several fiat currencies that are legal tender, one or several commodities or one or several cryptoassets, or a combination of such assets.

[68] According to article 3(1)(4) of MiCA, electronic money token is a type of cryptoasset the main purpose of which is to be used as a means of exchange and that purports to maintain a stable value by referring to the value of a fiat currency that is legal tender.

cryptoassets.[69] Asset-referenced tokens and electronic money tokens were introduced for the emergence of Stablecoins. Dual regulation is necessary for the reason that Stablecoins can be used as a means of payment, but also as a means of storing value.[70] MiCA introduces additional rules in respect of significant asset-referenced tokens and significant electronic money tokens. These significant tokens are a special subcategory in the basic division. Additional rules are set due to financial stability and increased risks if transactions with said tokens reach a large scale.[71] The remaining category of cryptoassets consists of utility tokens,[72] but also any other cryptoassets within the scope of MiCA that are not asset-referenced tokens or electronic money tokens.[73] Finally, in the context of the topic of this paper, it should be pointed out that the MiCA does not bring anything revolutionary in terms of defining the legal nature of cryptoassets. Given that civil law issues are not within the competence of the Union, the regulation of the private law aspect of cryptoassets is left to the Member States.[74]

3 The Legal Nature of Cryptoassets

Both legal scholars and practitioners have long been concerned with the question of the legal nature of cryptoassets, whether a cryptoasset is a thing (*res*), a right or something else. In an effort to qualify cryptoassets as correctly as possible, attempts are often made to address legal gaps in the regulation of legal orders by analogy. When considering the implementation of the right to cryptoassets, we start from the normative regulation of shares, bonds, notes and other securities and intellectual property rights.[75] For example, Japan defines cryptocurrencies as means of payment, while the United States of America has a wide range of definitions given the variety of legal orders, and considers cryptocurrencies as money, things or commodities. In the People's Republic of China cryptocurrencies have the legal status of virtual assets.[76] The United Kingdom originally considered cryptocurrencies as data, until a court applied the rules of ownership, i.e., the rules of property law, to such cryptocurrency in a case when it ruled on the prohibition of the sale of cryptocurrencies.[77]

[69] Maia and Dos Santos (2022), p. 62.

[70] Ibid, p. 61.

[71] Ibid, p. 62.

[72] According to article 3(1)(5) of MiCA, utility token is a type of cryptoasset which is intended to provide digital access to a good or service, available on DLT, and is only accepted by the issuer of that token.

[73] Maia and Dos Santos (2022), p. 62.

[74] Ferreira et al. (2021), p. 24.

[75] Cooper (2021), p. 624.

[76] Korobeinikova (2020), p. 232.

[77] Ibid., p. 233.

In continental Europe, Liechtenstein has made a step forward in defining the legal nature of cryptoassets from a private law perspective.[78] Liechtenstein law stipulates that the provisions on civil qualification apply to all tokens, regardless of whether they represent any rights, if the tokens are generated or issued by a TT service provider with its registered office or place of residence in Liechtenstein, or if the parties have expressly stated that the relevant Liechtenstein law applies.[79] The qualification of tokens is very general, because tokens are considered assets located in Liechtenstein, if Liechtenstein law applies.[80]

As already mentioned, the TVTG provides a very broad definition of a token, because it is defined as a piece of information on a TT System which can represent claims or rights of memberships against a person, rights to property or other absolute or relative rights.[81] Given the definition of a token, it is not surprising that the TVTG contains the rules of property law, law of obligations and securities law applicable to tokens. In the context of the qualification of the token in terms of property law, not the representation of rights through tokens, it is important to draw attention to the provisions of the TVTG on the power of disposal (*Verfügungsgewalt*) and the right of disposal (*Verfügungsberechtigung*) over the token. According to the TVTG, the disposal power belongs to the TT key holder, and the presumption is given that a person who has the power of disposal over a token has the right of disposal over the token.[82] Furthermore, it is presumed that any previous holder of the power of disposal had the right of disposal at the time of its ownership.[83] This legal construction points to the conclusion that the token is suitable to be the object of ownership, which is explicitly mentioned at the end of the previous sentence. It could be concluded that the power of disposal is synonymous with the concept of possession, while the right of disposal should be understood as the content of the ownership in the context of tokens. This is to be understood because Liechtenstein law recognises only corporeal things as objects of the rights *in rem*.[84] However, the general definition of ownership in the Rights *In Rem* Act of Liechtenstein indicates the right of disposal as the fundamental content of ownership.[85] Furthermore, what points to the conclusion that the legislator in Liechtenstein used the rules of property law by analogy is the previously mentioned presumption of the right of disposal with regard to the power of disposal. The stated presumption would be equivalent to the presumption of the possessor's ownership of the movables according to the

---

[78] Lehmann (2021), p. 152.

[79] Art. 3 of the TVTG.

[80] Art. 4 of the TVTG.

[81] Art. 2(1)(c) of the TVTG.

[82] Art. 5 of the TVTG.

[83] Ibid.

[84] Allen (2021), p. 316.

[85] Art. 20(1) of the Righs *In Rem* Act (Sachenrecht (SR) vom 31. Dezember 1922, Liechtensteinisches Landesgesetzblatt 1923.004).

Liechtenstein Rights *In Rem* Act.[86] This also applies to Croatian property law,[87] as well as Scottish, French and German.[88] But as noted earlier, Liechtenstein property law only recognises corporeal things as movables.

The German Electronic Securities Act (*Gesetz über elektronische Wertpapiere*—eWpG) is much more specific in defining incorporeal objects as it introduces the possibility of issuing a security as an electronic security.[89] The eWpG stipulates that an electronic security is considered a thing within the meaning of §90 of the German Civil Code[90] (hereinafter: BGB).[91] However, §90 of the BGB defines that only corporeal objects are things.[92] This leads to the conclusion that an electronic security, although in fact incorporeal, is legally considered as a corporeal thing. An additional significance of the eWpG is that in addition to the central register security, the concept of a crypto security is introduced, which is defined as an electronic security entered in the crypto register of security.[93] The eWpG does not mention DLT or similar technologies related to the crypto register, but only stipulates that the register must be kept on a forgery-proof recording system in which data is logged in chronological order and stored protected against unauthorised deletion and subsequent modification.[94] The holder of an electronic security (including crypto) is a person who is registered in the electronic securities register and considered the owner of the electronic security as long as the person is registered as the holder, in accordance with the explicit presumption of ownership.[95]

That crypto securities fall under the property law regime, since they are defined as things, is further emphasised with regard to the transfer of electronic securities. The eWpG explicitly stipulates that the transfer of electronic securities results in the transfer of ownership of the security and that the right from the security is transferred with the transfer of ownership of the security.[96] The rule on the transfer of securities traditionally follows the legitimation function of securities. According to this, the

[86] Art. 509(1) of the Righs *In Rem* Act (Sachenrecht (SR) vom 31. Dezember 1922, Liechtensteinisches Landesgesetzblatt 1923.004).

[87] Art. 11(3) of the Ownership and Other Rights *In Rem* Act, Official Gazette No. 91/96, 68/98, 137/99, 22/00, 73/00, 129/00, 114/01, 79/06, 141/06, 146/08, 38/09, 153/09, 143/12, 152/14.

[88] Carr (2019), p. 192.

[89] §2(1) of the Act on Electronic Securities of 3 Jun 2021, Federal Law Gazette I, p. 1423 (Gesetz über elektronische Wertpapiere vom 3. Juni 2021, BGBl. I S. 1423).

[90] German Civil Code (BGB) (Bürgerliches Gesetzbuch in der Fassung der Bekanntmachung vom 2. Jan 2002 (BGBl. I S. 42, 2909; 2003 I S. 738), das zuletzt durch Artikel 2 des Gesetzes vom 21. Dezember 2021 (BGBl. I S. 5252).

[91] §2 (3) of eWpG.

[92] §90 of the BGB.

[93] §4(2)(3) of eWpG.

[94] §16(1) of eWpG.

[95] §3(1), §27 of eWpG.

[96] § 25 of eWpG.

right incorporated in the security belongs to the person who has the right to the security, as a right *in rem*.[97]

This equating of electronic securities (and crypto security) with things represents a revolutionary legal solution of German civil law, which is otherwise based on the Pandecten system, according to which only physical (corporeal) objects can be considered things.[98] However, the German legal solution did not fully regulate the legal nature of cryptoassets, as it was limited to crypto securities only. Can other types of cryptoassets, such as virtual currencies and other tokens, analogously qualify as things? The answer to this question should be negative, given that German law, like Swiss law, only recognises corporeal objects as things.[99] Other European countries like Portugal, Hungary, Greece, and the Netherlands, do not recognise incorporeal objects as things either.[100] Thus, for example, it is considered that cryptoassets could be recognised as an object of fewer property rights. However, since it is not a thing, it is not capable of being an object of ownership.[101] There is no answer to the legal nature of cryptoassets. Nevertheless, it is considered that the provisions on the purchase of goods should be applied analogously when buying virtual currencies, given that the German Civil Code itself refers to such application when buying rights and other objects.[102]

Given that Swiss law accepts only corporeal objects as things and the consequent inadmissibility of the existence of ownership rights over incorporeal objects, cryptoassets in Switzerland are regulated within the framework of securities law.[103] A new type of ledger-based securities has been introduced which include various types of tokens. These tokens must contain a certain right of an obligatory nature, which on the other hand excludes cryptocurrencies such as Bitcoin.[104] Regarding the character of ledger-based securities, no revolutionary solution was introduced as in the previously mentioned German law. Ledger-based securities are defined under Swiss law as rights over which the creditor has the right of disposal.[105] They are defined as rights and cannot be the object of ownership rights which are immanent only over things. But, this does not mean that certain limited rights *in rem* cannot exist over ledger-based securities. Swiss law allows ledger-based securities to be collateral and pledged.[106]

---

97 Klarić and Vedriš (2014), pp. 659–660.

98 Low and Hara (2022), pp. 1, 5.

99 Garcia-Teruel and Simon-Moreno (2021), p. 4.

100 Allen (2021), p. 315.

101 Ibid.

102 Garcia-Teruel and Simon-Moreno (2021), pp. 4–5.

103 Zellweger-Gutknecht and Seiler (2021), p. 6.

104 Ibid., p. 7.

105 Art. 973.d of the Federal Act of 30 March 1911 on the Amendment of the Swiss Civil Code (Part Five: The Code of Obligations), SR 220.

106 Art. 973.g of the Federal Act of 30 March 1911 on the Amendment of the Swiss Civil Code (Part Five: The Code of Obligations), SR 220.

Certain normative activities are underway at EU level dealing with cryptoassets, but the proposed acts have not specifically defined the legal nature of cryptoassets in terms of private law. It is therefore appropriate to rely on the case law of the Court of Justice of the European Union to define the legal nature of cryptoassets by analogy, where such analogy is actually justified.

In *Skatteverket v. David Hedqvist*,[107] a case involving a reference for a preliminary ruling on the interpretation of the provisions of Council Directive 2006/112/EC on the common system of value added tax[108] (the VAT Directive), the Court of Justice of the European Union took certain legal positions with respect to cryptocurrencies that may also be relevant with respect to a broader interpretation of EU secondary legislation. The factual context of the case is that the party to the proceedings wanted to buy and sell Bitcoin online through a company, in exchange for the Swedish krona as a traditional currency, with the specific price of Bitcoin based on an exchange rate published on the Internet with a certain percentage markup or markdown in exchange for consideration. The legal issue raised is, *inter alia*, whether such a transaction should be considered as a supply of services for consideration within the meaning of the relevant provisions of the VAT Directive.[109] The Court's legal opinion is that transactions for the exchange of units of the Bitcoin virtual currency for traditional currency and vice versa against payment of an amount equal to the difference between the purchase price paid by the operator and the sale price obtained by the operator, constitute the provision of services for consideration within the meaning of the relevant provision of the VAT Directive.[110,111] The importance of this judgement lies in the fact that, in addition to the qualification of the legal relationship within the meaning of the VAT Directive, the Court took other important legal positions in relation to cryptocurrencies. Namely, the Court considered that Bitcoin, as a cryptocurrency, cannot be characterised as a tangible asset because it has no purpose other than that of a means of payment. The Court emphasised that this also applies to traditional currencies as long as they are money that is legal tender.[112] Thus, the Court indicated that it is not a tangible asset, which *a contrario* leads to the conclusion that virtual currencies could be considered intangible assets. The additional significance of the ruling is that the Court indicated

[107] Judgment of 22 October 2015, Skatteverket v David Hedqvist, C-264/14, EU:C:2015:718.

[108] Council Directive 2006/112/EC of 28 November 2006 on the common system of value added tax, OJ L 347, 11.12.2006.

[109] Judgment of 22 October 2015, Skatteverket v David Hedqvist, C-264/14, EU:C:2015:718 paras 10, 13, 14, 58(1).

[110] The qualification of a legal relationship as the provision of services is relevant only in the context of the VAT Directive because Art. 14(1) of the VAT Directive stipulates that 'supply of goods' means the transfer of the right to dispose of tangible property as owner, while Art. 24(1) of the VAT Directive stipulates that 'supply of services' means any transaction which does not constitute a supply of goods.

[111] Vlček (2019), p. 53.

[112] Judgment of 22 October 2015, Skatteverket v David Hedqvist, C-264/14, EU:C:2015:718, paras 24–25.

that the Bitcoin virtual currency cannot be considered a security either.[113] The statement that the Bitcoin virtual currency is not a security is significant because of its digital nature. This position was taken by the Court and it follows that it is not a security in either materialised or dematerialised form.[114] The Court's view that the Bitcoin virtual currency is not a security in terms of the VAT Directive is also acceptable in a wider context because virtual currencies are not compatible with the incorporation principle. According to this principle, certain rights that are inextricably linked to a security are derived from securities.[115] An important feature of securities is that, from the debtor's point of view, they contain a certain obligation that has to be fulfiled towards the creditor as the legal holder of the security. From the creditor's point of view, this represents his right or claim, regardless of whether it is a security in materialised or dematerialised (electronic) form.[116] This shows the incompatibility of virtual currencies with securities, since Bitcoin or any other virtual currency, even if in electronic form, does not embody a right that would correspond to a specific obligation. The holder of a virtual currency, by the mere fact of possession, has no right to require anyone to fulfil a specific obligation. Such a right is not even embodied in virtual currencies for the holder, and consequently there is no obligation of a specific issuer as debtor. As can be seen from the abovementioned decision of the Court, virtual currencies fulfil their function only in exchange transactions, i.e., in bilaterally binding legal transactions in which virtual currencies are a means of payment for a specific consideration.

The next case from the Court of Justice of the European Union does not specifically refer to cryptoassets, but it is important to properly qualify the legal nature of cryptoassets because of certain findings of the Court that can be applied by analogy to cryptoassets. In *The Software Incubator Ltd v. Computer Associates (UK) Ltd* case,[117] the Court of Justice was asked, in the context of a reference for a preliminary ruling on the interpretation of the provisions of Council Directive 86/653/EEC on the coordination of the laws of the Member States relating to self-employed commercial agents, whether the concept of sale of goods can be interpreted, within the meaning of the relevant provisions of that Directive, such that it includes the supply, in return for payment of a fee, of computer software to a customer by electronic means where the supply is accompanied by the grant of a perpetual licence to use that software.[118] The Court's ruling is relevant to this paper

[113] Ibid, para 55.

[114] Dematerialised form is the fact that a financial instrument exists only as a book entry record. Article 2(1)(4) of the Regulation (EU) No 909/2014 of the European Parliament and of the Council of 23 July 2014 on improving securities settlement in the European Union and on central securities depositories and amending Directives 98/26/EC and 2014/65/EU and Regulation (EU) No 236/2012, OJ L 257, 28.8.2014.

[115] Slakoper (2017), p. 207.

[116] Ibid., pp. 207–208.

[117] Judgment of 16 September 2021, The Software Incubator Ltd v Computer Associates (UK) Ltd, C-410/19, EU:C:2021:742.

[118] Ibid., para 26.

for two reasons. Namely, in defining the concept of goods, the Court referred to its previous case law and indicated that goods should be understood as any product that can be valued in money and is capable of being the subject of a commercial transaction. So the Court concluded that computer software can be classified as goods because it has a commercial value and is capable of being the subject of a commercial transaction.[119] No less important is the Court's position regarding the qualification of the concept of sale. The Court considered that a sale is an agreement by which a person transfers his ownership rights in a tangible or intangible property belonging to him to another person for consideration.[120] In conclusion, the Court answered the question posed by stating that the concept of "sale of goods" should be interpreted within the meaning of the relevant provisions of the aforementioned Directive such that it covers the supply of computer software to a customer by electronic means for consideration if that supply is accompanied by the grant of a perpetual licence to use that software.[121]

Although cryptoassets are not licences, their creation is based on various types of software solutions, because cryptoassets are the result of the operation of software.[122] In this sense, the significance of the Court's decision is that computer software is classified as a good. Moreover, property is divided into intangible and tangible, and the ownership right is transferred after the sale. Therefore, if the ownership right to computer software is transferred, it is necessary that the transferor's ownership right to it exists immediately before the transfer. It is necessary to remind that the concept of good is a broad concept and may or may not correspond to the concept of thing (*res*) in the sense of civil law. However, legal trends in certain legal systems indicate that certain types of cryptoassets could be equated with things. Simply put, applying the Court's position by analogy, it can be concluded that cryptoassets might be the subject of the ownership right inherent in things. This kind of interpretation is only possible by analogy, because cryptoassets are not software,[123] nor do they have the purpose of software. Therefore, the aforementioned decision of the Court was considered through certain similarities between software and cryptoassets. The software in the case was delivered in electronic form, and the Court indicated that there are ownership rights over this intangible asset as well. Thus, as a conclusion, the possibility of the existence of ownership rights over cryptoassets is imposed, considering that cryptoassets exist exclusively in an intangible form.

Moreover, it is important to note that cryptocurrencies and other tokens were created as part of computer software intended for widespread use in the market and are not characterised as the subject matter of intellectual property law.[124] In this

[119] Ibid., paras 34–35.

[120] Ibid., para 40.

[121] Ibid., para 52.

[122] Bartle (2004), p. 22.

[123] Boehm and Pesch (2014), p. 49.

[124] Kharitonova (2021), p. 21.

sense, it is necessary to distinguish rights over cryptoassets, such as ownership rights, from intellectual property rights that may exist over software or databases.[125] For example, cryptocurrencies are not the result of anyone's intellectual work, nor are they software, rather cryptocurrencies are a kind of software product.[126] According to the Directive 2009/24/EC of the European Parliament and of the Council of 23 April 2009 on the legal protection of computer programs, "the function of computer programs is to communicate and work together with other components of a computer system and with users (...)".[127] It is clear that cryptocurrencies cannot perform such a function as computer programs. Therefore, cryptoassets cannot even be the subject matter of intellectual property law, because it requires that the subject matter of protection should be the result of direct human action.[128]

A further contribution to this hypothesis is made by the UNIDROIT Working Group on Digital Assets and Private Law. It states in its study LXXXII as one of its general principles that a state's law should provide that digital assets may be the subject of proprietary rights.[129] In the commentary, UNIDROIT defines proprietary rights as rights or interests that persons have in digital assets, and these rights or interests may be enforced against third parties or persons who are not necessarily contracting parties.[130] From such a definition of *proprietary rights*, it is clear that the rights associated with digital assets are intended to have an *erga omnes* effect. This effect is inherent in the private law principle of power over things as one of the fundamental principles of property law in continental European legal systems.[131] In support of this statement, it should be recalled that rights of obligatory nature always act *inter partes*, while the *erga omnes* effect is characteristic of rights *in rem* and personality rights.[132]

Moreover, the introductory part of the paper gives the definition of digital assets developed by UNIDROIT, according to which digital assets are electronic records capable of being subject to control, where electronic records are information that cumulatively meets two criteria, i.e., that this information is stored in an electronic or other intangible medium and that it is capable of being retrieved.[133] The significance of this definition is that it emphasises the necessity that as an electronic record, digital assets must be, *inter alia*, capable of being subject to control. The concept of

[125] Dickinson (2019), p. 128.

[126] Boehm and Pesch (2014), p. 49.

[127] Recital 10 of the Directive 2009/24/EC of the European Parliament and of the Council of 23 April 2009 on the legal protection of computer programs (Codified version), OJ L 111, 5.5.2009, pp. 16–22.

[128] Perkušić (2020), pp. 281–282.

[129] UNIDROIT (2022), p. 11.

[130] Ibid.

[131] Gavella (2007), p. 21.

[132] Klarić and Vedriš (2014), p. 69.

[133] UNIDROIT (2022), p. 7.

being *capable of being subject to control* suggests that digital assets are subject to a property law regime, which means that digital assets should be considered as a thing.

UNIDROIT removes any doubts about this by defining the content of digital asset control in the following way:

> A person has control of a digital asset if:
>
> (a) the digital asset or the relevant protocol or system confers on that person:
>
> (i) the exclusive ability to change the control of the digital asset to another person (a "change of control");
> (ii) the exclusive ability to prevent others from obtaining substantially all of the benefit from the digital asset; and
> (iii) the ability to obtain substantially all the benefit from the digital asset; and
>
> (b) the digital asset or its associated records allows that person to identify itself as having these abilities.[134]

It is clear from the above definition of control that it includes the *de facto* control over digital assets. In the continental European legal context, this definition corresponds to the concept of possession in property law. This is explicitly stated by UNIDROIT in its accompanying explanatory notes, pointing out that the concept of control is the functional equivalent to possession of movables.[135] The functional equating of control over digital assets with possesion finds its meaning in the fact that digital assets recorded on the blockchain can only be disposed of with a private key.[136] Therefore, there are considerations that the private key is actually a link between possesion and the owner of the digital asset.[137]

Furthermore, equating intangible or incorporeal entities with things is not unknown to civil law. For example, the Croatian Ownership and Other Rights *in Rem* Act defines things as the corporeal parts of nature, distinct from and used by people, and a legal fiction further emphasises that anything recognised by law as having the same value is also considered a thing.[138] Furthermore, when it comes to the issue of distinguishing between immovable and movable assets, this Act sets a presumption that, in case of doubt, a thing is to be considered a movable asset.[139] This suggests that Croatian property law also recognises intangible entities if they are recognised as things by law. In this case, such a thing would be considered a movable asset, unless such an incorporeal thing were characterised differently by law.

---

[134] UNIDROIT (2022), p. 19.

[135] UNIDROIT (2022), p. 19.

[136] De Vauplane (2017), p. 50.

[137] De Vauplane (2017), p. 50.

[138] Art. 2(2) of the Ownership and Other Rights *in Rem* Act, Republic of Croatia, Official Gazette No. 91/96, 68/98, 137/99, 22/00, 73/00, 129/00, 114/01, 79/06, 141/06, 146/08, 38/09, 153/09, 143/12, 152/14.

[139] Art. 2(7) of the Croatian Ownership and Other Rights *in Rem* Act.

In support of the application by analogy of the provisions of Croatian property law, attention should also be drawn to the decision of the French *Conseil d'Etat* (ruling as the Supreme Administrative Court).[140] In the case of taxation of profits from the sale of Bitcoin, *Conseil d'Etat* considered, *inter alia*, the legal nature of Bitcoin in the sense of the French Civil Code. *Conseil d'Etat* draws attention to the provisions of the French Civil Code under which all assets are movable or immovable. Furthermore, it is explicitly stated that Bitcoin does not meet the definition of immovable assets and must therefore be treated as intangible movable assets.[141] It should be noted that the French Civil Code recognises various types of incorporeal objects that are characterised as movables, such as bonds, shares in companies, etc.[142]

The next, more recent court case also comes from France. In the case of *Bitspread v Paymium* before the Commercial Court of Nanterre, the legal question was whether a loan in Bitcoin should be considered as a loan for the purpose of use or consumption?[143] The factual context of the case is that Bitspread borrowed 1,000 Bitcoins from Paymium and a hard fork followed, so the Bitcoin blockchain is separated into two different blockchains and each continues to evolve independently.[144] Paymium considered itself the owner of the Bitcoins loaned to Bitspread, but Paymium also considered itself the owner of the 1,000 Bitcoin Cash that Bitspread received as a result of the hard fork, as these are the fruits of Bitcoin.[145] Although the French Court did not specifically indicate whether cryptocurrencies should be considered as things, it is significant that the Court applied the rules of the loan of things of the French Civil Code.[146] The French Court decided that the Bitcoin Cash belongs to Bitspread. The reason for that was that Bitcoin is consumable and fungible by nature, and Bitspread acquired ownership of Bitcoin based on the loan agreement, while the Bitcoin Cash is fruit.[147]

Furthermore, the Digital Assets Act of the Republic of Serbia states that digital assets, including cryptoassets, are capable of being the object of rights *in rem*.[148] This Act regulates two types of assets, i.e., virtual currencies and digital tokens. In the context of this consideration, it is important to note that the Act allows digital assets to be a means of securing claims by the institutes of pledge and fiduciary ownership.[149] These are undoubtedly entities in which ownership and other rights *in rem* can be exercised if one analyses relevant provisions on fiduciary ownership of

[140] *Conseil d'Etat*, Nos. 417809, 418030, 418031, 418032 and 418033, 26 Apr 2018.

[141] *Conseil d'Etat*, Nos. 417809, 418030, 418031, 418032 and 418033, 26 Apr 2018, para 13.

[142] Allen (2021), p. 315.

[143] Lee and Van de Looverbosch (2021), pp. 14–15.

[144] Ibid., p. 14.

[145] Ibid.

[146] Low and Hara (2022), p. 6.

[147] Ibid.

[148] Digital Assets Act, Official Gazette, Republic of Serbia, No. 153/2020.

[149] Ibid., Arts 98-121.

digital assets. Indeed, a fiduciary agreement on digital assets obligates a debtor to a creditor to transfer ownership of digital assets to the creditor, to secure a claim, and the creditor is obligated to return the received assets to the debtor upon satisfaction of the secured claim.[150] In support of the thesis about the existence of rights *in rem* over digital assets, it should be pointed out that the pledger can only be a person who has the right of ownership or a person who is the holder of digital assets which he can freely dispose of.[151] However, in the case of an involuntary sale of a pledged digital asset due to non-payment of a debt, the Act expressly stipulates that the buyer of such digital asset acquires the right of ownership of the digital assets.[152] Given that the Digital Assets Act does not define whether cryptocurrency or other type of token can be considered as a thing, but only defines that the right of ownership of such assets is acquired, it is necessary to consider the relevant provisions of general property law. According to the Serbian Basis of Ownership and Proprietary Relations Act, natural persons and legal entities may have the ownership right only over movables and immovables, while the pledge right can also exist on rights.[153] From the aforementioned provisions, it can be concluded that digital assets could be considered as a kind of thing according to general property law. The reason for that is that the object of ownership rights can only be movable and immovable things, but not rights.

Considering the disparity in qualifying cryptoassets, there is an opinion that cryptocurrencies, and thus cryptoassets, are an unregulated set of information or data.[154] As already mentioned, cryptocurrencies fulfill their primary function as a means of payment. Namely, the property benefit for the holder depends on the value on the cryptocurrency markets, which in turn is conditioned by trust in the system of other participants in the cryptocurrency market.[155] Therefore, it can be concluded that cryptocurrencies as data have a certain material benefit for their holder.[156] The British Law Commission is also on the trail of qualifying cryptoassets as a set of data. It is based on the fact that crypto tokens consist of data structures that realize their functionality exclusively within a certain crypto system, which is maintained and managed by the users themselves.[157] Accordingly, the Law Commission proposes the introduction of data objects as a special (third) category of personal property, different from rights of an obligatory character or rights *in rem*. An object would be included in a special category of personal property if: “1) it is composed of

[150] Ibid., Art 121.

[151] Ibid., Art 105(1).

[152] Ibid., Art 114(1).

[153] Art. 1 and Art 61(1) of the Basis of Ownership and Proprietary Relations Act, Republic of Serbia, Official Gazette SFRY, No. 6/80, 36/90; Official Gazette FRY No. 29/96; Official Gazette RS No. 115/05.

[154] Perkušić (2020), pp. 283–284.

[155] Ibid., p. 284.

[156] Ibid., p. 284.

[157] Law Commission (2022b) Summary of consultation paper, p. 8.

data represented in an electronic medium, including in the form of computer code, electronic, digital or analogue signals; 2) it exists independently of persons and exists independently of the legal system; and 3) it is rivalrous".[158]

The first criterion, the existence of an object in an electronic medium, aims to make a distinction in relation to physical things, which consist of physically composed particles.[159] The second criterion requires the independent existence of data objects in relation to people, but also in relation to the legal system.[160] Separation from people wants to emphasize the independence of data objects in relation to people, i.e. the concrete definiteness of data objects.[161] The criterion of independent existence in relation to the legal system aims to exclude rights of an obligatory character from the scope of application of this criterion.[162] Namely, rights of an obligatory character can be realized exclusively through legal procedures, and claims or debts exist based on legal regulations. On the other hand, data objects exist independently of the legal order.[163] Finally, the rivalry criterion dictates that the data object can be used by a certain person at a certain time, limiting its use by other persons, i.e. the use of such an object is not unlimited.[164] According to the Law Commission, the third category of personal property in the context of cryptoassets would allow the application of property law or law of obligations by analogy, depending on the appropriateness.[165] However, at the same time, it would be possible for certain types of crypto assets not to fall under the rules of property law or law of obligations. Therefore, it would be possible to apply law to specific types of cryptoassets depending on their characteristics.[166] Finally, the Law Commission concludes that crypto tokens meet the criteria of data objects and are appropriate objects of property rights.[167] Similar to UNIDROIT, the Law Commission proposes the qualification of the interaction between a person and a data object through the concept of factual control, which would be equivalent to possession.[168] Therefore, it is clear that with the design of data objects as a new category of personal property, solutions are sought in the analogical application of already known concepts.

[158] Law Commission (2022a), pp. 78–79.

[159] Ibid., p. 79.

[160] Ibid., p. 82.

[161] Ibid., p. 82.

[162] Ibid., p. 85.

[163] Ibid., p. 85.

[164] Ibid., p. 87.

[165] Ibid., p. 69.

[166] Ibid.

[167] Law Commission (2022b) Summary of consultation paper, p. 3.

[168] Ibid., p. 9.

4 Concluding Remarks

Considering the legal nature of cryptoassets, the disparity of normative solutions is obvious, both in terms of the regulation itself or the absence of adequate regulation of private law relations with regard to cryptoassets and in terms of the fundamental principles on which the selected civil law systems are based. It is difficult to take an unequivocal position on the characterisation of cryptoassets. The buyer of an exchange token, such as Bitcoin, does not acquire the right of an obligatory character that would arise from such a token. However, the fact is that a certain person invested part of his assets and acquired such a token. A person's assets therefore changed their form. For example, part of the assets no longer exists in the form of money, but in the form of a certain cryptotoken. Therefore, it is impossible to deny the existence of such assets and consider that no right exists over such a token. It follows that certain types of cryptoassets such as cryptocurrencies should certainly be regarded as incorporeal objects to which ownership rights and other rights *in rem* may exist.

In the context of utility tokens and security tokens, the situation is more complex. Such types of tokens nevertheless incorporate certain obligatory rights for their holder. From the aforementioned comparative solutions, it is evident that two approaches are possible. It is possible to consider such tokens as things, as in the case of German crypto securities, over which ownership and other rights *in rem* exist, or as obligatory rights, as in the case of Swiss ledger-based securities. The token as a right is acquired for the purpose of requiring the issuer to fulfill a certain obligation. Therefore, as a legal relationship *inter partes*, it is not necessary to consider it as an incorporeal thing on which ownership rights would exist. On the other hand, the right of disposal over cryptoassets is realised exclusively with a private key, which supports the thesis that cryptoassets can be considered an incorporeal thing over which there are ownership rights. The reason for this is that with a private key real control over digital assets is achieved, which is close to the concept of possession of things. Otherwise, as a rule, there is no real control similar to possession over obligatory rights.

Finally, if the differences between endogenous and exogenous tokens are removed, then the proposal of the Law Commission is imposed as the most logical solution. Any crypto token that meets the criteria should be considered a data object, as a special category of personal property. In that case, property rights would be acquired on such data objects. The type of rights that would be acquired over data objects would lean more towards real rights. As a reason for this, it should be pointed out that the considered solutions focus on issues of factual control over cryptoassets. It is the equivalent of possession, which is, after all, an institute of property law. Also, the introduction of the concept of a data object enables the legal recognition of cryptoassets, without violating the fundamental principles of civil law regarding what can be considered as a thing. In order to strengthen legal certainty in private law relations, it is desirable to adequately regulate the legal nature of cryptoassets as soon as possible. The application of analogy, as a legal technique, always leaves a grain of doubt as to whether a certain legal norm has been correctly applied by analogy. Also, legal certainty regarding the legal qualification of cryptoassets would certainly contribute to greater investor interest in participating in the European cryptoasset market.

References

Act No. XXX of 2018 – Virtual Financial Assets Act, 2018, Government Gazette of Malta No. 20,028 – 20.07.2018

Act on Ownership and other Real Rights, Official Gazette No. 91/96, 68/98, 137/99, 22/00, 73/00, 129/00, 114/01, 79/06, 141/06, 146/08, 38/09, 153/09, 143/12, 152/14

Allen JG (2021) Cryptoassets in private law. In: Chiu IH-Y, Deipenbrock G (eds) Routledge handbook of financial technology and law. Routledge, Abingdon, pp 309–323

Allen JG et al (2020) Legal and regulatory considerations for digital assets. CCAF Publications, Cambridge

Allen JG et al (2022) Cryptoassets in Private Law: Emerging Trends and Open Questions from the First 10 Years. SMU Centre for AI & Data Governance Research Paper No. 06/2022. https://papers.ssrn.com/sol3/papers.cfm?abstract_id=4206250. Accessed 20 Sept 2022

Bartle AR (2004) Pitfalls of Virtual Property. The Themis Group white paper. https://www.academia.edu/13016129/Pitfalls_of_Virtual_Property. Accessed 15 May 2022

Binder JH (2022) Cryptocurrencies - Country Report Germany. https://doi.org/10.2139/ssrn.4019514

Boehm F, Pesch P (2014) Bitcoin: a first legal analysis. In: Böhme R et al (eds) Financial cryptography and data security. FC 2014. Lecture notes in computer science, vol 8438. Springer, Berlin, Heidelberg, pp 43–54

Bürgerliches Gesetzbuch in der Fassung der Bekanntmachung vom 2. Jan 2002 (BGBl. I S. 42, 2909; 2003 I S. 738), das zuletzt durch Artikel 2 des Gesetzes vom 21. Dezember 2021 (BGBl. I S. 5252)

Carr D (2019) Cryptocurrencies as property in civilian and mixed legal systems. In: Fox D, Green S (eds) Cryptocurrencies in public and private law. Oxford University Press, Oxford, pp 177–198

Conseil d'Etat, Nos. 417809, 418030, 418031, 418032 and 418033, 26 Apr 2018

Conway H, Grattan S (2017) The 'New' new property: dealing with digital assets on death. In: Conway H, Hickey R (eds) Modern studies in property law, vol 9. Hart Publishing, Oxford, pp 99–116

Cooper GQC (2021) Virtual property: trusts of cryptocurrencies and other digital assets. Trusts Trustees 27(7):622–631. https://doi.org/10.1093/tandt/ttab027

Council Directive 2006/112/EC of 28 November 2006 on the common system of value added tax, OJ L 347, 11.12.2006

De Vauplane H (2017) Blockchain and conflict of laws. Revue Trimestrielle de Droit Financier (RTDF) 4:50–52

Dickinson A (2019) Cryptocurrencies and conflict of laws. In: Fox D, Green S (eds) Cryptocurrencies in public and private law. Oxford University Press, Oxford, pp 93–137

Digital Assets Act, Official Gazette of the Republic of Serbia, No. 153/2020

Directive (EU) 2019/713 of the European Parliament and of the Council of 17 April 2019 on combating fraud and counterfeiting of non-cash means of payment and replacing Council Framework Decision 2001/413/JHA, PE/89/2018/REV/3, OJ L 123, 10.5.2019, pp 18–29

Directive 2009/24/EC of the European Parliament and of the Council of 23 April 2009 on the legal protection of computer programs (Codified version), OJ L 111, 5.5.2009, pp 16–22

European Law Institute (2022) ELI Principles on the Use of Digital Assets as Security. Report of the European Law Institute. https://www.europeanlawinstitute.eu/fileadmin/user_upload/p_eli/Publications/ELI_Principles_on_the_Use_of_Digital_Assets_as_Security.pdf. Accessed 10 May 2022

Federal Act of 30 March 1911 on the Amendment of the Swiss Civil Code (Part Five: The Code of Obligations), SR 220

Ferreira A et al (2021) Cryptocurrencies, DLT and crypto assets – the road to regulatory recognition in Europe. In: Thai M et al (eds) Handbook on Blockchain. Springer (in press) https://papers.ssrn.com/sol3/papers.cfm?abstract_id=3891401. Accessed 22 Sept 2022

Garcia-Teruel RM, Simon-Moreno H (2021) The digital tokenization of property rights. A comparative perspective. Comput Law Secur Rev 41:1–16. https://doi.org/10.1016/j.clsr.2021.10554

Garcimartin Alferez FJ, Sanchez Fernandez S (2020) Is private international law tech-proof? Conflict of laws and FinTech: selectes issues. In: Thomas J et al (eds) The Elgar companion to the Hague conference on private international law. Edward Elagar Publishing, Cheltenham, pp 406–415

Gavella N (2007) Stvarnopravno uređenje. In: Gavella N (ed) Stvarno pravo, vol 1, 2nd edn. Narodne novine, Zagreb, pp 5–54

Gesetz über elektronische Wertpapiere vom 3. Jun 2021, BGBl. I S. 1423

HCCH (2022) Developments with respect to PIL Implications of the Digital Economy. Prel. Doc. No 4 REV of January 2022. https://assets.hcch.net/docs/b06c28c5-d183-4d81-a663-f7bdb8f32dac.pdf. Accessed 15 May 2022

Huang RH (2021) Fintech regulation in China. Principles, policies and practices. Cambridge University Press, Cambridge

International Bar Association. A French point of view: from crypto assets to digital assets. https://www.ibanet.org/article/f59c675e-e95e-4c74-bdc3-ea5a42e8ef9c. Accessed 20 May 2022

Judgment of 16 September 2021, The Software Incubator Ltd v Computer Associates (UK) Ltd, C-410/19, EU:C:2021:742

Judgment of 22 October 2015, Skatteverket v David Hedqvist, C-264/14, EU:C:2015:718

Kharitonova JS (2021) Digital assets and digital inheritance. Law Digital Technol 1:19–26. https://doi.org/10.18254/S123456780015732-6

Klarić P, Vedriš M (2014) Građansko pravo. Narodne novine, Zagreb

Korobeinikova TS (2020) Digital Rights as an Object of Civil Rights. In: Nazarov AD (ed) Proceedings of the 2nd International Scientific and Practical Conference "Modern Management Trends and the Digital Economy: from Regional Development to Global Economic Growth" (MTDE 2020). 2nd International Scientific Conference "Modern Management Trends and the Digital Economy: from Regional Development to Global Economic Growth" (MTDE 2020), Yekaterinburg, April 2020. Advances in Economics, Business and Management Research, vol 138. Atlantis Press, Dordrecht, pp 230–234

Kreditwesengesetz in der Fassung der Bekanntmachung vom 9. September 1998, BGBl. I S. 2776, das zuletzt durch Artikel 3 des Gesetzes vom 23. Mai 2022, BGBl. I S. 754

Law Commission (2022a) Digital assets: Consultation Paper (Consultation Paper 256). https://www.lawcom.gov.uk/project/digital-assets/. Accessed 20 Sept 2022

Law Commission (2022b) Digital assets: Summary of consultation paper. https://www.lawcom.gov.uk/project/digital-assets/. Accessed 20 Sept 2022

Law of 3 October 2019 on Tokens and TT Service Providers (Token and TT Service Provider Act; TVTG) (Gesetz vom 3. Oktober 2019 über Token und VT-Dienstleister (Token- und VT-Dienstleister-Gesetz; TVTG)), Liechtensteinisches Landesgesetzblatt, 2019.301

Lee J, Van de Looverbosch M (2021) Property and data: a confused relationship. In: Lee J, Darbellay A (eds) Data Governance in AI, FinTech and RegTech: Law and Regulation in the Financial Sector (2022) Cheltenham. Edward Elgar Publishing. Available at SSRN: https://ssrn.com/abstract=3995492. Accessed 20 June 2022

Lehmann M (2017) Financial instruments. In: Basedow J et al (eds) Encyclopedia of private international law. Edward Elgar Publishing, Cheltenham, pp 739–747

Lehmann M (2021) National Blockchain laws as a threat to capital markets integration. Uniform Law Rev 26(1):148–179. https://doi.org/10.1093/ulr/unab004

Low KFK, Hara M (2022) Cryptoassets and property. In: Van Erp S, Zimmermann K (eds) Edward Elgar Research Handbook on EU Property Law (Forthcoming), Available at SSRN: https://ssrn.com/abstract=4103870. Accessed 20 June 2022

Low KFK, Mik E (2020) Pause the Blockchain legal revolution. Int Comp Law Q 69(1):135–175. https://doi.org/10.1017/S0020589319000502

Maia G, Dos Santos JV (2022) MiCA and DeFi ("Proposal for a Regulation on Market in Cryptoassets" and "Decentralised Finance"). Revista Electrónica de Direito 27(2):57–82. https://doi.org/10.24840/2182-9845_2022-0002_0004

National Conference of Commissioners on Uniform State Laws (2015) Revised Uniform Fiduciary Access to Digital Assets Act. (hereinafter: RUFADAA). https://www.uniformlaws.org/HigherLogic/System/DownloadDocumentFile.ashx?DocumentFileKey=112ab648-b257-97f2-48c2-61fe109a0b33&forceDialog=0. Accessed 10 May 2022

Perkušić M (2020) Pravo elektroničkog plaćanja. Školska knjiga, Zagreb

Perkušić M, Slakoper Z (2017) Novac. In: Slakoper Z (ed) Bankovni i financijski ugovori. Narodne novine, Zagreb, pp 62–92

Proposal for a Regulation of the European Parliament and of the Council on Markets in Crypto-assets, and amending Directive (EU) 2019/1937, COM/2020/593 final

Regulation (EU) No 909/2014 of the European Parliament and of the Council of 23 July 2014 on improving securities settlement in the European Union and on central securities depositories and amending Directives 98/26/EC and 2014/65/EU and Regulation (EU) No 236/2012, OJ L 257, 28.8.2014

Sachenrecht (SR) vom 31. Dezember 1922, Liechtensteinisches Landesgesetzblatt 1923.004

Slakoper Z (2017) Vrijednosni papiri. In: Slakoper Z (ed) Bankovni i financijski ugovori. Narodne novine, Zagreb, pp 204–239

The Law on the Basis of Ownership and Proprietary Relations, Republic of Serbia, Official Gazette SFRY, No. 6/80, 36/90; Official Gazette FRY No. 29/96; Official Gazette RS No. 115/05

UNIDROIT (2022) Study LXXXII – W.G.5 – Doc. 3: Master Copy of the Principles, plus Commentary (with Questions). https://www.unidroit.org/wp-content/uploads/2022/03/W.G.5.-Doc.-3-Master-Copy-Principles-plus-Comments-with-Questions.pdf. Accessed 14 May 2022

Vlček F (2019) Virtual currencies: a new challenge for tax law and monetary law, Master's Thesis. Masaryk University

Walker MD (2017) The new uniform digital assets law: estate planing and administration in the information age. Real Prop Trust Estate Law J 52(1):52–78

Wu TH (2020) Trustees' investment duties and cryptoassets. Trusts Trustees 26(2):183–194. https://doi.org/10.1093/tandt/ttz117

Zellweger-Gutknecht C, Seiler B (2021) Country Report Switzerland – the law of crypto assets. In: Maume P et al (eds) The law of crypto assets. Bloomsbury Publishing. Available at SSRN: https://ssrn.com/abstract=3708316 or https://doi.org/10.2139/ssrn.3708316. Accessed 25 June 2022

MIX
Papier aus verantwortungsvollen Quellen
Paper from responsible sources
FSC® C105338

If you have any concerns about our products,
you can contact us on
ProductSafety@springernature.com

In case Publisher is established outside the EU,
the EU authorized representative is:
Springer Nature Customer Service Center GmbH
Europaplatz 3, 69115 Heidelberg, Germany

Printed by Libri Plureos GmbH
in Hamburg, Germany